A MODERN ARCADIA

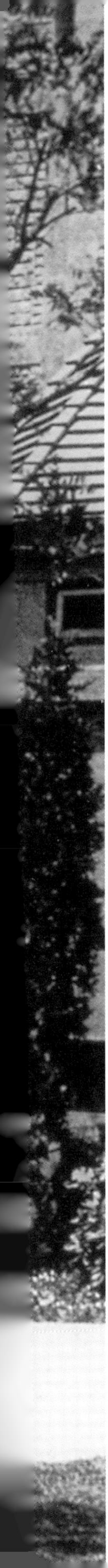

A MODERN ARCADIA

Frederick Law Olmsted Jr. & the Plan for Forest Hills Gardens

SUSAN L. KLAUS

UNIVERSITY OF MASSACHUSETTS PRESS AMHERST & BOSTON

in association with

LIBRARY OF AMERICAN LANDSCAPE HISTORY AMHERST

Printed in China
LC 2001007538 ISBN 1-55849-314-X (cloth) ISBN 978-1-55849-443-5 (paper)
Designed by Mary Mendell Set in Galliard
Printed and bound by C&C Offset Printing Co., Ltd.

Library of Congress Cataloging-in-Publication Data
Klaus, Susan L.
A modern Arcadia : Frederick Law Olmsted Jr. and the plan
for Forest Hills Gardens / Susan L. Klaus.
p. cm.
"In association with Library of American Landscape History, Amherst."
Includes bibliographical references and index.
ISBN 1-55849-314-X
1. Planned communities—New York (State)—New York—Case
studies. 2. Olmsted, Frederick Law, 1870–1957—Contributions in city
planning. 3. Forest Hills (New York, N.Y.) I. Olmsted, Frederick Law,
1870–1957. II. Title.
HT169.57.U62 N75 2001 307.1'216'09747243–dc21 2001007538

British Library Cataloguing in Publication data are available.

All photographs credited to Fairsted are courtesy National Park Service, Frederick Law Olmsted National Historic Site.

PAGE ii Wrought-iron entrance to Tea Garden from Greenway Terrace. Courtesy Frances Loeb Library, Graduate School of Design, Harvard University.
iii Logo of the Sage Foundation Homes Company combining their initials with Forest Hills Gardens.
viii Sign for Forest Hills Gardens Station, 2001. Photograph by Carol Betsch.
2 Running commuter lamp, Station Square. Forest Hills Gardens Corporation Records (no. 2775, box 30, glass neg. no. 85). Courtesy Division of Rare and Manuscript Collections, Cornell University Library.
6 Dense plantings at Forest Hills Gardens rail station. From *American Homes and Gardens,* February 1915.
16 Steps to lower gardens at Fairsted. Courtesy Library of Congress, Prints and Photographs Division, Historic American Buildings Survey, HABS, MASS, 11-Brok, 6, 7.
30 Arch bridge at Station Square. Courtesy Frances Loeb Library, Graduate School of Design, Harvard University.
54 Atterbury's sectional concrete construction. From *Concrete Cement Age,* 1910. Courtesy Rockefeller Archive Center.
84 Climbing roses, Greenway Terrace. Courtesy Rockefeller Archive Center.
110 Fourth of July poster, 1917. Courtesy Forest Hills Gardens Corporation.
120 The Village Green, 2001. Photograph by Carol Betsch.
146 Light at Station Square, 2001. Photograph by Carol Betsch.
208 Mature trees on Olivia Place, 2001. Photograph by Carol Betsch.

For Nathalie and Phil

Nancy, Philip, and Jim

Ashley, Joel, Will, Nathalie II,

and …

CONTENTS

FOREST HILLS

PREFACE

THE LIBRARY OF AMERICAN LANDSCAPE HISTORY publishes the Designers and Places Series to illuminate the significance of practitioners and sites of particular importance to the field. *A Modern Arcadia* by Susan L. Klaus is the third volume in the series, which includes *The Muses of Gwinn* by Robin Karson and *The Gardens of Ellen Biddle Shipman* by Judith B. Tankard. These richly illustrated books are intended for both professional and general readers.

THE SUBJECT OF THIS BOOK is Forest Hills Gardens, a 142-acre planned community in Queens, fifteen minutes from Manhattan on the Long Island Rail Road. The pioneering commuter suburb was designed in 1909 by landscape architect Frederick Law Olmsted Jr. and architect Grosvenor Atterbury and inspired by English garden cities and modern American planning methods. The suburb still exists today, distinguished by a parklike ambience, rich architectural detail, and a sense of quality and permanence.

Susan L. Klaus begins her story in the twentieth century's first decade, when great numbers of immigrants poured into cities ill-equipped to provide for them. As urban conditions deteriorated and the elite moved to country estates, middle-class workers came to covet country life, too—for both its salutary and its culturally legitimizing effects. Forest Hills Gardens, the first project of the newly formed Russell Sage Foundation, was conceived as the answer to their dreams. The Progressive Era housing experiment was greeted with immediate, almost universal acclaim.

Klaus's book traces the suburb from conception to construction to daily life in the community, as recorded by resident shopkeepers, artists, businessmen, and housewives who enthusiastically planted trees, bird-watched, and staged patriotic pageants on the village green. The author integrates the story of young Olmsted's discovery of his professional calling with that of the birth of the new science of city planning and weaves together several strands of planning, social, and landscape architectural history. An urban historian and the leading authority on Olmsted Jr., Klaus provides particularly insightful analysis of Olmsted's plan. She makes a compelling case that his layout of streets, parks, and public and private spaces was a stroke of genius and the reason that Forest Hills Gardens thrives today—a green oasis that supports a vital, diverse community of six thousand residents.

It is our hope that *A Modern Arcadia* will contribute to a wider understanding of the principles of suburban planning and that this understanding will bear fruit in the work of developers, planners, architects, and landscape architects. We hope, too, that the book will encourage efforts to renew the historically momentous landscape of Forest Hills Gardens and to protect it for future generations.

RESEARCH, PHOTOGRAPHY, and design for *A Modern Arcadia* were supported by generous grants from the Rockefeller Archive Center, Graham Foundation for Advanced Studies in the Fine Arts, and Furthermore, a program of the J. M. Kaplan Fund.

Robin Karson, Executive Director
Library of American Landscape History
Amherst, Massachusetts

LIBRARY of AMERICAN LANDSCAPE HISTORY

Library of American Landscape History, Inc., a nonprofit organization, produces books and exhibitions about North American landscape history. Its mission is to educate and thereby promote thoughtful stewardship of the land.

ACKNOWLEDGMENTS

THIS BOOK HAS BEEN so long in the making, I fear that many who have been so helpful may have forgotten me! But I remember them, and thank those named below, as well as the many librarians and archivists who have assisted me over the past decade.

That *A Modern Arcadia* exists at all is a tribute to the patience, enthusiasm, and stubbornness of Robin Karson, executive director of the Library of American Landscape History. After meeting Robin at a landscape symposium at Bryn Mawr College, I invoked "the kindness of strangers," sending her an article I had written on the Olmsteds, father and son, and asking for her advice. What I received in return was encouragement, kindness, and unflagging support. It is Robin's vision of how to make the Forest Hills Gardens story accessible and interesting to a broad audience that has shaped this book. It has been Robin's friendship and resolve that have helped me finish it.

Carol Betsch joined our team several years ago. She has used the tact of a diplomat and the skill of a surgeon in editing my prose, politely but relentlessly pointing out those places where I was too tired or too lazy to write clearly. Carol's artistry is visible as well in her striking photographs of Forest Hills Gardens today.

My thanks to my thesis advisers at The George Washington University, Howard Gillette Jr., who was the first to inform me that there *was* a Frederick Law Olmsted Jr., and Richard Longstreth, who has continued to encourage me and critique my work. I am also grateful for the inspiration and assistance of other Olmsted scholars and enthusiasts, particularly Charles Beveridge and Charles McLaughlin. I have very much enjoyed my association with those I have met through the National

Association of Olmsted Parks, and thank them for their friendship and interest in my work.

Anyone who works with manuscript collections generally acknowledges that your research will be as good as the archivist who assists you; I have been fortunate to work with some of the most professional and helpful. My thanks to those who staffed the Manuscript Reading Room at the Library of Congress during the nearly two years I spent working with the Olmsted collections. They truly made me feel that I was in my "home away from home." I am especially indebted to Joyce Connolly, former archivist at the National Park Service Frederick Law Olmsted Historic Site (Fairsted), and Melissa Smith, former archivist at the Rockefeller Archive Center. I worked with both women for many years; they were unfailingly helpful and never once asked, "Haven't you finished that book yet?" I am also grateful to the archivists currently in those positions, Michele Clark at Fairsted, and Tom Rosenbaum and Michele Hiltzik, picture archivist, at RAC. Ann Whiteside, former visual resources librarian at the Frances Loeb Library, Graduate School of Design, Harvard University, helped me obtain illustrations, and Herbert Finch, formerly at the Carl A. Kroch Library at Cornell University, guided my work in the Forest Hills Collections housed there.

At Forest Hills Gardens itself, resident and "town historian" William Coleman kindly showed me around the community and introduced me to the Forest Hills Gardens Corporation archives. Cathy Eiring, manager of the Forest Hills Gardens Corporation office, provided illustrations and graciously answered last-minute inquiries.

Landscape designer Carolyn Mullett studied the Olmsted planting plans for private residences and parks at Forests Hills Gardens with me, helping me understand the plant material and providing interesting insights into some differences between planting conventions then and now.

Crucial support was provided early in my research by the Rockefeller Archive Center and the Graham Foundation for Advanced Studies in the Fine Arts.

Finally, it's your friends who get you through. To Mike, Popie, Sue, and my other long-suffering friends (all of whom know how to spell Olmsted), my heartfelt thanks for your support and your faith in me. Thanks to Steven, whose daily email pep talks were better than a shot of caffeine. To my oldest friends, seven special St. Catherine's classmates who encircle me with love and acceptance, I could not have finished this without the positive energy you continue to provide.

A MODERN ARCADIA

INTRODUCTION

That's what I'll do after college! I'll get my hands on one of these prairie towns and make it beautiful!... Why should they have all the garden suburbs on Long Island?—Carol Kennicott in Sinclair Lewis's Main Street *(1920)*

MAROONED IN GOPHER PRAIRIE, Minnesota, in 1912, newly wed Carol Kennicott dreams of transforming "the unsparing unapologetic ugliness and the rigid straightness" of her village into something like the new "fairy-book suburb" of Forest Hills Gardens on Long Island, pictures of which had already found their way to her tiny public library on the American plain. When *Main Street* was published, Forest Hills Gardens was barely eight years old. Yet Sinclair Lewis could assume with some confidence that its name would convey to his readers, as it did to Carol, the image of an American community that was "lovely, as well as useful." What made this early twentieth-century suburban community so newsworthy? Why did it catch the public's imagination?

Conceived in 1909, Forest Hills Gardens was the collaborative creation of the landscape architect and planner Frederick Law Olmsted Jr. and the architect and housing reform activist Grosvenor Atterbury. It was widely publicized in newspaper stories, professional journals, and popular women's magazines as America's first garden city, a place where people of "moderate income and good taste . . . might find some country air and country life within striking distance of the active centers of New York."[1] Underwritten by the Russell Sage Foundation, a new philanthropic organization dedicated to improving social and living conditions in the United States, Forest Hills Gardens was an experiment in applying the new "science" of city planning to a suburban setting. Its sponsors and designers hoped to demonstrate both the practicality and the profitability of good design and comprehensive planning.

Forest Hills Gardens appeared at the height of the Progressive Era, those decades in pre–World War I America when experimentation, scientific reform, pragmatism, and professionalism were the watchwords of the day. Responding to the overcrowding, squalor, and chaos of an increasingly urbanized and industrialized country, to the problems of absorbing an immigrant population rapidly expanding in both size and diversity, and to the corruption of big city political machines, an array of reform-minded men and women gathered under the progressive banner. They espoused a wide-ranging, sometimes conflicting, set of proposals to address social and political concerns. Most agreed on the importance of revitalizing family, school, and community as socializing institutions.

Forest Hills Gardens, the era's most notable experiment in planned suburban development, was rooted in a faith in human ability to shape the environment and its confidence in the power of technology and professional expertise. Journalists lauded Forest Hills Gardens for giving the country a vision of suburban living "the like of which is not to be found at all in America." They deemed it a modern Arcadia, a place that "smashes all the convention of commonplace suburban building."[2]

Early photographs captured its charm: an arresting entrance plaza—inspired by medieval college towns as well as the new Hampstead Garden Suburb, then under development outside of London—leading to a traditional town green; quiet shaded neighborhood streets; distinctive architecture rich in color, texture, and detail; and a richly planted landscape that melded private gardens and lawns with public spaces. These were the qualities that captivated Carol Kennicott and those like her who looked around their own towns and villages and yearned for order and beauty.

Some ninety years later Forest Hills Gardens still surprises the first-time visitor. Just two blocks from the subway stop at 71st Street and Continental Avenue down a busy Queens commercial street, one passes under the railroad tracks into the enclosed, brick-paved Station Square plaza, the entrance into Forest Hills Gardens—and into another world, one that is quiet, green, and serene.

I CAME TO FOREST HILLS GARDENS in the course of my research on the career of Frederick Law Olmsted Jr. As an urban historian with a particular interest in the early twentieth century, I had been looking at Olmsted's critical, yet largely forgotten, role in the development of the profession of city planning in the United States. Like his acclaimed father, Olmsted saw suburbs as an integral part of the urban fabric. Olmsted Sr. had observed that "no great town can long exist without great suburbs," and he applied the principles that he had developed in creating major urban parks and regional park systems to the suburban landscape of the post–Civil War period.[3] In the early twentieth century, Olmsted Jr. warned that the overcrowding and blight plaguing American cities would soon overwhelm suburban areas "with belching chimneys' soot-laden air, clanging noises, and landscape blighted with flaming billboards," unless measures were taken to control new development.[4] He believed that the emerging field of city planning could provide tools for shaping suburban growth and designing superior residential subdivisions. At the same time that he was preparing reports for improving and beautifying established cities and planning for their future growth and development, Olmsted was applying these urban planning principles to suburban enclaves, most notably at Forest Hills Gardens.

I was astonished to find that Forest Hills Gardens looks exactly like the original renderings of Olmsted and Atterbury's 1909 plan. Here was a community that was actually built as designed and had maintained its integrity for nearly a century. As I walked its streets, I was struck by how much Forest Hills Gardens appears to embody what we often speak of as our suburban ideal. It is a community with a distinctive town center, pleasant public spaces, a varied yet logical street plan, sidewalks that invite walking, and a luxuriant landscape setting for homes whose lively variety and fine craftsmanship still impress.

Forest Hills Gardens was not Arcadia. Like the Progressive Era itself, its legacy is a mixed one, reflecting both the possibilities and limitations of planning and design. But Olmsted and his colleagues did create a community that set a new standard for suburban development. That it remains today a desirable place to live is one measure of their success. That it still has much to teach about creating and maintaining a high-quality suburb is another. A landmark in community planning in this country and a major project in the career of a distinguished landscape architect and planner, Forest Hills Gardens is a living lesson in planning history.

I

"A Garden City for America"

In November 1910 more than one hundred fifty newspapers—ranging across the country from the *Atlanta Constitution* to the *Peoria Star*, from the *San Diego Sun* to the Denison, Texas, *Herald*—carried stories about plans to build a model suburban community called Forest Hills Gardens. "A garden city for America," announced the *New York Sun*. It would be "a conventionalized and modern Garden of Eden," said the *New York Tribune*, "a fairy tale too good to be true." Dubbing the proposed development "Sageville" in honor of its patron, Mrs. Russell Sage, the Portland, Maine, *Eastern Argus* summed up the venture with Yankee succinctness: "It will be a Community of Quality." Some of the news accounts mentioned the name of the new town's site planner, Frederick Law Olmsted Jr., referring to him variously as architect, landscape architect, landscape designer, and "Mrs. Sage's own landscape gardener."[1]

The occasion for this extraordinary nationwide press was the announcement by the Russell Sage Foundation of a new venture in suburban land development. Under its sponsorship, a community was taking shape on 142 acres in the borough of Queens, nine miles from Manhattan, a commute now possible in just fifteen minutes via the newly inaugurated line of the Long Island Rail Road. The country's preeminent landscape architect, Frederick Law Olmsted Jr., and the distinguished New York architect Grosvenor Atterbury had been retained by the foundation to prepare site plans and architectural designs for the town.

The *Atlanta Constitution* praised the venture as "Philanthropy with a

Portrait of Olivia Sage by Cecilia Beaux. Courtesy Russell Sage Foundation.

Brain." It applauded the Sage Foundation's intent "to establish near New York City a 'Spotless Town' where people of small means may buy homes within reach of their pockets. . . . The growing congestion of Manhattan Island, ascending rents and the extreme difficulty under which adults, no less than little children, may live in a sanitary fashion will make the Sage project a Godsend to even the limited number able to avail themselves of its provisions."[2]

The *Grand Rapids Press* pointed out that the new suburb would be the first American residential experiment based on the principles of the English garden city, which, the paper marveled, had produced "small floral paradises" for factory workers in the company-built towns of Bournville and Port Sunlight.[3] The Sage Foundation's town-building project would "show that those who work in the big cities need not live in their ugliness and grime, but may secure beauty, fresh air and the healthful benefits of the open spaces in suburbs." The Washington, D.C., *Times* agreed that the experiment's most far-reaching benefit would be educational: "The most important feature of the development . . . is that it is intended to demonstrate what can be done anywhere. . . . [I]f it proves that the talent of a landscape architect like Frederick Law Olmsted, of Boston, and of an architect like Grosvenor Atterbury, of New York, can be utilized on a suburb of this kind, giving it the intelligent study which is now given only to much more pretentious and more expensive places, and that the money laid out for that sort of advice is money well expended, a most useful service will have been performed."[4]

But some cautionary notes were sounded as well. Several reporters expressed skepticism about the concept of creating "model towns" for Americans. The *Seattle Times* flatly predicted failure: "[Mrs. Sage] is having her houses built by her own architect and her lawns and parks laid out by her own landscape gardener—something which is bound to result in trouble at the first meeting of the 'Mrs. Sage Sewing Circle.'" The paper also observed that the mere idea of a model town was "too proper and too much cut and dried" to appeal to American individualists. Under the headline "Model Cities Need Model Men," the Pueblo, Colorado, *Chieftain*, alluded to the kinds of problems that had arisen in the company towns established by the not so benign paternalism of some late nineteenth-century American capitalists. "In Gary, Indiana, for example," the story reported, "the workmen who live in the model houses have been using their bathtubs for coal bins."[5]

A few papers questioned why the development of a suburb for people of modest means should be deemed a newsworthy event. As a Cleveland reporter put it: "In Mrs. Russell Sage's model town the streets will be cleaned after heavy snowstorms, there will be enough street cars for all and gas will be reasonable. Otherwise it will be much like Cleveland." Some wondered with the Saginaw, Michigan, *Herald*, why the year-old Russell Sage Foundation had chosen as its first major undertaking a project that would benefit "those who are struggling but who are still able to secure something more than the bare necessities of life. . . . [T]his does not constitute the most serious problems of great cities." Surely the Sage millions could be more usefully applied to "far more important work among those who both through ignorance and through actual inability to secure more sanitary homes . . . are now quartered in filthy, vastly overpopulated and destructive tenements."[6]

It was a fair question to address to the Russell Sage Foundation. Established in 1907 with a $10 million endowment from the widow of financier Russell Sage, the Sage Foundation was the forerunner of the modern, multipurpose philanthropic institution, and a pioneer in supporting both social research and social action. At the time there were only eight similar endowed funds in the country, none of which had the broadly based social purpose that the Sage Foundation took as its mission, namely, to help ameliorate "social and living conditions in the United States."[7]

The guiding force of the foundation was Robert de Forest, the Sage family lawyer. A prominent member of New York society, de Forest was well known for his activism in the city's major philanthropic and cultural institutions. In a 1906 memorandum to the recently widowed Mrs. Sage which contained "suggestions for a possible Sage Foundation," de Forest listed a number of areas that he believed were in line with Mrs. Sage's inclination toward "social betterment—improvement of the hard conditions of our working classes, making their homes and surroundings more healthful and comfortable and their lives happier; giving more of opportunity to them and their children." Any one of these, he assured Mrs. Sage, would be worthy of the proposed foundation's support.[8]

Among de Forest's suggestions was the development of model "tenements in the city and small houses in the suburbs—for the working class on a business basis."[9] The creation of a model suburban community did become the first major project of the Russell Sage Foundation, which was incorporated in a bill submitted to the state legislature and signed into law on 11 April 1907.

In 1909 the foundation purchased a tract of land on which they planned to create a garden city, made "somewhat attractive by the treat-

Portrait of Robert de Forest, ca. 1914. Courtesy Rockefeller Archive Center.

ment and planting of our streets, the possibility of little gardens, and possibly some public places." While this project, foundation officials later noted, grew out of "Mrs. Sage's express wish" to improve housing conditions, it complemented de Forest's own long-standing interest in housing reform for the working classes and in good housing for all.[10] Addressing the press's criticism that this garden city experiment would not directly benefit the poorest and most needy, de Forest claimed that the "Sage Foundation has not forgotten the laboring man. It may be ready to announce something for his benefit later on. But the cost of the land at Forest Hills Gardens, and the character of its surroundings, preclude provision there for the day laborer."[11]

The Sage Foundation's goal, de Forest declared in announcing the Forest Hills Gardens project, was to "set an example to the growing suburban districts of New York and other cities of how the thing can be done tastefully and at the same time with due regard for profit."[12] By showing that it was possible to make money on an attractive suburb, intelligently designed according to the most modern town-planning principles, the foundation hoped that their experiment would be widely imitated. Thus Forest Hills Gardens was intended to be a demonstration as much in the economics of suburban development as in community planning and building techniques.

The creators of Forest Hills Gardens believed that the primary importance of the project was educational, that it would set a new national standard for design and development for suburban enclaves springing up across the country. "It is so seldom that an American town plans its growth with an idea of future development," one of the first visitors to the Gardens underscored, "that the example of Forest Hills Gardens is noteworthy."[13] Some contemporary critics did recognize that this, in fact, was the most significant aspect of the Sage Foundation's experiment. An editorial in *The American Architect* praised Forest Hills Gardens as "perhaps the first example in America where a barren site has been treated along the lines of modern methods of Town Planning." At Forest Hills Gardens "there is nothing haphazard. It is thoughtfully studied."[14]

De Forest assembled a design and management team for the project exhibiting his preference for collaborating, where possible, with people already known to him or the other trustees. He was well acquainted with Atterbury and Olmsted, both because of their shared interest in civic improvement and housing reform and through projects each had undertaken at various de Forest family properties.[15] The Sage Founda-

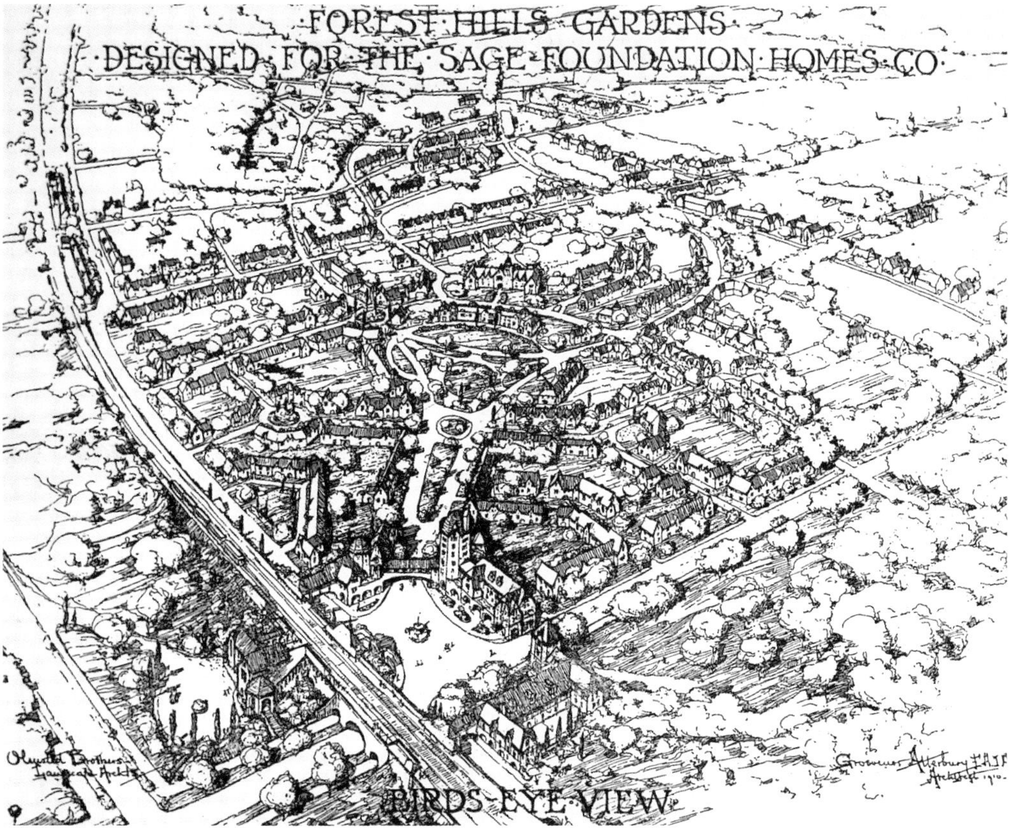

Bird's-eye view of Forest Hills Gardens, 1910. Courtesy Rockefeller Archive Center.

tion was already funding Atterbury's experiment in prefabricated construction methods, and the architect's well-known interest in low-cost housing made him the ideal architectural consultant for the project.

Olmsted had been engaged in professional practice for just over a decade when de Forest invited him to join the venture, but he was, arguably, already the most visible member of his profession. In addition he was emerging as the chief public spokesman of the nascent American city planning movement, whose goal was to bring into harmony a myriad of "enormously complex forces which"—he readily admitted—"no one clearly understands and few pretend to." But the "appalling breadth and ramifications of real city planning," he maintained, was no excuse for not attempting to take control of these forces.[16]

America's crowded, chaotic, and unhealthy cities were testaments to the effects of the uncontrolled, unplanned urban growth of the nineteenth century. Prevention is cheaper than the cure, Olmsted argued. Planners must look to "the outskirts of the city," he said, "where the

Frederick Law Olmsted Jr., ca. 1910. Courtesy U.S. Commission of Fine Arts.

major part of the city's growth is bound to occur, and where the city plan is daily taking shape out of nothing, whether it is intelligently designed or not."[17] Since suburban expansion promised to be a dominant feature of the early twentieth century, it should be planned and guided by professionals, not left to the vagaries of real estate speculation. The Forest Hills Gardens project would demonstrate that this could be done, and even be done profitably.

By 1909 Olmsted had completed or was working on comprehensive planning reports for the cities of Detroit; Utica, New York; Boulder, Colorado; Pittsburgh; New Haven; Rochester; and Newport, Rhode Island. Olmsted had a remarkable facility for grasping the essential character of a city even on short acquaintance. His plans emphasized the importance of preserving the individuality of each locale. Another hallmark of an Olmsted plan was its often startling prescience about the direction that future development of the locale under study would take.[18] In Detroit, for example, Olmsted pushed for private–public cooperation in rebuilding the waterfront and drew attention to the likely importance of the Great Lakes area as a summer resort. In the reports for Utica and Boulder, he suggested improvements that would preserve the unique scenery and pleasant aspects that gave each city its distinctive appeal. His reports for Pittsburgh, New Haven, and Rochester exhibited an increasing sophistication in data collection and analysis as the nascent planning profession continued to broaden its agenda and improve its techniques.

When he joined the Forest Hills Gardens project, Olmsted was serving a term (1908–1909) as president of the American Society of Landscape Architects. As one of the authors of the 1901 McMillan plan, a comprehensive blueprint for transforming the monumental core of Washington, D.C., and for guiding the future development of the nation's capital, Olmsted had recently been appointed by President Taft to the new Fine Arts Commission, which was given oversight authority in aesthetic, architectural, and planning matters in the federal city. Olmsted was also lecturing at Harvard, where he had helped create the first university courses in both landscape architecture and city planning. These positions of national importance attest to his preeminence in both planning and landscape architecture. De Forest had no doubt that Olmsted was the man to advise on the site plan and landscaping of the new suburb.

City planning reports by Olmsted. Author photograph.

2

All in the Family

OLMSTED'S EARLY CAREER

FROM A YOUNG AGE Olmsted was marked as the "heir apparent," schooled by his famous father to take up the profession that the elder Olmsted had labored to create.[1] While Olmsted's decision to follow in his father's footsteps seemed fitting, if not inevitable, the family saga was far from simple. The responsibility of inheriting both his father's name and his professional mantle dominated the formative years of the son's life.

On 24 July 1870 Frederick Law Olmsted, at the age of forty-eight, celebrated the birth of a son at his Staten Island, New York, home. He and his wife Mary had endured the loss of two children: their firstborn had succumbed to illness at two months of age and a second male baby had survived for only six hours. Neither infant had been given his father's name; nor was this newborn, whose birth name was recorded as Henry Perkins Olmsted, after his maternal grandfather. Several years would pass before the little boy became his father's namesake, when Olmsted Sr. renamed his only natural son Frederick Law Olmsted Jr.[2]

"Rick," as he was known in the family, was the youngest child in a large and complex household. In 1859 Olmsted Sr. had married Mary Perkins Olmsted, the widow of his younger brother, John Hull Olmsted. Olmsted Sr. thus became stepfather to his nephews and niece—John Charles (age eighteen when Rick was born), Charlotte (fifteen), and Owen (thirteen). Olmsted Sr. and Mary had one other child of their own, Marion, who was nine when her baby brother was born.

In 1872 the family moved to 209 West 46th Street, a four-story New

Fairsted, the Olmsted home and office. Courtesy Fairsted.

York City brownstone that served as both residence and office. Olmsted Sr. was now well-established as a landscape architect, a career auspiciously launched by his award-winning collaboration with the architect Calvert Vaux on the design for Central Park (1853). With the Olmsted–Vaux partnership nearing its amicable end, this was very much a family business. Professional and personal life intermingled at home, and from his earliest years Rick was exposed casually to the workings of the office. Olmsted Sr. took over the dining room for his study; Mary Olmsted copied out her husband's reports; and John Charles was in training as his stepfather's field assistant and draftsman.

In 1881 the family moved to the elite suburb of Brookline, Massachusetts, a town Olmsted Sr. deemed the "most civilized community in America."[3] Two years later he bought an old farmhouse at 99 Warren Street, and here, too, the family home was both residence and workplace. Olmsted Sr.'s office was in the north parlor, which maintained its ambience of a comfortable Victorian sitting room. Over the years, wings and additional stories were added onto the house, providing drafting, reproduction, and storage spaces for the growing business. The house, known as Fairsted, remained the headquarters of the Olmsted firm for nearly a century.[4]

In 1890 Rick entered Harvard, where he chose his course of study, he said, "with the definite expectation from the first of going into the profession of landscape architecture." During Rick's college days, Olmsted Sr. began to voice the concern that would become the obsession of his final years. "Now in nearly all our work," he told his son, "I am thinking of the credit that will indirectly come to you. . . . How is Rick to be best prepared to take advantage of what in reputation I have been earning? Reputation coming as the result of what I shall have done, but not coming in my time."[5]

Wanting to include his son in the culminating projects of his career, Olmsted Sr. took Rick on site visits to the visionary "White City" of the 1893 Chicago World's Columbian Exposition, and to Biltmore, the vast estate under construction for George Vanderbilt in Asheville, North Carolina. Rick also helped out in the Brookline office during school vacations and spent the summer following his freshman year in Chicago working at the World's Fair site under the supervision of his father's colleague on the project, the architect Daniel Burnham. In 1892 Olmsted Sr.

Rick possibly costumed for a play at Roxbury Latin School. Courtesy Fairsted.

combined business for the exposition with the opportunity to guide Rick on his first European tour, a five-month-long exploration of parks and country estates in England and France.

Although Rick Olmsted was twenty-four when he graduated from Harvard in 1894, there was no immediate invitation to join the family firm. Instead, Olmsted Sr. posted him to Biltmore, so that he could be a part of the most important job that the firm had ever undertaken for a private client. Suffering from insomnia, physical ailments, and increasing mental confusion, the elder Olmsted recognized that this would most likely be his career finale. For both these reasons he was determined that Rick be associated with the project. "I am anxious," he told his son, "to use any advantage that I may have for getting you established favorably. . . . The time may come when the fact of your having been engaged [at Biltmore] from the start . . . will give you some prestige."[6]

Olmsted Sr. made it clear that this was Rick's postgraduate course, his final apprenticeship. The firm (Olmsted, Olmsted and Eliot at this date) would be observing as Rick undertook his "first serious professional responsibilities. . . . According to the way in which you meet them," his father warned, "the place that you will be able to fill in our organization must be judged." In deciding whether to take Rick into

Olmsted Sr.'s plan for 10,000-acre Biltmore estate. Courtesy Frances Loeb Library, Graduate School of Design, Harvard University.

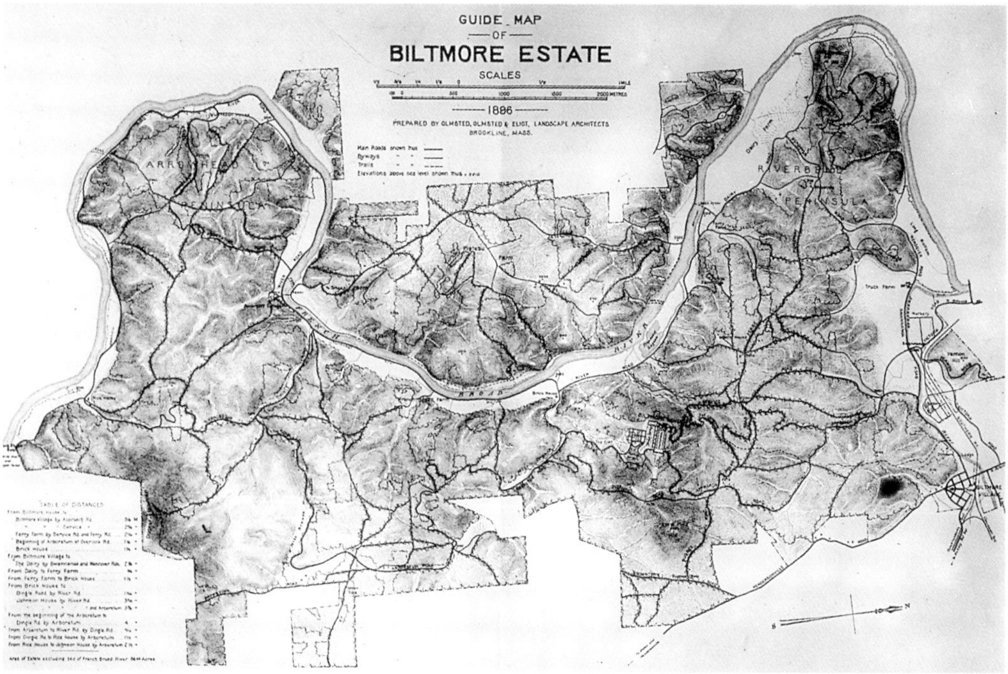

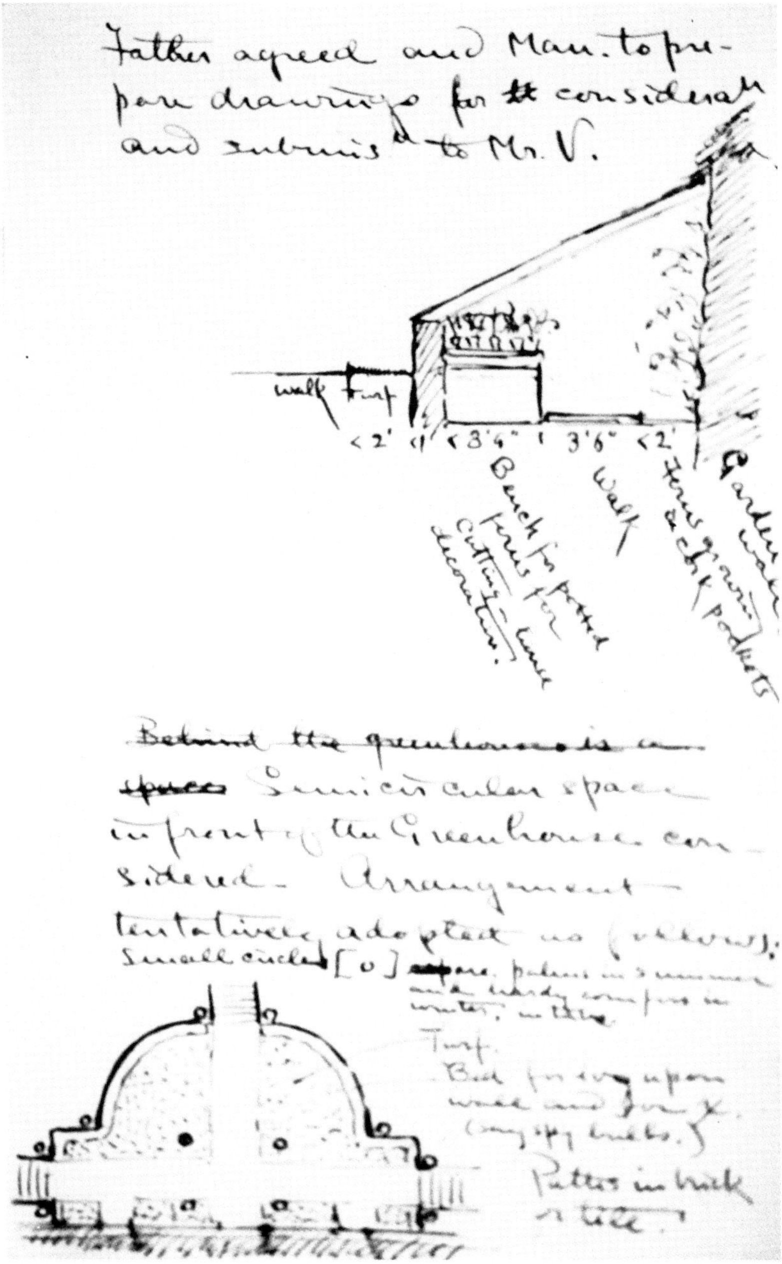

Rick's sketch of Olmsted Sr.'s ideas for walled and greenhouse gardens. Courtesy Library of Congress, Manuscript Division, Biltmore scrapbooks.

the firm, Olmsted Sr. emphasized that he and John Charles would defer to their partner Charles Eliot. "That is to say," he informed Rick, "you are not to consider it in the least as a family matter." But, of course, a family matter it was. Rick Olmsted's thirteen-month stay at Biltmore was a time of emotional turmoil for both father and son, intensified by the inseparability of familial and professional concerns.[7]

The younger Olmsted's position on the project was ambiguous. He was not an official employee, indeed, he was not on the firm's payroll; instead he received a living allowance from his father. Nevertheless, he inevitably became involved in day-to-day operations. He prepared studies on-site and made drawings to scale of landscape elements in response to requests from Brookline. When Olmsted Sr. visited, his son acted as personal assistant and secretary, taking field notes and transcribing letters. The majority of his time was spent in the Biltmore nursery, where he worked on cataloguing the estate's plants and trees and, at his father's insistence, on honing his botanical knowledge.

Seventy-five letters written by an increasingly distraught Olmsted Sr. came to Rick during his year at Biltmore. In these rambling epistles the aging father was by turns loving and stern, affectionate and threatening. Olmsted Sr.'s many successes over his long career had not mitigated a painful sense of how much more he might have accomplished: he believed that his lack of formal botanical, horticultural, and technical training had forced him to rely too much on others in the execution of his work, and he wished to spare his son similar feelings of inadequacy and regrets over unfulfilled potential. During this volatile period the elder Olmsted displayed an unusually intense identification with his son. "You seem to me to have very much of my character," he told Rick; "you are weak where I am weak, you are strong where I am strong."[8] Acutely aware of his own mortality, Olmsted Sr. seemed to be looking for solace in the knowledge that he would live on in the work of his namesake and professional heir.

Olmsted Sr. was determined that his son have the advantage of both the Olmsted name and excellent training. He exhorted Rick to become better grounded in botanical knowledge than anyone else in the firm. "I *insist* on your making yourself an expert nursery man," Olmsted Sr. flatly decreed, or "I shall not take you into this office." "If you think it is impracticable," he admonished, "the sooner you give up the profession the better."[9]

To this point in his life Rick had accepted that following in his father's

Frederick Law Olmsted Jr., ca. 1890. Author collection.

footsteps was the inevitable, as well as the wisest, course to follow: "I have generally come to the conclusion that it would be sheer folly" to enter any other profession. Now, under the strain of his father's unceasing emotional barrage, Rick's doubts and anxieties about becoming a landscape architect, repressed "ever since I entered college," spilled out. He had "lain awake at night many times," he confessed, trying to "thrust aside or outgrow" them. But if his father felt that he did not measure up, if more was to be demanded of him than of any other member of the firm, then "with pain and regret, after the most serious and thorough thought," he wrote, "I believe I would better enter upon another career."[10]

Having finally admitted to himself and to his father his anxieties about the responsibility of carrying on both the family name and business, Olmsted pondered other options. He had thought of teaching mathematics or physics, he told his father. He might study engineering or zoology. He invoked the authority of his Harvard professors, who thought he had the talent to succeed as an architect.[11]

Frederick Law Olmsted Sr. Courtesy The Papers of Frederick Law Olmsted.

In the midst of his struggle for independence and to define his own identity, Olmsted recognized that as his father's mental and physical condition deteriorated, "his deeply affectionate nature made him desperately anxious and worried, in a confused way, about the future of the youngest and least mature of his family."[12] Thus, as the parent-child relationship began its inevitable reversal, Rick Olmsted's long adolescence came to an end. The highly charged emotional situation was defused as the young Olmsted, with pain and a sense of helplessness, faced the mental illness that would cloud his father's last eight years. At Biltmore, Olmsted reconciled himself to the inevitable comparisons to his father. Indeed, for the rest of his life he took pride in acknowledging his professional legacy, fondly quoting his father and frequently alluding to Olmsted Sr.'s influence on his work.[13]

Over the summer Olmsted Sr.'s condition worsened, and the brothers agreed that their father was no longer able to direct work. In November 1895 John Olmsted and Charles Eliot formally invited twenty-five-year-old Frederick Jr. to join the firm, at a salary of $1,200 a year. On Eliot's sudden death the following year, John made his brother partner and joint owner, without, Olmsted appreciatively noted, "my contributing one cent of capital." The practice continued under the name Olmsted Brothers for the next sixty-three years.[14]

By all accounts, the brothers appear to have enjoyed a congenial relationship in circumstances replete with the possibility of personal and professional conflict. During the 1890s and in the early years of the twentieth century, both brothers' initials often appear on office correspondence, indicating that each made an effort to keep abreast of all business. Although the usual practice was for one to act as principal for a project, both might contribute. This was often the case on jobs that went on for several years, such as municipal park systems or residential developments.

Each brother traveled extensively, although John spent comparatively more time in Brookline attending to office management.[15] In the late 1880s he had assumed the role of the firm's managing partner and had put the practice on a business footing, aided by his "uncanny memory for details, for conversations, and instructions," as well as his intimate knowledge of his stepfather's working methods and design.[16] Neither Olmsted styled himself "senior partner" on office letterhead, preferring to emphasize the work of the firm rather than an individual designer. Within a few years of entering the practice, however, Rick Olmsted had become the firm's more visible partner. While he was highly respected

Rick plotting the 39th Parallel through the Rockies, 1894. Courtesy The Papers of Frederick Law Olmsted.

within in the profession, John was a shy man, seemingly content to let Rick assume the firm's public face. And the fact that the younger brother bore the name of the famous father clearly carried weight with some clients.

Early in his career Rick Olmsted was a key participant in two events that signaled both the maturation of the profession of landscape architecture and his own steadily growing prominence within the field: the founding of the American Society of Landscape Architects in 1899 and the inauguration of the first university course in the discipline, at Harvard in 1901.[17] Also in 1901, Olmsted was appointed to the commission assembled by Michigan senator James McMillan to plan for the growth and development of Washington, D.C. The nation's capital had been spared the scars of industrialization that marred the landscape of most metropolitan areas; nevertheless, at the dawn of the twentieth century the city gave Americans little occasion for civic pride. Pierre L'Enfant's 1791 design had conceived of the new federal city on the banks of the Potomac River "as a work of civic art," but much of the substance and the symbolic intent of L'Enfant's plan had been lost over the years, obscured by the accretion of mediocre architecture and haphazard maintenance of public spaces.[18] The city's centennial motivated civic leaders, politicians, architects, and artists to restore L'Enfant's vision.

How better to accomplish this transformation than by reassembling the team responsible for the 1893 Chicago World's Columbian Exposition, which had exposed millions of Americans to a classically inspired urban splendor previously identified with the venerable cities of Europe? And so, at the age of thirty-one, Olmsted stepped into what would have been his father's place, had he been well, and joined the aging deans of the architectural profession, Daniel Burnham and Charles McKim, in producing the country's first comprehensive planning document.[19] With its visionary rhetoric and seductive illustrations of a cityscape graced by classical architecture, statuary, and parks, the widely publicized McMillan plan captured the public imagination and inspired a national enthusiasm for bringing order and beauty to cities and towns across the country.[20]

The younger Olmsted found himself in the vanguard of the new discipline of urban planning.[21] The emergence of a profession of comprehensive planning at the beginning of the twentieth century was a natural progression from the earlier efforts of Olmsted Sr. and others to redress

Model of conditions on the Mall in 1901. Courtesy U.S. Commission of Fine Arts.

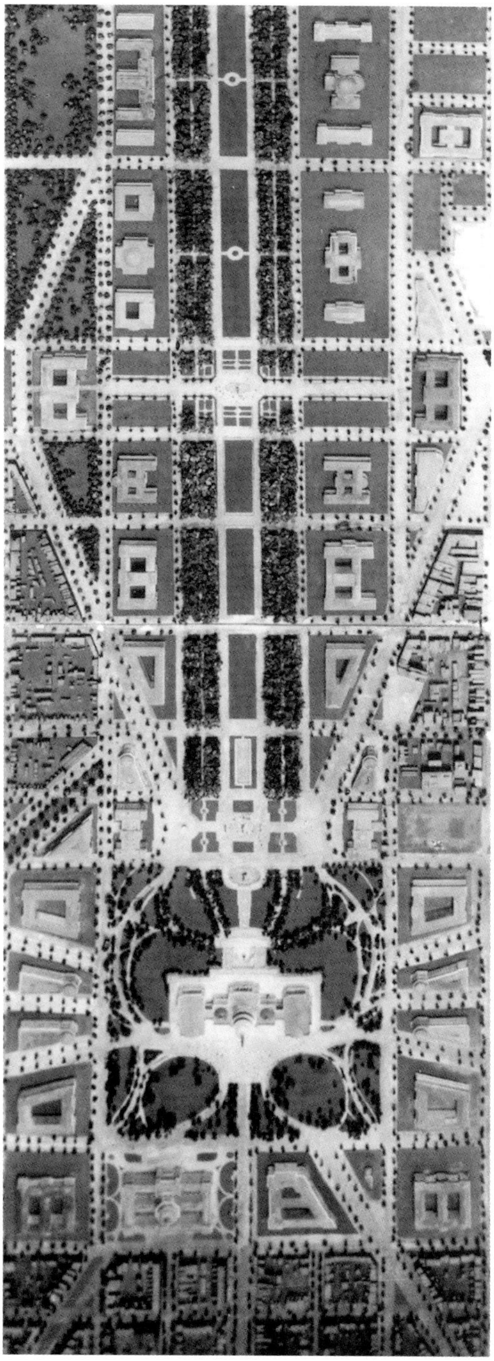

Model of Mall improvements proposed by McMillan Commission. Courtesy U.S. Commission of Fine Arts.

problems resulting from urbanization and industrialization. Olmsted Sr. believed that the designed environment, the consciously planned landscape, could influence civilized behavior. In his plans and writings he envisioned an ideal cityscape, a harmonious assemblage of buildings, civic art, park systems, and parkways that would promote a sense of community and civic responsibility. Equally important, Olmsted Sr. believed that residential suburbs could be designed to support family values and the virtues of domestic life.[22]

Early twentieth-century planners like Olmsted Jr. were less inclined than their nineteenth-century progenitors to see planning as the means of realizing some conception of an ideal city. Although their social philosophy may have been less visionary, their belief in the capacity of planners to shape the growth and development of cities was far more sweeping. These pioneering city planners proclaimed that a new "science of modern city-making" made it possible to address all the major physical needs of the city at once. Born of an era of optimistic faith in the human capacity to control the environment, a faith that was the legacy of visionaries like Olmsted Sr., highly publicized grand schemes such as the 1901 plan for Washington and Burnham's 1909 proposal for transforming Chicago marked a transition from the piecemeal approach of nineteenth-century planning.

But confidence in the largely aesthetic emphasis of these City Beautiful plans—with their focus on civic centers, grand boulevards, and municipal art—quickly gave way to public demand for a more practical, permanent, and institutionalized approach to planning. Even Charles Mulford Robinson, whose writings had helped popularize the City Beautiful movement across the country, agreed that the achievement of "utilitarian and social benefits," rather than the noble adornment of public buildings and parks, must be the paramount goal of planning efforts.[23] No longer could city planning be the province of businessmen, leading members of society, and other well-intentioned volunteers. Population growth, industrialization, and the sheer complexity of modern life demanded that the comprehensive city plan be developed by trained professionals and carried out as a regular function of city government.[24]

Olmsted served as chief spokesman for the planning movement during its formative years.[25] In the decade following the publication of the McMillan plan, Olmsted focused on comprehensive planning, an area in which he believed Americans had much to learn "from the example of progressive European cities." In November 1908 he embarked on a three-month-long study trip of planned communities and company towns in Germany, France, and England. He was eager to learn more about the tools Europeans had developed for "the systematic control of urban development for the greater well-being of the people" and to see firsthand their "radical work in controlling suburban growth." He also looked forward to revisiting "with new ideas" the nineteenth-century English model industrial villages of Port Sunlight and Bournville, and to seeing the "celebrated Garden City [Letchworth]."[26]

It was on this European tour that Olmsted received a letter from Robert de Forest, vice president of the Russell Sage Foundation, asking if he would be interested in undertaking the landscape work in a new venture in suburban development—one that its sponsors hoped would bring the garden city to the United States.

3

"A Suburban Town Built on Business Principles"

THE FOUNDATION'S EXPERIMENT

IT TOOK TWO WEEKS FOR Robert de Forest's letter, forwarded from the Brookline office, to catch up with Olmsted at the Bristol Hotel in Berlin. "If I mistake not," de Forest wrote on 7 December 1908,

> you are interested on the social as well as the aesthetic side of landscape gardening, and this is to ask whether you are, in your judgment, equipped . . . both with knowledge and interest so as to be able to take the part of advising landscape gardener in the following project, which I wish to be at this stage strictly confidential. . . . We are proposing to go into housing on a fairly large scale, in the suburban district of New York. Our plan is not merely to give houses but to lay out these tracts in some way different from the abhorrent rectangular city block, and to make our garden city somewhat attractive by the treatment and planting of our streets, the possibility of little gardens, and possibly some public places. We would like to set an example to the growing suburban districts of New York and other cities of how the thing can be done tastefully and at the same time with due regard for profit.

De Forest already had selected a consulting architect and a real estate expert. Now he wished "to bring someone in on the landscape garden side" to complete the team. "Is this congenial to you?" he asked. "Can you undertake it promptly?"[1]

Olmsted immediately replied that nothing could interest him more.

Commercial buildings at Hampstead Garden Suburb. From Raymond Unwin, Town Planning in Practice *(1909).*

Coincidently, he told de Forest, the chief purpose of his European trip was to meet with German, French, and English planners, architects, and municipal officials and visit some of those countries' fledgling garden cities and model industrial villages. "I am, in my own judgment, equipped . . . with a modicum of knowledge, which I am diligently striving to increase. In fact I know very little about it; but I cannot think of any landscape man in America who knows any more, if as much."[2]

Faced with congestion and overcrowding in urban industrial centers, Europeans were pursuing new ways to provide better housing for workers and enacting legislation to regulate suburban development. Planners and architects drew on the theories of Viennese architect and planner Camillo Sitte, whose treatise *Town Planning* (1889) emphasized the importance of visual effect in city and town planning and drew attention to the design and placement of medieval streets, squares, and buildings. Sitte saw in the organic development of these old settlements not the apparent irrationality but rather an intuitive and artistic approach to city growth. He believed that modern planners could learn from these time-honored planning traditions and principles to fashion urban centers that were functional and aesthetically pleasing and could help to foster community.

Olmsted began his three-month study tour in Germany, where efforts directed toward housing reform, city planning, and regulating land use were the most advanced on the continent. "A city plan in Germany," Olmsted marveled, "included in one unified project not only . . . the layout of street . . . but the whole code of building regulations, health ordinances, police rules, and system of taxation in so far as they have a direct influence upon the physical development of the city."[3]

Continuing through Holland into France, Olmsted's trip culminated in England, home to the other great social and urban theorist of the late nineteenth century, Ebenezer Howard. Howard's concept of a network of comprehensively planned "garden cities" captured the imagination of the founding generation of town planners, initially in England, which was the first country to experience the full impact of the industrial revolution, and then abroad. Howard published his ideas in 1898 in a book called *Tomorrow: A Peaceful Path to Real Reform*. It was reissued in 1902 as *Garden Cities of Tomorrow,* the new title a testament to the rapidity with which the garden city concept was spreading, and to its popular appeal.

Responding to the blight and squalor afflicting England's urban centers, Howard envisioned the development of a cluster of new towns, dispersed throughout the countryside and contained by greenbelts of agricultural land that would both limit their size and form a protective buffer against encroaching sprawl. These garden cities—economically, politically, and socially self-sufficient—would attract residents from overcrowded older urban areas (which could then be redeveloped), thus redistributing the population. The land on which the towns were built would be cooperatively owned, and the appreciated land values resulting from development would accrue to the community (rather than to developers or speculators) and be used for further improvements. When a garden city reached its optimum population of about thirty thousand, expansion would cease; new cities would be started as needed. These

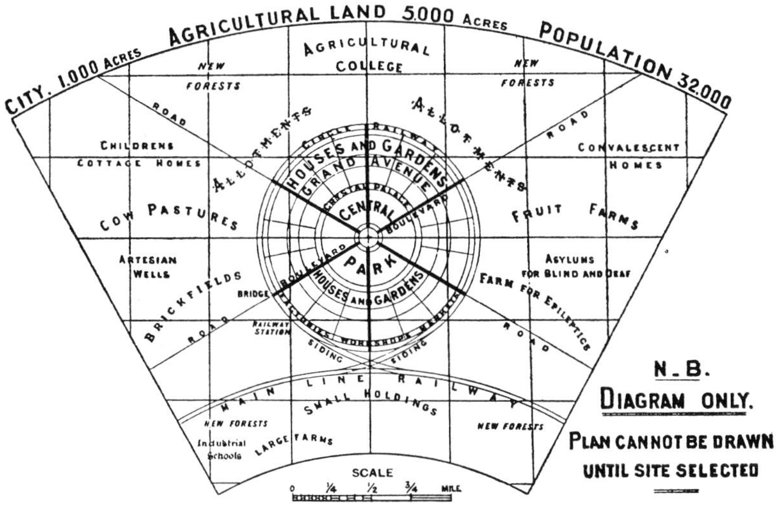

GARDEN CITY AND RURAL BELT

Schematic diagram of the garden city. From Ebenezer Howard, Garden Cities of Tomorrow *(1902).*

Evocation of the old English village. From Unwin's Town Planning in Practice.

communities would be linked to one another and to older city centers by rapid transit.[4] Thus, Howard's treatise offered an approach to managing growth and development that addressed population decentralization, urban renewal, and preservation of farmland and open space.

Howard's unique contribution was in realizing that the problems of urban and rural improvements had to be addressed together. His vision was not anti-urban: the garden city was to be a self-sustaining precinct, not just an enclave of suburban residences. Nor was he harking back to some nostalgic view of agrarian life in the pre-industrial era. Howard believed that the new planned communities would draw residents precisely because they offered the benefits of *both* town and country. The liveliness and stimulation of shops, restaurants, and entertainment venues as well as the social and economic opportunities associated with city life all would be provided in a healthy and attractive landscape setting.

Ironically, as British planning historian F. J. Osborn has observed, although Howard's work "endowed all modern languages with a new term (Garden City, Cité-Jardín, Gartenstadt, Ciudad-jardín, Tuinstad) and though this term was given a most precise meaning by Howard, everywhere it has been used persistently in a sense entirely different from, indeed opposed to, the author's definition."[5] Howard's garden city model was theoretical, not physical. The schematics illustrating his concepts noted that each garden city would be site specific, designed according to the requirements of the land. In fact, Howard was interested in design only as a means to facilitate social and economic change. It was the English architect and planner Raymond Unwin and his architect partner, Barry Parker, who gave the garden city its visual identity.[6] And it was Parker and Unwin's planning concepts and appealing Arts and Crafts aesthetic, not Howard's social and economic theories, that became popular throughout Europe and America.[7]

Howard's garden city looked to the future; it was a new approach to metropolitan development. However, Parker and Unwin's three-dimensional interpretation of Howard's garden city theory was tied to the past, to the physical forms and social relationships of the traditional English

Plan of Hampstead Garden Suburb. From Unwin's Town Planning in Practice.

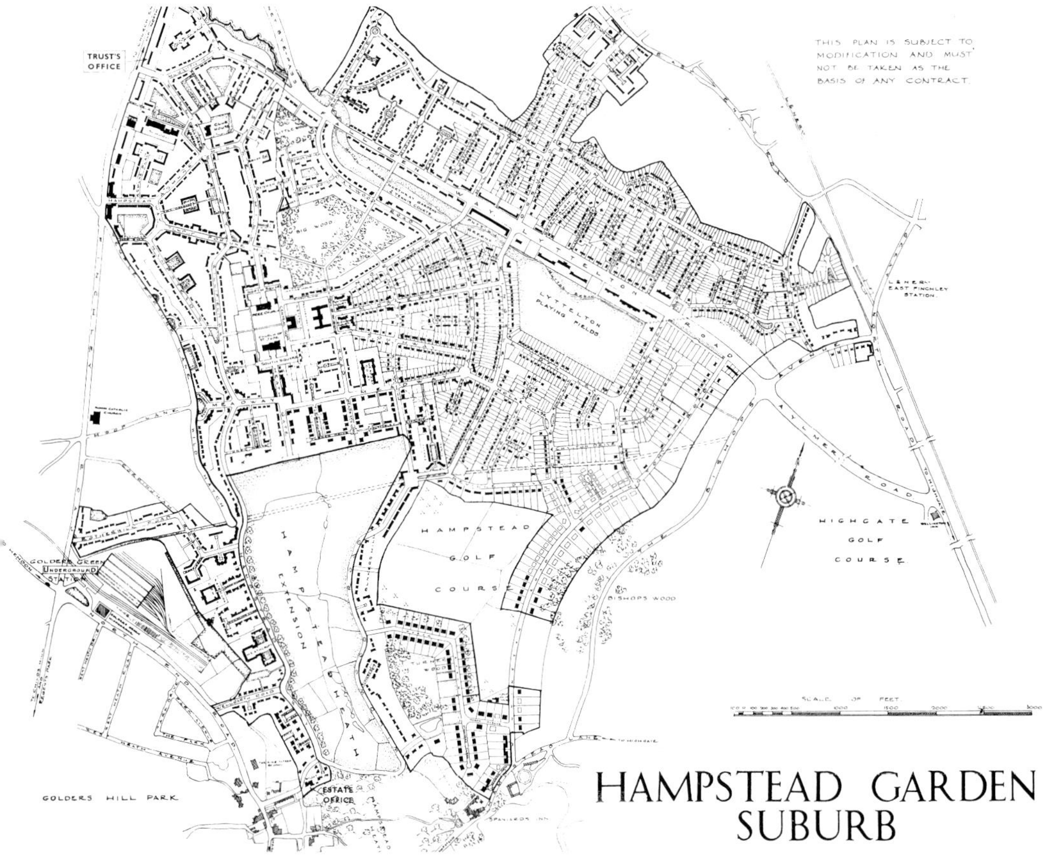

Attached house around a green. From Unwin's Town Planning in Practice.

village. Unwin observed that it was the village's "organized life of mutual relations, respect or service" which gave a feeling "of being an organic whole, the home of a community, to what would otherwise be a mere conglomeration of buildings."[8] The use of local building materials in harmonious, attractive groups of houses, shops, and public buildings and a respect for vernacular building forms and crafts also contributed to this strong connection to place. Thus, Parker and Unwin wedded reformist ideals about worker housing and the new science of comprehensive planning to the communal and architectural heritage of England's past. It was their masterly amalgam of planning, incorporating sophisticated ideas of site design, circulation systems, and housing density, with charming assemblages of architecture and landscape which gained international attention.

De Forest had this image of the garden city—a community of shaded streets, shared parks and village greens, attractive homes, and well-tended private gardens—in mind when he invited Olmsted to join the Sage Foundation's real estate venture. De Forest was a pragmatist and an entrepreneur. He knew that Howard's idea of land held in common, with income deriving from capital improvement returned to and used for the benefit of the community as a whole, was too radical for the United States.[9] Stripped of its political ideology, however, the English garden city could appeal to American private enterprise because it was intended to return a fixed yield on investment. De Forest recognized that an experiment to demonstrate higher standards in community planning and design would have to be an economically sound and profitable venture if it was to have significant impact on suburban real estate development.

Like others of his generation, educated and well-to-do civic leaders and activists who espoused at least some of the diverse social, political, and economic reform initiatives flying under the banner of progressivism, de Forest saw no incongruity in pursuing the public good and private gain simultaneously. "There's money to be had in taste," he concluded in his letter to Olmsted. Fortunately, de Forest, catalyst for the Forest Hills Gardens project, was amply endowed with both.

Robert W. de Forest, a seventh-generation New Yorker, born in 1848 in Greenwich Village and later living on Washington Square, personified the "gentleman-activist" of the Progressive Era. Over the course of an extremely prosperous business career that involved banking, insurance, and legal representation of railroad interests, de Forest assumed a leadership position in every major philanthropic, charitable, and cultural orga-

A street vista. From Unwin's Town Planning in Practice.

nization in the city, earning him the sobriquet "First Citizen of New York."[10]

De Forest had considered becoming an artist like his younger brother, landscape painter Lockwood de Forest (father of the future landscape architect Lockwood de Forest Jr.), but instead had entered the family law firm after receiving degrees from Yale and Columbia. He maintained a lifelong interest in the arts, however, which was reinforced by his "marrying into" the Metropolitan Museum of Art; his engagement to Emily Johnston, daughter of the Metropolitan's first president, John Taylor Johnston, was announced on the day the museum was incorporated in 1870. The de Forests were among the first to appreciate American antiques and decorative arts. Mrs. de Forest was a passionate collector of Tiffany flower-form vases (Louis Comfort Tiffany was de Forest's boyhood friend) and presented the museum with its first American period room in 1910. The couple would later endow the Metropolitan's American Wing.[11] As museum trustee (from 1883) and president (1913–1931), de Forest was particularly interested in the Metropolitan's educational function. He believed that art should be part of daily life and that everyone should have the opportunity to view masterpieces of painting and sculpture. In support of these goals, he also served as president of the American Federation of Arts, which sent traveling exhibitions to small towns and rural communities, and of the New York Municipal Art Committee.

De Forest's other philanthropic activities encompassed the broad range of social problems that an increasingly urban America was beginning to confront. In 1882 he became a founder of the Charity Organization Society of New York, whose purpose was to coordinate the work of various relief agencies in the city; and later served as president of that organization, as well as the New York Welfare Society and the National Conference on Charities and Corrections. De Forest was particularly active in housing reform, asserting that "houses are quite as much needed to make good citizens as to make good men." He chaired the New York State Housing Commission (1900), which established minimum standards for light and ventilation in tenement housing, and was the city's first Tenement Housing Commissioner (1902–1903). Working with one of the most prominent advocates of housing reform, Laurence Veiller, de Forest coedited an influential two-volume work on the subject.[12]

A pioneer in promoting "scientific" charity work, de Forest became a founder of the New York School of Social Work (1898). By the turn of the century, social welfare agencies were intent on "helping the poor to help themselves" through education and by example. Much of the working-class poor population was now composed of immigrants, who crowded into America's deteriorating urban centers. Rather than be given charity outright, it was thought that they needed to learn self-reliance and moral responsibility and be introduced to traditional American values. As the motto adopted by de Forest's Charity Organization Society made clear, the mission was to provide "not alms, but a friend." The city's working poor would be taught and inspired by friendly, albeit paternalistic, helpers.

De Forest's active engagement with the critical problems of the day was shared by many of his class. Inspired by feelings of moral superiority, by a sense of noblesse oblige, and, too, by a genuine concern about the social ills they saw around them, young middle- and upper-class men and women volunteered in their communities.[13] For women in particular, the 1890s were a time when opportunities for higher education began to open. Many women ventured into the civic arena, reasoning that women's "natural" function as homemaker could be extended to include "municipal housekeeping." Just as women worked at home to create the "house beautiful," they could be active in their communities to turn their city into "a Home, clean and beautiful." Across the country women formed groups that addressed local sanitation, health, and housing problems and joined garden clubs, recreation groups, civic improvement societies, and municipal art organizations to cultivate and enhance their own communities.[14]

Many college-educated women were drawn to neighborhood settlement houses, where they lived among the poor, acting as role models and "friendly visitors" to their neighbors.[15] These innovative residential communities were based on the social settlement philosophy that had spread from England (where the first settlement house, Toynbee Hall, had been founded in London's East End in 1884), carrying with it the idea that university students could use the neighborhood as a base for working toward social reform. By actually living in working-class quarters, the residents of the settlement houses could begin to diagnose and overcome some of the problems of urban life. The settlement philosophy differed from (and sometimes came into conflict with) that of traditional charitable organizations. Rather than provide relief from the end products of poverty—destitution, unemployment, disease—the settlements wanted to study and ameliorate their underlying social and economic causes. The idea of living and working in poor urban neighborhoods had tremendous appeal for idealistic American college students of the time, and especially for newly educated young women, many of whom saw

Olivia Sage. From Outlook Magazine, *July 1907. Courtesy Rockefeller Archive Center.*

settlement house work as a way into professional careers. By 1900 there were more than one hundred social settlements in working-class districts across the United States, by 1910 more than four hundred.[16]

Life in social settlements provided the residents with an opportunity to offer more than simple charity, the chance to effect change in the urban social environment itself. This philosophy was shared by de Forest's client Margaret Olivia Slocum Sage, who believed that it was as important to educate and foster independence in the working classes as it was to relieve poverty. Further, she maintained that women, as the morally superior sex, were particularly suited to act as role models for the lower classes. Like other benevolent Victorian ladies, Mrs. Sage regarded the support of missions, hospitals, and schools as women's work, a natural extension of their role as homemaker and helpmeet.[17] Her many charitable interests centered on these accepted areas of women's philanthropy, but she also supported the cause of women's suffrage and patronized civic institutions including the Metropolitan Museum of Art and the American Museum of Natural History in New York, as well as the city's zoo and botanical garden.

The daughter of a successful merchant, Olivia Slocum was born in Syracuse, New York, and, like de Forest, could trace her American ancestors back to the seventeenth century. After graduating from the Troy (New York) Female Academy (later Emma Willard School), she taught for several years at the Chestnut Street Seminary in Philadelphia; the cause of education for women always remained one of her strongest interests. Her future husband, Russell B. Sage, got his start in business in Troy as an employee in his brother's grocery store. He started trading in the stock market at an early age and bought out his brother's business by the time he was twenty-one.[18] Sage moved to New York City in 1863, where he soon became one of the country's wealthiest men. In 1869 Sage, a widower, married Olivia Slocum, aged forty-one, who had been a Troy schoolmate of his first wife. The marriage produced no children.

Sage made his fortune in the railroad, telegraph, and lumber industries and added to it through stock and commodity trading on Wall Street. He became as renowned for his determination to retain money as he was for his ability to make it, and his success in both endeavors was confirmed by an estate approaching $65 million left to his widow at his death in 1906 at the age of ninety. The money passed to Mrs. Sage with no restrictions, and having been largely unable to interest her husband in philanthropy during his lifetime, she devoted the last twelve years of her life to giving away the fortune he had amassed.

Olivia Sage became one of America's preeminent philanthropists, dispensing more than $35 million during the next twelve years and leaving charitable bequests of over $36 million at her death in 1918. This work certainly made her the equal of the Rockefellers, Carnegies, and Morgans, but because she refused to associate her gifts with her own name, because the majority of her giving was concentrated in New York and New England, and probably because as a proper Victorian woman she would have considered publicity unseemly, she never received the public acclaim enjoyed by her male peers.

In the first six months after Russell Sage's death, more than twenty thousand letters asking for money found their way to the Fifth Avenue brownstone opposite Saint Patrick's Cathedral, where his widow tried to cope with the deluge of requests.[19] For advice on structuring her philanthropic endeavors, Mrs. Sage turned to the family lawyer and confidant, Robert de Forest. De Forest canvased academics as well as men active in welfare and social reform for advice on how the Sage millions could be applied "to accomplish the most good." He found consensus that there was a critical need to support research and education about social problems. Accordingly, de Forest proposed the establishment of the Sage Foundation for Social Betterment, which would have a mandate to carry out "research, study, teaching, publication, [establish] necessary agencies and institutions, [and aid] such efforts already existing and such agencies

Bird's-eye view of Forest Hills, Queens, showing proposed development. Courtesy Rockefeller Archive Center.

or institutions already established."[20] Olivia Sage was receptive to de Forest's suggestion that she endow such a foundation to carry out her interest in, as she put it in her letter of gift, "improving the hard conditions of our working classes, making . . . their lives happier; giving more opportunity to them and to their children."[21]

The Russell Sage Foundation was incorporated on 11 April 1907 by an act of the state legislature. The half million dollars in income that was expected to be generated annually from the foundation's ten-million-dollar endowment would be dispensed under the broad mandate of improving social and living conditions in the United States. One-quarter of the money was designated for projects in New York City.[22]

Opening the foundation's first board meeting of the five men and four women trustees with a prayer, Olivia Sage confessed her excitement, exclaiming: "I am nearly eighty years old and I feel as if I were just beginning to live."[23] The new trustees shared her enthusiasm, telling de Forest afterward that they were "exhilarated" and "stunned" by the possibilities of the unprecedented venture.[24] The aging Mrs. Sage attended board meetings infrequently, leaving the management of the foundation to the trustees. It appears that her role in day-to-day operations was slight. De Forest observed that she had her definite views and she made them known; however, her only express request to the trustees was that an office building be designed for the foundation headquarters.[25] The foundation's bold and innovative approach in its beginning years surely came from de Forest and the board of trustees.[26]

The first grants made by the foundation went to prevent tuberculosis and provide education about the disease; to support schools of social work; to support the research and underwrite the publication of six volumes of the Pittsburgh Survey, a landmark study of living and working conditions in that city undertaken in 1906–1907; and to help fund the nationwide playground and supervised recreation movement being organized by the newly formed Playground Association of America. The Forest Hills Gardens project was the first direct work the foundation itself undertook for the improvement of social and living conditions. It was also the foundation's first attempt to achieve a return on its investment. The foundation supplied the capital for the purchase of land and the development of the suburb. It incorporated and financed a separate entity, the Sage Foundation Homes Company, to carry out day-to-day operations.

When Olivia Sage endowed the foundation, the trustees debated whether they should limit their investments of part of the principal to income-producing securities. "I have had some hesitation," Mrs. Sage said, "as to whether the Foundation should be permitted to make investments for social betterment which themselves produce income, as for instance small houses or tenements. . . . I realize [such investments] may not produce a percentage as large as that produced by bonds or like securities, and that the income of the Foundation might be therefore diminished by such investments." Eventually it was agreed that up to one-quarter of the foundation's principal could be invested in a profit-making venture at any one time, "provided that such investments shall, in the opinion of the trustees, be likely to produce an annual income of not less than 3%."[27]

The trustees began to look for a suitable site for development in the rapidly expanding suburban areas of New York City. De Forest's December 1908 letter to Olmsted indicated that the foundation had purchased a tract of about fifty acres in Jamaica, an area in the borough of Queens. A few months later the *New York Times* announced that this purchase had been made by "Mrs. Russell Sage and other capitalists" with the intent to "transform it into a miniature city, teaming with life," modeled after philanthropic housing projects in England. However, the article noted, word of this transaction had "caused values to soar in the neighborhood," so inflating land prices that it "defeated the plan of Mrs. Sage and her associates to buy more property."[28] The search for a larger site continued in the Queens area.

With the consolidation of the boroughs of Manhattan, Brooklyn, the Bronx, Queens, and Staten Island in 1898, New York City became the second largest metropolis in the world; only London boasted a larger population. The borough of Queens was the largest of the five in land mass, yet through the early years of the twentieth century it remained the most sparsely settled, retaining its rural character of cultivated fields, gentle meadows, and woodland tracts.[29] One reason was its isolation from Manhattan. At the beginning of the century, the Brooklyn Bridge (erected in 1883) and the Williamsburg Bridge (built in 1903) were the only links across the river. To reach Queens, Manhattan travelers had to take the ferry, disembarking at the Long Island Rail Road terminal in Long Island City. A New Yorker considering a move to the suburbs then might climb aboard the horse-drawn coach provided at the terminal by the eponymously named Cord Meyer Development Company and take the three-mile journey along a two-lane country road, grandly named Hoffman Boulevard (today's Queens Boulevard), to inspect that company's growing development of Elmhurst.[30]

In 1905 the newly electrified Long Island Rail Road began extending its routes within Queens, and in 1906 Meyer broke ground for a new subdivision, which he named Forest Hills, alluding to Forest Park, a 536-acre public park nearby.[31] The company was planning to erect 6,000 houses on standard 25-by-100-foot rectangular lots laid out on a conventional street grid.[32] A promotional brochure promised "high class residences" in a community whose character would be guaranteed "by the adoption and enforcement of sensible restrictions regarding the class of buildings which can be erected in its limits." The company promised to remain involved with Forest Hills for the fifteen to twenty years it would take to complete the subdivision. "With an inseparable bar to deterioration, furnished by the policy of the Company, Forest Hills' investors will enjoy the full benefit of those many contributory factors in the advancement of values."[33]

Cord Meyer's advertisements were designed to persuade residents of dark, crowded city apartments to consider purchasing one of these suburban houses. The homeowner's investment, the company proclaimed, would be "constantly growing in value for a monthly payment which is no more than the rent of a flat in the city." Recent advances in transportation to the city meant that Forest Hills would become "practically a Manhattan point," only fifteen minutes away. By 1908 commuters could flag down one of three daily Manhattan-bound steam trains from a little wooden station on the Cord Meyer property, and prospective suburbanites could anticipate the opening of the Queensboro Bridge in 1909, which would link Queens to Manhattan at 59th Street.[34]

Because of these new connections to Manhattan and improvements in transportation within Queens itself, residential development was gaining momentum. Throughout the borough, farmland and flower-filled meadows rapidly were being plowed under to accommodate as many as fifty new residential enclaves.[35] By 1909 a Queens resident and nature enthusiast, John H. Hendrickson, was bemoaning the fact that "our beaches and meadows, formerly the home of the plover or meadow hen, are now being occupied for residential purposes at a rate that dazes the lover of nature."[36]

The Russell Sage Foundation was exploring the Queens real estate market during this heated period of speculative development and realized that no site would be had cheaply. In May 1909 the foundation made a deal with Cord Meyer to buy 142 acres adjacent to his Forest Hills property for the remarkable price of $6,000 per acre (well over $100,000 per acre in today's dollars).[37] With the site in hand, the trustees created the Sage Foundation Realty Development Committee to oversee its suburban development experiment; they later incorporated the Sage Foundation Homes Company to be the project's operating arm. Heading both groups was foundation vice president de Forest.

In every public statement regarding the Forest Hills Gardens project, the principals involved, whether from the design or the marketing end, took care to emphasize that the development was conceived as a business proposition. Despite the astronomical cost of the land, the Homes Company intended to realize a profit on its suburban venture and to pay back the Sage Foundation's capitalization loan with interest. The foundation was investing a part of its capital in a suburban land development company to earn "income which it uses in various lines of philanthropic work," Olmsted explained in an article titled "A Suburban Town Built on Business Principles."[38] By proving that it was possible to make money on an attractive suburb, intelligently designed according to the most modern town planning principles, the Sage Foundation believed that Forest Hills Gardens would inspire widespread imitation.

The Forest Hills Gardens experiment, like many undertakings during the Progressive Era, was an exercise in practical idealism. Some scholars, while they acknowledge that there was also a genuine impulse to ameliorate working and living conditions, have argued that business, civic, and political leaders of the time were primarily concerned about the seemingly out of control effects of urbanization and industrialization and the swelling immigrant population that was fueling them. Progressivism was undeniably propelled by the middle and upper classes, who had a vested interest in preserving and promulgating their interpretation of "American values" in the face of unprecedented immigration, and in restoring order to the modern city. By supporting municipal reform and urban planning, many people hoped to regain a social cohesiveness that they saw threatened in an increasingly diverse and class-conscious society, as well as to protect property values and preserve the capitalist ethic. Their emphasis was on improving municipal government, promoting its efficiency and professionalism, and boosting civic pride and community spirit. Progressive activists supported efforts to rationalize and enhance the physical environment and to make changes in the organization of municipal government, but few were interested in examining the core political, social, and economic tenets of American life.[39]

Progressivism and the planning profession grew side by side. The involvement of the nonprofessionals was a distinctive feature of the early years of both, but, as was true in the helping occupations such as social work, specialization and the importance of formal training increasingly prevailed. New jobs such as city manager and municipal planner appeared at the same time that architects and landscape architects were seeking to validate their roles in the planning process. Designers and planners held several common goals: both wanted a larger role in addressing social and political reform; both wanted to widen their area of professional interests; and both wished to confirm their positions as credentialed specialists. If the question of professional legitimacy was still an issue for architects and landscape architects, it was even more crucial for the nascent planning profession. All three professions had to convince the public of the necessity of their special services in redesigning cities and creating new towns. All three advanced their scientific and technological expertise as well as their capacity to take the wider view of problems of urban growth and development.

The aesthetic emphasis—promoting the city as a work of civic art—that was the hallmark of the City Beautiful Era, was superseded within a decade by a new focus on the practical arrangement of the individual elements of the city: streets, public transit, grouping of public buildings, provision of open space and park land, and regulation of activities permitted in different parts of the city—guided by a master planning document. By the second decade of the twentieth century, the role of the design professionals was reduced as lawyers, civil engineers, and municipal officials assumed the lead in urban planning. The City Beautiful approach failed, it was said, because it was too expensive, because in most cases there was no one public authority with enough money and political influence to implement a comprehensive plan, and because the movement had not gotten sufficient backing from the business sector. The new approach to planning championed the "City Practical," the "City Scientific." As planning became more technical and legalistic, many of the social concerns shared by the initially diverse group of professional and amateur reform activists disappeared from the planning agenda.[40]

Like many of the initiatives associated with the Progressive Era, the Sage Foundation's model suburb project was innovative in its planning and design but conservative in its business philosophy. Forest Hills Gardens would showcase modern principles of town planning as well as inventive building technology, but its sponsors did not intend to challenge the standard financial and marketing practices of conventional real estate development. In contrast to the English garden cities and European model industrial housing projects, lots at Forest Hills Gardens would be sold to individuals instead of being held in common; homes would be owned, not rented. As Olmsted conceded, Forest Hills Gardens' creators did not expect "or attempt to do anything revolutionary or epoch-making." Rather, their main objective was to demonstrate that planning and building a modern residential suburb could be "reduced to science in this era of great projects," with the hope of educating the public, as well as developers, about what was possible.[41]

It was clear to all the participants that the undertaking was a business investment, and Forest Hills Gardens was always promoted and marketed as such. Nevertheless, it would prove difficult for the public—and for many in the press—to associate the idea of profit with a philanthropic institution and to absorb the fact that this housing demonstration sponsored by the Sage Foundation would not be for the benefit of "the laboring man, whose wages are small," because the high cost of the land made it impractical. Confusion over the goals and purpose of Forest Hills Gardens would persist.[42]

FOREST HILLS GARDENS was a collaborative effort, a true partnership of architectural, landscape, and real estate professionals, who were known to one another and most of whom had already worked together in a professional context or through their shared interest in progressive causes. To join Olmsted and Atterbury and advise on the business side of the project, de Forest turned to William E. Harmon, a real

Grosvenor Atterbury. From Notable New Yorkers, 1896–1899.

estate developer he had come to know as a cofounder of the National Child Labor Committee. Harmon also was acquainted with Olmsted, sharing his interest in the parks and playground movement, and like him was active in the National Recreation Association. Harmon was a pioneer in marketing suburban developments. He believed that offering "thrifty artisans" the opportunity to own property was important "from the standpoint of social stability." In the 1880s he introduced an installment plan for purchasing property in Cincinnati's first subdivision, offering buyers low down payments and low monthly installments. He popularized the concept of a land sales contract in which the developer (rather than a bank or lender) retained deed to the property until payments were complete. By the early 1900s, his firm, Wood, Harmon and Co.,was promoting itself on its letterhead as the "Developers of over 100 Suburbs in 26 Cities." Harmon brought to the Sage Foundation's venture his expertise in setting prices for lots and homes, establishing terms of sale, and developing restrictive covenants.[43]

De Forest selected his design team on the basis of nearly a decade of social and professional links to Olmsted and Atterbury. The three had much in common. All were born into comfortable circumstances, grew up on the East Coast, attended Ivy League schools, and were well traveled. They held similar views on professional duties and civic responsibilities. They belonged to the same clubs. The Atterburys and the de Forests summered near each other in the Hamptons, on Long Island. All three men participated in the same voluntary groups committed to housing reform and urban betterment. And, most significantly, de Forest had experience in working with both designers: Atterbury was the architect of Robert de Forest's country place, Wawapek Farm, in Cold Spring Harbor; Olmsted had designed gardens for de Forest's brother Henry at his Cold Spring Harbor estate, Nethermuir, and on the adjoining property of their sister Julia.[44]

Born in 1867 in Detroit but reared in New York, Grosvenor Atterbury attended Yale and Columbia University's architectural school, trained in Paris at the Ecole des Beaux-Arts, and started his career with the preeminent firm of the day, McKim, Mead, and White. Like de Forest, Atterbury had a talent for painting, and he spent several summers studying with the American impressionist William Merrit Chase at his Shinnecock Hills Art School. Taking advantage of family connections both in New York City and in the Hamptons, Atterbury made his name on Long Island, building homes for wealthy clients at the start of what has come to be called the Country Place Era, America's golden age for the creation of harmonious assemblages of houses and landscape.

But Atterbury always was more interested in architecture for social purposes than for socialites. He shared de Forest's concern for improving worker housing and was a founding member of the National Housing Association. Atterbury joined other classically trained architects of his generation, including Ernest Flagg and I. N. Phelps Stokes, in asserting that professional architects should apply their expertise to problems of housing production and tenement design (even William Rutherford Mead participated in tenement design competitions). Atterbury, Flagg, and Stokes all served on the New York Tenement Housing Commission. They entered competitions on tenement housing design sponsored by the Charity Organization Society and created prototypes to conform with the provisions of new housing regulations proposed in the wake of de Forest and Veiller's landmark book on the subject. These architects looked beyond individual buildings to consider site planning for entire blocks. Rather than trying to force as many tenements as possible onto a site, the reformers pondered building placement in relation to air circulation, natural lighting, and sanitation. Atterbury designed two innovative housing projects in New York City, the first Phipps Model Tenement (1906) and the Rogers Model Dwellings (1913).[45] He believed that working-class housing should be attractive as well as sanitary and economical, and his plans included areas for gathering and recreation such as reading rooms, roof gardens, and playgrounds. He used the idea of a central courtyard to orient buildings, and children, away from the filthy, crowded streets.

Atterbury spent many years and much of his own money testing new building materials and construction methods. Since 1904 he had been developing innovative techniques for manufacturing prefabricated concrete slabs, with the aim of making it possible to build better quality, permanent worker housing at lower cost by using a limited number of mass-produced structural components. The Sage Foundation began funding this work in 1907 and maintained their support through the 1920s.

Atterbury extended his experiments in working-class housing as consultant on a number of company-sponsored new towns, including Indian Hill in Worcester, Massachusetts, for the Norton Company; Dundalk, Maryland, for Bethlehem Steel; and Mocanaqua, Pennsylvania, for the West End Coal Co.[46] He also became known as a preservation architect, working on the New York City Hall for a number of years (Olivia Sage paid for the restoration of its historic Governor's Room in 1907). In 1919 de Forest engaged Atterbury to plan the American Wing at the Metropolitan Museum of Art; it is the only section of the museum designed by an architect selected by its donor.[47]

Olmsted and Atterbury relished the unique opportunity they were given at Forest Hills Gardens to create a grand harmony "which is possible only where the entire scheme of development is laid out and executed" by a team of cooperating experts.[48] Their similar training and flexibility made for an extraordinarily compatible and inventive partnership.

Both men came to professional maturity at a time when two important design schools held sway: the classical formalism of the City Beautiful movement and the vernacular tradition and hand-craftsmanship that inspired Arts and Crafts architecture and decorative arts. Although expressed in fundamentally different stylistic vocabularies, the two approaches had much in common. They had developed in response to the chaotic, unhealthy, and blighted urban landscape that was an ever-increasing by-product of the Industrial Revolution, and they both embraced the idea that the designed environment could improve the lives of individuals and society as a whole. Both espoused architectural eclecticism, combining historical forms and elements in new ways and for new uses. They each championed the idea of collaboration among artists and design professionals. Both emphasized the interrelationship between building and landscape and the importance of the passage from inside to the outdoors. And, perhaps most crucial, they both espoused the principle that design could be a tool for solving social problems.

The City Beautiful movement produced classically inspired compositions of buildings, art, and landscapes in a celebration of urban culture. Planners, design professionals, and civic leaders believed that it was their responsibility, indeed their duty, to bring their taste and moral vision to the task of manipulating the physical fabric of the urban landscape for the public good. Many of the architects and artists associated with City Beautiful projects had studied in Paris at the Ecole des Beaux-Arts. The technical expertise and historically based design eclecticism they learned there were ideally suited to the lofty vision of making America's cities worthy of an emerging world power.[49]

Arts and Crafts adherents, in contrast, looked to everyday life rather than ancient imperial splendor to inform architecture and the decorative and fine arts. The family home and appropriate furnishings were celebrated here. Like the proponents of the City Beautiful, the supporters of the Arts and Crafts movement were reformers, steeped in the social and aesthetic doctrines of John Ruskin and William Morris. Ruskin and Morris wanted to restore the dignity of labor, strip away Victorian artifice and excess in arts and architecture, and wed the beautiful with the useful in design. In England, Scotland, and throughout Europe, architects and designers sought to preserve and rejuvenate the old ways while taking advantage of modern advances in planning and technology.[50]

The Arts and Crafts ambience is most immediately apparent at Forest Hills Gardens, but adaptations of City Beautiful formality in planning can also be discerned. Yet it was not a particular theory or style that most influenced Olmsted and Atterbury. Rather, they were guided by a principle common to both design movements: namely, that there be a

Frontispiece by Walter Crane. From Howard's Garden Cities of Tomorrow.

clear, central, controlling idea underlying every project. Details, whether in architectural features or landscape setting, should contribute to the design's overall intended effect.

Progressive Era politics, garden city planning principles, and Arts and Craft design were widely embraced internationally at the turn of the twentieth century, but in the wake of World War I all three movements lost energy and soon fell from favor. These concepts were templates, abstractions interpreted by politicians and citizen activists, architects and designers to reflect ideas and concerns specific to their own country. In the United States, this meant progressive reform politics stripped of European socialism, garden city planning divorced from Howard's social and economic theories, and Arts and Crafts design that accepted the technological and economic advantages of the machine. In short, reformist politics, planning, and design adapted to American democratic and capitalist traditions.

Forest Hills Gardens was conceived in a time when hopes for political, social, and artistic reform ran high, and it was hailed as an emblem of that hope. The inspired design partnership of Olmsted and Atterbury created an environment so different from "the rigid, monotonous effect of the typical American suburb" that charmed contemporary visitors wondered whether they had not been "transported by magic to some romantic realm of another country. . . . For it is not like America."[51]

4

"The Thoroughness with Which Things Are Done Here"

PLANNING AND CONSTRUCTION

SOMETIMES A PARTICULAR year stands out as a benchmark for an era. Nineteen-nine was such a milepost in American planning history. That year the aging Daniel Burnham, still working on a grand scale, presented his comprehensive plan for the Chicago metropolitan region. A model of beauty, harmony, and order, it was the last of the classic City Beautiful schemes. For by the second decade of the twentieth century, the emphasis in the planning movement had shifted from urban design to urban management. Laws and administrative policies, rather than physical design, took precedence, as city planning began to be institutionalized both as a professional discipline and as a function of municipal government.[1]

Other events of 1909 were harbingers of this change. Raymond Unwin published his monumental *Town Planning in Practice: An Introduction to the Art and Design of Cities and Suburbs*. This influential volume successfully bridged the two phases of the city planning movement, combining a narrative sensitive to the importance of beauty and design with practical detail and technical information. The New York social activist Benjamin Marsh summarized current advances in city planning in both Europe and the United States in his *Introduction to City Planning: Democracy's Challenge to the American City*, a book that proclaimed that "a city without a plan is like a ship without a rudder." *American City*, a journal covering municipal improvement projects and other urban developments around the country, made its debut. In the legal arena, the Supreme Court affirmed the right of communities to

Construction under way in 1910. Courtesy Forest Hills Gardens Corporation.

restrict building height and to zone property for specific use. Wisconsin became the first state to grant municipalities the right to establish city planning commissions as official, continuing entities, backed by political authority. In Los Angeles a land-use zone ordinance was applied for the first time to undeveloped land.

In May of 1909 the first National Conference on City Planning and the Problems of Congestion, which chose Olmsted as its president, convened in Washington, D.C. It brought together social reformers, design professionals, and representatives of many civic and philanthropic organizations, all of whom were excited by the possibilities that comprehensive planning presented for remaking the American city. These activists, community leaders, and planners believed that the expertise and technology that had created the modern city, with all its attendant ills and inconveniences, could be harnessed and rechanneled to achieve "perfect efficiency" in running the new metropolis.

Finally, in November 1909 *Architectural Record* reported that Harvard would be offering the first university course in city planning, to be taught by Frederick Law Olmsted Jr. and James Sturgis Pray. Expressing the confidence of the era, the course prospectus stated that students would consider the "modern city as a living organism, the perfect efficiency of which demands attention to the best service of many separate functions."[2]

THE DESIRE TO SHAPE well-ordered, functional communities was not new. Colonial towns had been laid out with forethought, mirroring religious ideals, legal traditions, and town planning features that dated from the Renaissance. Spanish explorers arriving in the Americas in the mid-sixteenth century established settlements that, although were often differentiated as military, civil, or religious settlements, shared the spatial organizing features of a central plaza and grid system of streets and rectangular plots of land. In the next century, newly established towns in New England used a similar block system to address both religious and civil requirements for land distribution. For instance, in 1641 the Puritan planners of New Haven located their meetinghouse on the central green of their nine-square-block town: God's house would be at the heart of their community, just as God was central to their lives. In contrast, in laying out Quaker Philadelphia in 1682, William Penn made secular public buildings for commerce, politics, and education the focal point of his plan, arranging them around a central town square. Plans for fledgling state capitals such as Annapolis and Williamsburg appropriated old world symbols of power and civic pride for the new American democracy, including central circles with radiating diagonal streets and formal axes terminated by public monuments and buildings.[3]

The town centers of colonial America were physical representations of the colonists' views about the nature of society and the positive role that a planned environment could play in community life. But as settlement pushed westward, social and religious theories about town planning gave way to practical necessity for managing rapid change and development. Most American communities founded during the period of western expansion were laid out pragmatically, according to the monotonous but easily replicated grid plan (which was also most spectacularly applied in 1811 to guide the extension of New York City).

In the nineteenth century, the American dream of domestic happiness began to take on a suburban image. Frederick Law Olmsted Sr. was among the first to recognize the importance that suburban communities would assume in the United States. "No great town can long exist without great suburbs," he wrote in 1868. The "strong tendency of people to flock together in great towns," he noted, had been one stage in civilization's march of progress. The next was the growing desire for neighborhoods that combined the "special charms and substantial advantages of rural conditions" with urban conveniences. Olmsted Sr. believed that these new suburbs, if well planned, would prove "the most refined and the most soundly wholesome forms of domestic life, and the best application of the arts of civilization to which mankind has yet attained."[4]

Pre–Civil War suburbs generally evolved by an informal process, following advances in transportation, and were the products of individual developers and builders. Architecturally, the "romantic cottage" or suburban villa was the popular residential choice. As cities grew and the urban environment deteriorated, the suburb became a place of refuge from the world of work, and the home was glorified as a domestic sanctuary. By the 1850s the idea of the romantic suburb began to be expressed in a more formal way. In Glendale, Ohio (1851), considered by some the first suburb to incorporate curvilinear streets in a plan, houses were set amid flowing lawns. In 1855 the developer Llewellyn Haskell offered "country homes for city people," in Llewellyn Park, New Jersey, thirteen miles from New York City. Here the architect Alexander Jackson Davis also used a curvilinear plan to situate picturesque suburban villas on large lots bordering on a fifty-acre communal park.

In 1869 Olmsted Sr. moved beyond Davis's romantic idea of the country villa set within an isolated park. His comprehensive plan for Riverside, a 1,600-acre suburb of Chicago, offered the advantages of town life in a scenic setting. He laid out curving roads to subtly foster a feeling of "leisure, contemplativeness and happy tranquility" as residents moved through the community. These tree-lined streets delineated elongated residential blocks, creating an appealing but very tightly organized landscape. Olmsted's plan treated private gardens and public open spaces, and the transitions between them, as equally important. While respecting the importance of family privacy, Olmsted believed that design could contribute to a sense of community and facilitate interaction among neighbors by providing informal parks and playgrounds, as well as areas for strolling, boating, skating, and other recreational activities. Although there was already a railroad station on the Riverside property, Olmsted Sr.'s plan called for a parkway (never built) to link the suburb to the city center, a pleasure drive that would afford the businessman "an opportunity incidentally to his necessary communication with his store or office" to enjoy "air and exercise in driving, riding, and walking."[5] Incorporating a novel feature from the Olmsted and Vaux plan for New York's Central Park, Riverside's approach road

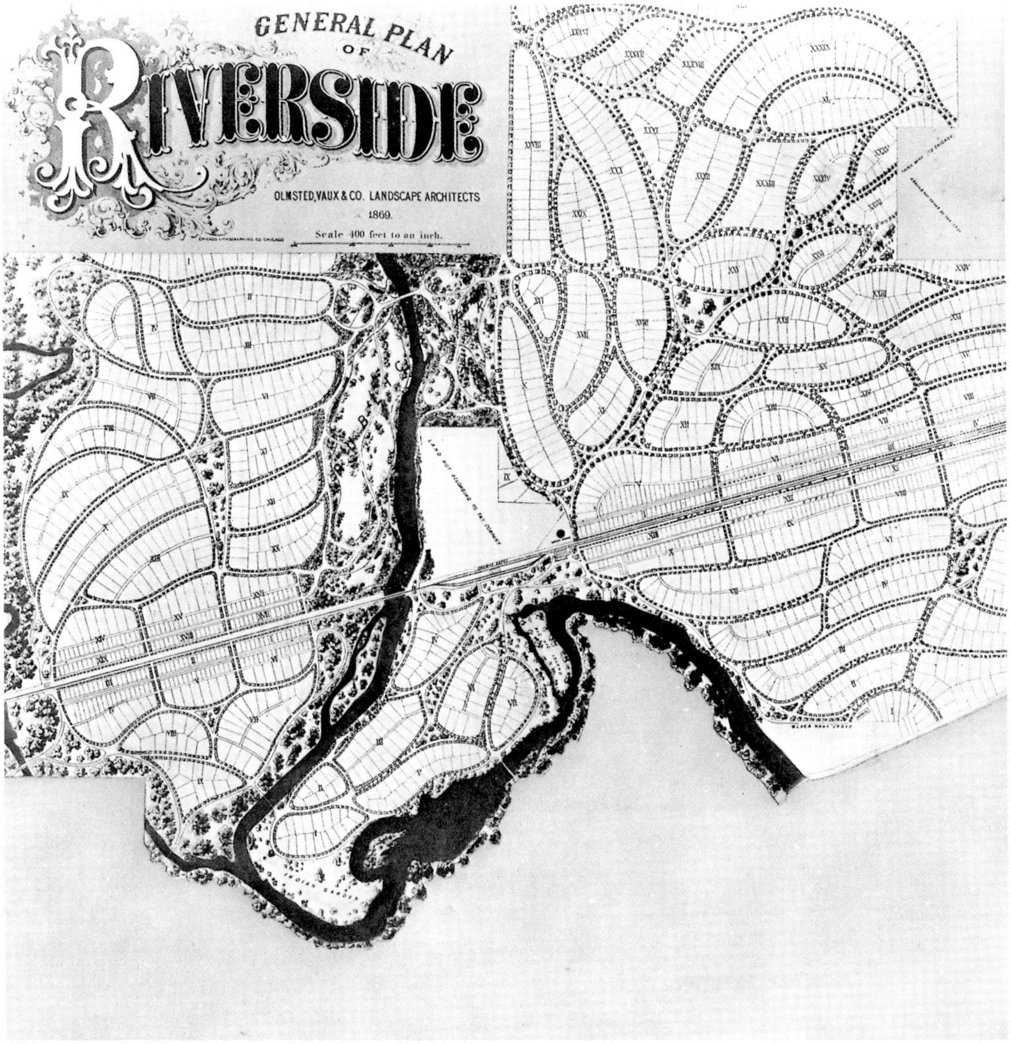

Olmsted Sr.'s plan for Riverside, Illinois, 1869. Courtesy Fairsted.

would have provided separate but adjoining lanes for each activity.

Olmsted's Riverside was designed for the middle class. But that same year Alexander T. Stewart, who made his fortune in his Manhattan department store, envisioned a model village suitable for a wider range of income levels on a 7,000-acre site on Long Island. Based on the gridiron plan, the community, which he called Garden City, featured lush landscaping and included both large homes to attract the city's affluent and rental housing that would be affordable to commuting clerks and shopkeepers. By the latter half of the nineteenth century the suburban ideal was affecting even model working-class housing in the development of planned industrial villages. An idea rooted in the early nineteenth century in towns such as Lowell, Massachusetts, the planned village was an improvement over the typical factory town, although the owner-developer often took advantage of the provision of housing and other community features to extend company control to the workers' private lives. Pullman, Illinois (1880), perhaps the best known of these industrial villages, marked the first collaboration between an architect and a landscape architect in executing a complete town.[6]

Like his father, Olmsted saw the growing suburban migration of the early twentieth century not as an anti-urban reaction but rather as a complementary and inevitable aspect of urban growth. Both Olmsteds presciently recognized that overcrowding and unplanned growth, which had taken its toll on America's cities, would spread to the suburbs as well, unless measures were taken to guide and control their development. Suburbs were "coming into existence almost daily on the outskirts of our growing cities," Olmsted Jr. saw, and they required the kind of professional planning until then seen only in city design and large-scale landscapes such as Central Park.[7] It was crucial, he and others maintained, to apply the new science of city planning to the suburban additions.

THE FIRST MEETING of the executive committee of the Sage Foundation Realty Development Committee—Olmsted, Atterbury, Harmon, and de Forest—was held on 29 April 1909 in Harmon's office on Lower Broadway and continued into the evening at de Forest's townhouse, where they were joined by foundation director John Glenn. Ten days later the group toured suburban developments in Brooklyn, including the resort communities that had grown up around Coney Island's seaside hotels in the 1880s and 1890s.[8]

On 20 May, Olmsted and Atterbury dined at the Century Association, the exclusive city club that was, in the words of the intellectual historian Thomas Bender, "a sanctuary for the city's artistic, political, and economic elite."[9] There the two roughed out the general architectural treatment and site layout of Forest Hills Gardens. They also discussed various housing types—attached, freestanding, and apartments—and the relative number of each to be included in the total housing mix. A site for a school was also approved; they would offer it rent-free to the city for a period of three years, with an option to buy. Only one week later, Olmsted was ready to present a preliminary street plan to the development committee.

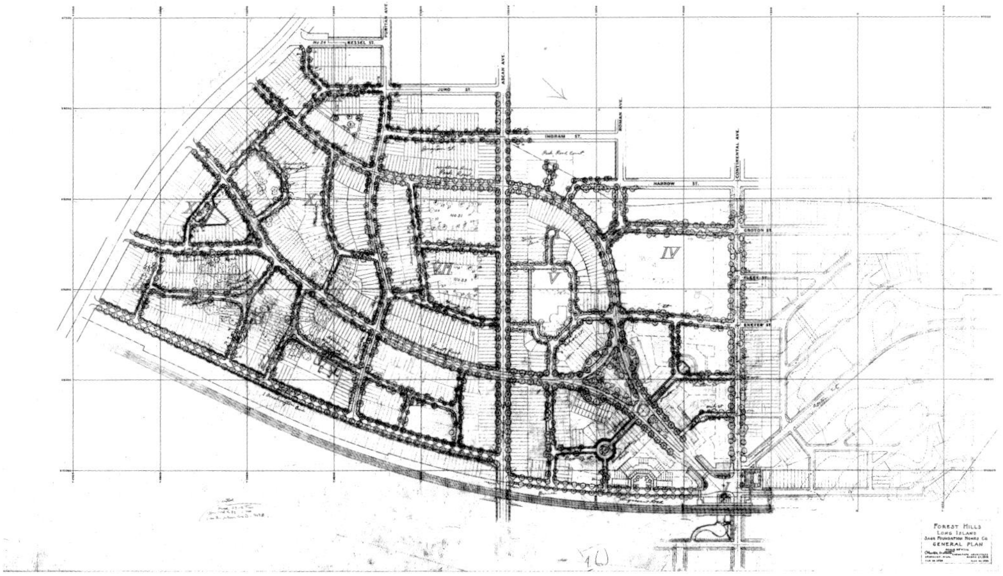

Forest Hills Gardens, preliminary street plan, 1910. Courtesy Fairsted.

The development committee met on 4 June to continue the discussion on the size and shape of house lots, using Olmsted's preliminary street plan as a guide. Olmsted and Atterbury worked late into the evening at the architect's townhouse on East 62nd Street, refining the site plan and architectural approach. They designated sites for special-use buildings, with offices, a public hall, a casino, a church, a library, and a club.[10]

Olmsted returned to Brookline and continued to experiment with the street plan. Since they were unfettered by topographical constraints or existing development, he suggested in a letter to Atterbury that they attempt "something rather strikingly different in kind as well as quality." The curvilinear roads of the nineteenth-century romantic suburb popularized by his father at Riverside were one possibility. But even more interesting, Olmsted thought, would be a free-form street design, "the kind of accidental plan which has generally resulted from unpremeditated city growth, combining straight streets with subtle deflections, bends and variations in width." This idea was directly inspired by his recent European trip, during which he had been much taken with what he described as the "picturesque irregularity based upon medieval examples." It would be difficult to do this convincingly, Olmsted acknowledged, but the results "could be charming."[11]

Atterbury diplomatically replied that either approach would be a "tour de force" that would no doubt succeed (and escape the danger of

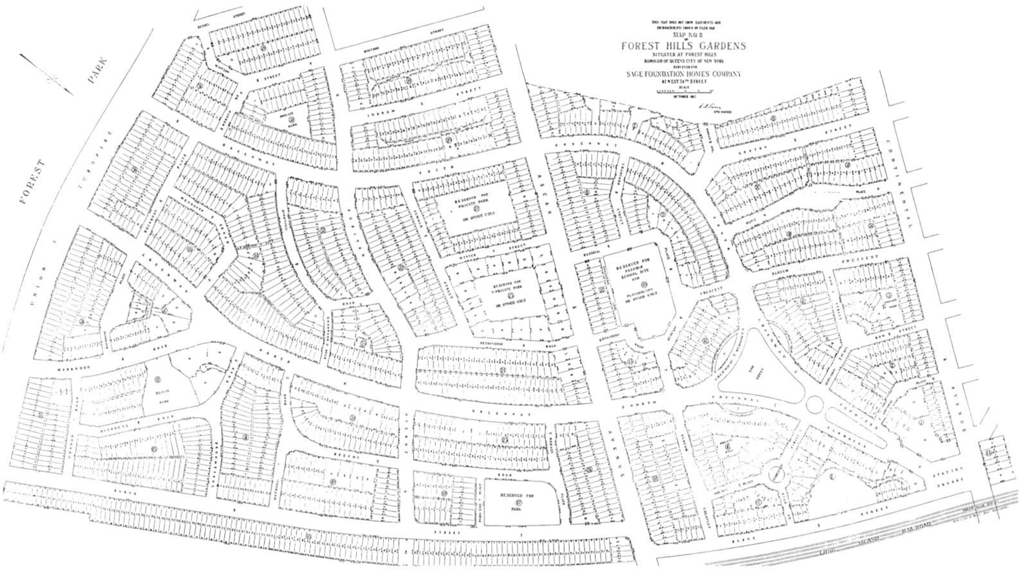

General plan of Forest Hills Gardens (map no. 2, October 1912). Courtesy Fairsted.

being criticized as an affectation) under Olmsted's skillful direction. But, the architect continued, "in as much as our work is primarily an educational one, I think it would be a very bad example to set to the public." Atterbury preferred "something distinctly reasonable and straightforward, relying upon the detail treatment and architectural effects for the variety and picturesqueness which we want to give to the development." He suggested a sequence of spaces, beginning with a rather formal geometric entrance, "a slightly less, but still distinctly practical and reasonable layout of the next zone adjoining, in which I take it the 'civic center' or 'mall' so called would lie, and a frankly curvilinear treatment in the remoter section where we are placing detached houses only and where such treatment would be largely suggested by the present irregular topography." He agreed with Olmsted that it would be "perfectly possible" to introduce some variety and artistry into the plan by incorporating "such features as you find in some of the foreign model towns, in the shape of circles, terraces and groups of houses" in that part of the development between the entry composition of buildings and "the absolutely informal domestic section devoted to detached houses only." Atterbury was confident that, even though there was nothing particularly novel in this solution, they should "be able to produce very different effects from what would ordinarily be expected and ordinarily result from such a general layout in this country today."[12]

Olmsted acquiesced and proceeded to finalize the street plan and arrangement of housing blocks along these lines.

At the 17 June meeting of the Realty Development Committee the Forest Hills Gardens project was officially funded with $1.5 million from the Sage Foundation. The goal was to initiate "a form, or forms, of development, which will set a standard for the production of more attractive, economic and sanitary suburban development. It will not only be the expectation of the Executive Committee to pay interest [to the foundation] at a reasonable rate on the entire investment, but to make profits."[13] Thus the foundation reaffirmed that the Forest Hills Gardens project was to be as much a demonstration in the economics of suburban development as it was in community design and building techniques.

In a letter to Olmsted summing up his own thoughts at the end of the first month of planning discussions, however, de Forest reiterated his own belief that "aesthetic success is quite as important as more commercial success." It would require, he acknowledged, "doing something a little different and involves the risk of perhaps not attracting would-be purchasers as the result of this difference." But, he stated, he was "quite ready to chance it." If it meant the adoption of unfamiliar or unpopular types of development, such as shallower and wider building lots than the standard 25 by 100 feet, then "let us teach people to like them and

Plan and elevation, Group II. From Architecture, *August 1916. Courtesy Rockefeller Archive Center.*

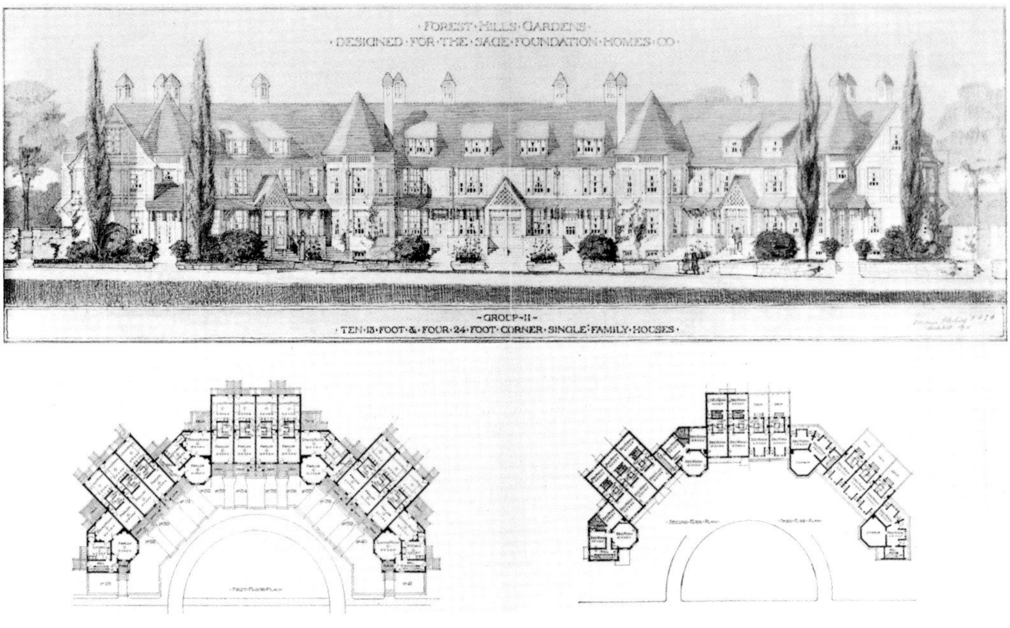

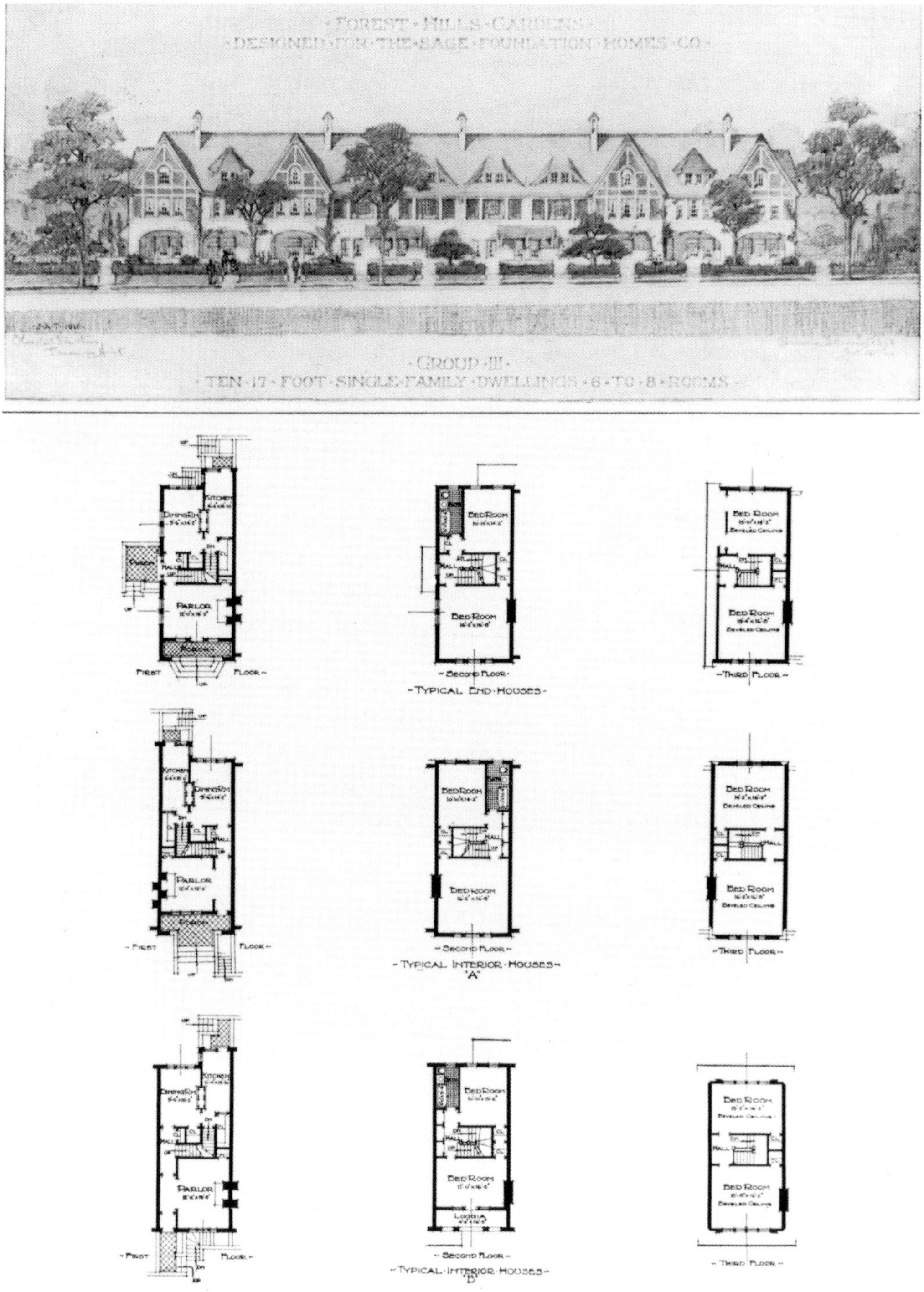

Plan and elevation, Group III. From Forest Hills Gardens, *1912.*
Courtesy Rockefeller Archive Center.

take some risk in doing so." De Forest also voiced his commitment to devoting a substantial amount of land to parks and playgrounds, even recognizing that in so doing "we decrease the amount of land we have for sale and decrease our profits from that point of view." He was convinced, however, that the loss would be made up in the enhanced value of the adjacent building lots.[14]

By July 1909 the executive committee was deciding on the types and cost of houses that the Sage Homes Company would build in the first stage of development. The least expensive house, with 5 or 6 rooms, would be offered at $3,000. It could be rented for $25 a month, which would be affordable to a worker making $1,000 to $1,200 a year. At the other end of the scale would be a three-story single-family home of 13 to 15 rooms, not to exceed $8,000 in construction cost. At a rent of $50 a month, it would be accessible to workers making $2,500 to $3,000 a year. The following week, however, Olmsted presented his cost estimates for the whole development project, which raised doubts that houses could be offered at those rates. The first phase of development was projected at $1,391,000, a figure that assumed a site plan yielding 1,670 building lots (of approximately 2,000 square feet), with the net cost per developed lot thus estimated at $836.[15]

Based on Olmsted's numbers, the development committee determined that it would not be possible to build a 5- or 6-room house for $3,000, given the purchase price of the property, the estimated construction and improvement costs, and "the class of tenants desired." They tentatively decided to build 74 units (either freestanding or semidetached) of 4 to 5 rooms with bath which would sell for $3,000; 114 units with 6 to 8 rooms and bath to sell for $4,000; and 59 units with 9 to 11 rooms and 2 baths selling for $8,000.[16] Harmon, the real estate expert, recommended increasing the price of the upper-level housing and substituting commercial real estate for residential housing on lots adjoining the entrance plaza, opposite the anticipated LIRR station. He also suggested building a three- or four-story apartment building at the head of the village green just inside the entrance to the community.[17]

With the initial planning well under way, Harmon continued to search for a general manager for the project. Olmsted arranged for Edward Bouton, general manager of the elite Roland Park suburb in Baltimore, to join the group for lunch at the 22 July meeting of the executive committee at the Hardware Club (a social club formed in the 1890s for members of the hardware and related trades) opposite City Hall in lower Manhattan.

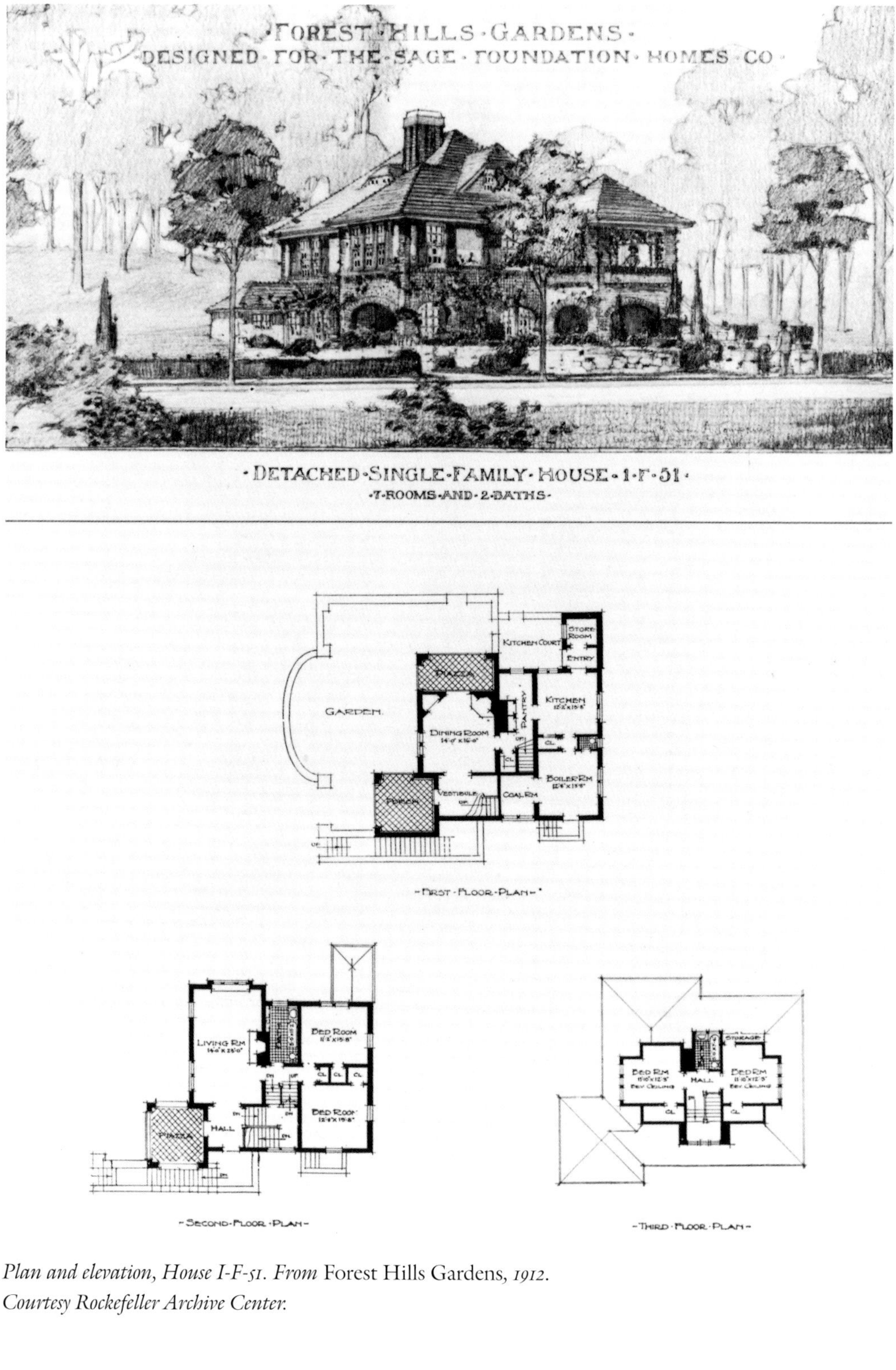

Plan and elevation, House I-F-51. From Forest Hills Gardens, *1912. Courtesy Rockefeller Archive Center.*

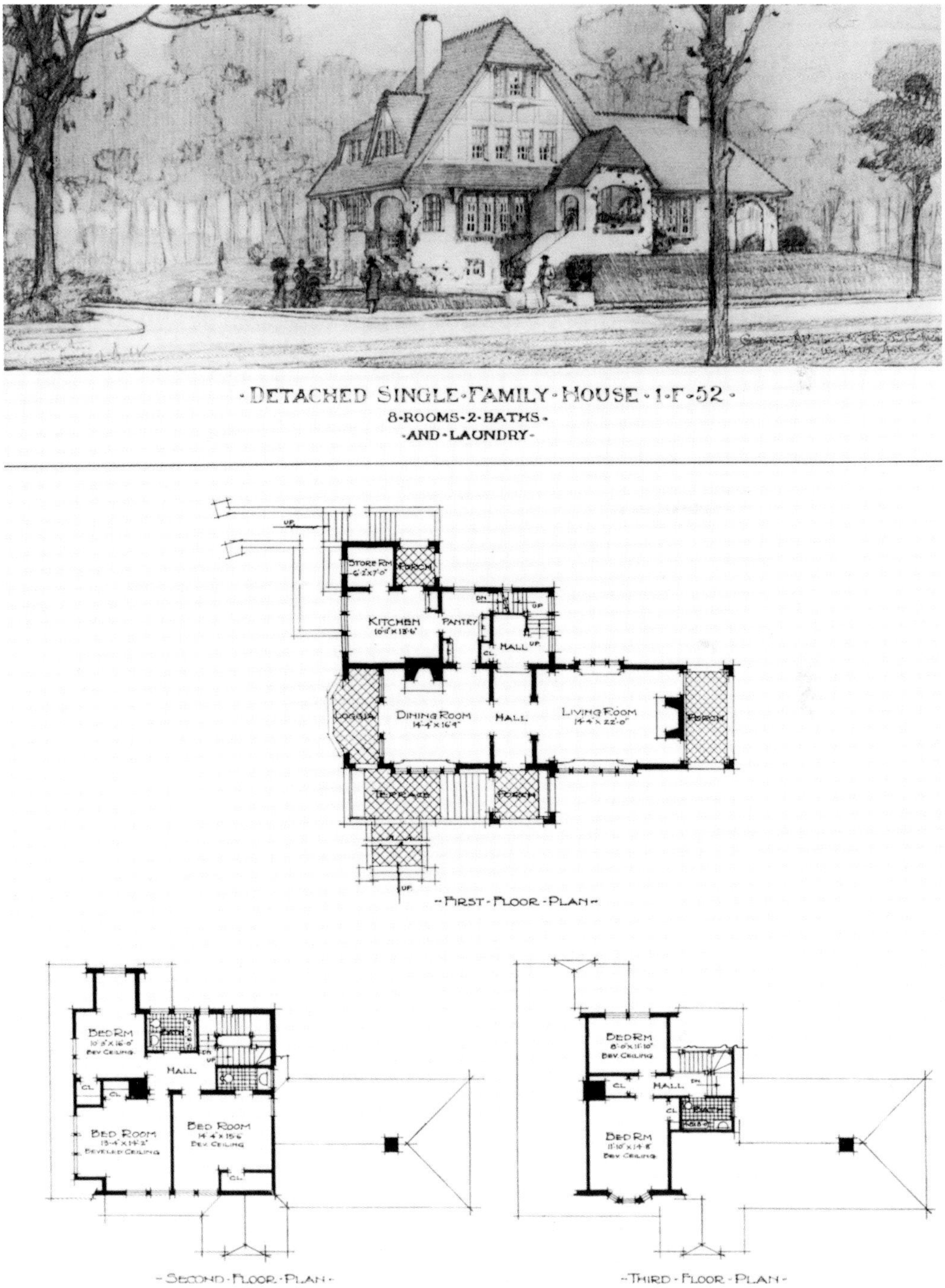

Plan and elevation, House I-F-52. From Forest Hills Gardens, *1912. Courtesy Rockefeller Archive Center.*

Edward Bouton (1858–1941) had come to Baltimore from his native Kansas City, Missouri, where he had been a subdivision developer, to promote the Roland Park tract. There he had instituted a number of practices that would become standard in upscale suburban developments in the United States. Bouton was among the first to incorporate land use restrictions within each individual property deed, thereby tying restrictive covenants to the land itself. He also established the idea of creating a separate maintenance corporation (to which residents would pay an annual assessment), controlled initially by the development company and eventually by the property owners, to ensure that the integrity of the development would be maintained over time. And he set up an architectural review board to approve building plans at Roland Park, thereby perpetuating aesthetic standards.[18] Bouton became known as the dean of American real estate developers, admired for "his exceptional integrity, gifted with artistic judgment, vision, respect for demonstrated competence and a strong interest in the well-being of his fellowman."[19]

In turning to Bouton for the position of general manager, the planning team once again selected someone well known to one or more of them. Olmsted knew him best, for the Olmsted firm and Bouton had been working together since 1897 on expanding Roland Park.[20] Olmsted expressed his high regard for the developer's "good taste and intelligent unremitting perseverance" and deemed him "one of the most satisfactory clients we have ever had, with an excellent appreciation of good work along all lines and a good judgement of artistic as well as business methods."[21] Bouton was hired at a salary of $10,000 a year, with the understanding that he would be spending most of his time in Baltimore, where Roland Park still demanded his attention. In October the executive committee would travel onboard a private railroad car to Baltimore to tour Roland Park.

In one of the last meetings of that busy summer the executive committee agreed that the name of the new development should include the words "Forest Hills" and be called something like Forest Hills Village or the Town of Forest Hills. (The name Forest Hills Gardens was approved formally the following March.) They also decided to begin improvements to the property in advance of the city's approval of the street layout, informing the authorities of their intentions. Anticipating that Olmsted and Atterbury would finalize their plans by early fall of 1909, the committee tentatively set a goal of having the property ready for the public sale of housing lots by the spring of 1911.[22]

Proposed Long Island Rail Road Station, 1910. Courtesy Rockefeller Archive Center.

Only the issue of the railroad station remained to be settled before the general plan could be completed. Olmsted and Atterbury viewed the station as a critical part of the overall plan. The building would set the architectural tone for the whole development, and so it deserved an appropriately detailed design. Moreover, Olmsted believed, this would be no mere suburban commuter station, but "an important gateway for the people of the city to a great park."[23] Since it was expected that most residents would be employed in the city, ease and speed of transit to and from Manhattan were to be major marketing themes as well.

The Sage Foundation agreed to contribute up to $5,000 for the station's construction if the LIRR would invest an equal amount. But LIRR president Ralph Peters balked at the cost, which soon escalated to an estimated $25,000 to $30,000. He protested that the railroad could not support "such extravagant structures," which would not only be too expensive in terms of operation and maintenance but also create unreasonable expectations of what the railroad would provide to subsequent developments.[24] It was finally agreed that the Sage Foundation, the LIRR, and the Cord Meyer Company would share in the cost equally. Olmsted returned to Brookline to prepare the detailed site plan, while in New York Atterbury worked out architectural designs for the ten housing groups that would be built during the first phase of development.

Olmsted's plan for Forest Hills Gardens was both a culmination and a beginning, wedding his father's principles of suburban design to twentieth-century expertise and technology. It furthered an evolution from the romantic conception of a suburban villa set in a park to a more modest and practical domestic enclave suited to the modern scientific era.[25] Soon after Forest Hills Gardens opened for public sale, *American Architect* hailed the suburb as "perhaps the first example in America where a barren site has been treated along the lines of modern methods of Town Planning." "It is the plan that naturally first invites attention," wrote another journalist. At Forest Hills Gardens, he marveled, "there is nothing haphazard. It is thoughtfully studied."[26]

The street plan, according to Olmsted, was "the foundation of all city planning."[27] In older urban areas planners were now attempting to revise street systems to make cities more efficient, convenient, and more beautiful. Olmsted maintained that the same care should be taken in creating new street systems for suburbs. The flat farmland site of Forest Hills Gardens presented few features or limitations, but Olmsted was faced with two existing constraints. Although the borough of Queens had not yet been incorporated into New York City's street plan, by 1909 the city had prepared tentative street maps for areas where development was expected, and a prudent developer had to take these plans into consideration.[28] Olmsted also had to incorporate two roads that Cord Meyer had laid out while he still owned the property (Ascan and Continental Avenues) because the Sage Foundation had agreed to keep them open to general traffic as part of its sales contract with Meyer. These straight, parallel roads (at eighty feet, they would be the widest streets in the suburb), Olmsted explained, "were fixed by the location of bridges under the railroad and in accordance with New York City's tentative street plan covering adjacent territory."[29]

Within these parameters, Olmsted devised a hierarchical circulation system. The north and south Greenways were laid out as the main arteries for internal traffic. These two avenues (one seventy feet and the other sixty feet wide) radiated from Station Square on direct but gently curving lines. Two other avenues, both sixty feet wide, were designed to carry through-traffic: Burns, paralleling the railroad tracks, and Puritan, curving through the rear of the property. Olmsted laid them out to connect with the adjacent street grid proposed by the city's tentative plan.

Neighborhood streets were narrower, averaging about forty feet, both to discourage through-traffic and, Olmsted commented, to permit

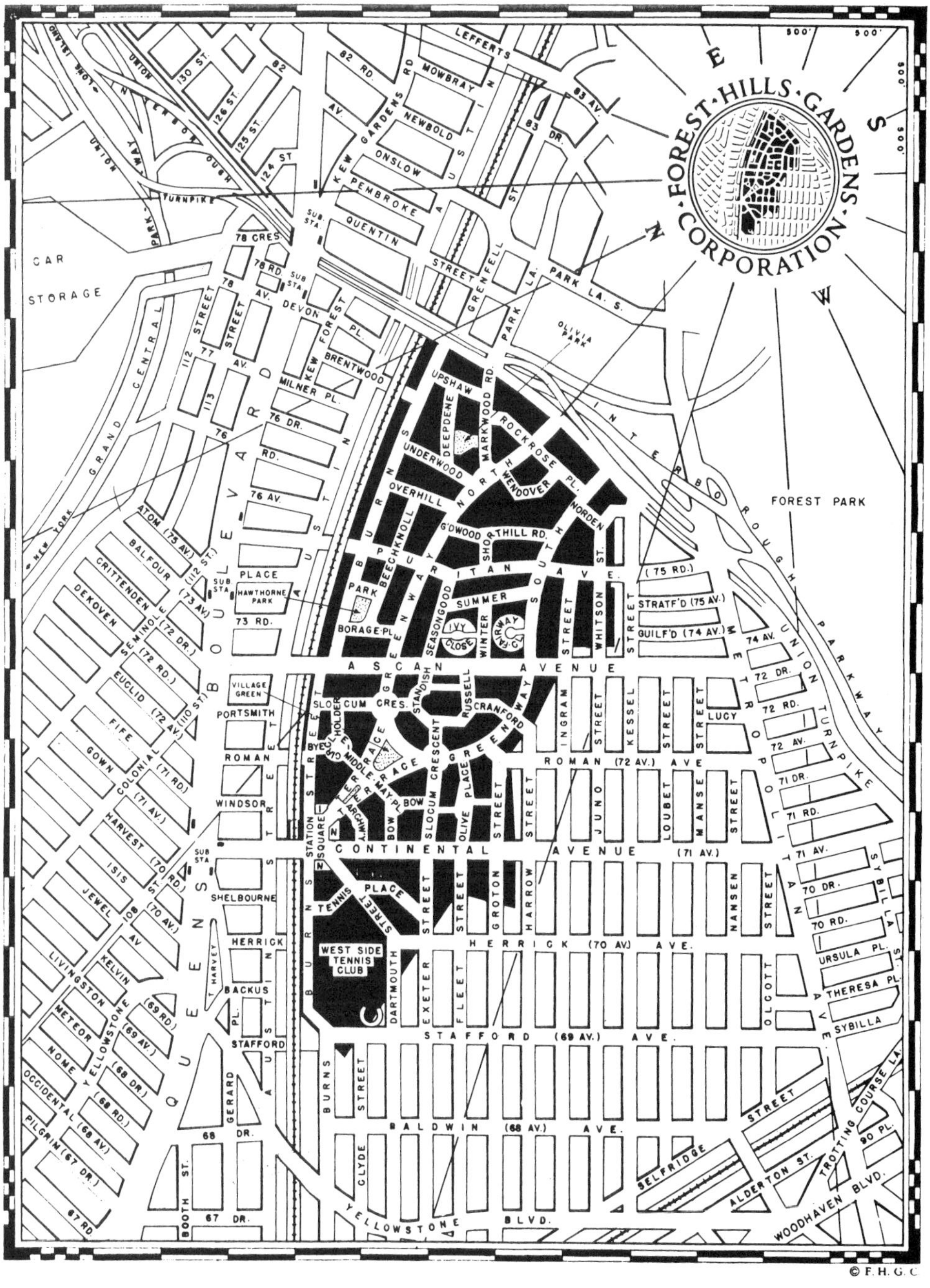

Current street map of Forest Hills Gardens. Courtesy Forest Hills Gardens Corporation.

Drawing of Station Square stores and apartments, 1910. Courtesy Rockefeller Archive Center.

"additional space to be devoted to the planting spaces and the front gardens which will be one of the characteristic features of the whole development." His design aimed for a middle ground between the free-flowing curvilinear streets of Riverside and the relentless but admittedly practical and economical grid that was favored by most speculative developers. "While not fantastically crooked," Olmsted explained, the neighborhood streets "are never perfectly straight for long stretches." As one contemporary critic observed, "one would have to search at some length to find one of the streets (the usual thing in a self-growing community) where the vista is neither terminated nor framed."[30] Believing that the "cozy, domestic character of these local streets" would be one of the suburb's most attractive attributes, Olmsted designed Forest Hills Gardens to a pedestrian scale.[31] His plan assumed that residents would use the conveniently located transportation and accommodated the automobile without giving it primacy.

Olmsted's modified grid plan followed the natural contours of the land, carving out forty-four blocks that were roughly rectangular yet varied enough in form to lend a distinctive character to each area. This variation also created a sequence of architectural massing, open spaces, and streetscapes that avoided the "deadly monotony" of conventional suburban sites and helped foster the illusion of a community developing organically, over time.[32] Atterbury's architectural groupings and his arrangement of freestanding houses on their lots added to the visual interest within the unified plan.

Olmsted sited the entrance so that it would be convenient for train passengers, for those traveling by car, and for pedestrians. Commuters would exit the LIRR train on a platform located on an embankment above street level. Twin staircases would lead them down to a brick plaza, Station Square, which Olmsted left open for pedestrian traffic and community gatherings; a small center island with a fountain was the only structure in the square. Plantings on the embankment and along the driveway in front of the station would soften the hardscape.[33] The red brick paving of Station Square, the texture and color of the concrete aggregate used for its sidewalks and curbs, the red terra-cotta roofs of Atterbury's arched and arcaded architectural complex, and his whimsical and elegant wrought-iron signposts and street lamps would provide a marked contrast to the Queens streetscape just across the railroad tracks.

In this most urban section of the Gardens, from Station Square to the major cross street Ascan Avenue, Olmsted adapted formal City Beautiful planning devices to create interesting street scenes and picturesque vistas. Passing through the arches of Station Square into the Gardens on foot or in a car, the visitor faces the principal public space, a small mall and green of about three and a half acres. Formally planted, this was to be the social gathering place for the community, in contrast to Station Square, its commercial hub. This centerpiece of Olmsted's

Station Square buildings in scaffolding. Courtesy Forest Hills Gardens Corporation.

street plan is bounded by the Greenways North and South, two roads that loop through the central section of the development. Atterbury planned clusters of terrace housing on either side of the Greenways, complementing the urban quality of the Station Square complex.

The view down the street to the left of the roundabout linking the mall and the green is punctuated by Middlemay Circle; a prominent housing group bounded by Bow Street terminates the vista to the right. At the top of the green the two arms of Slocum Crescent define a roughly square section, which is distinguished by shorter street segments and a higher housing density than are found as one moves farther from the community's entrance. Olmsted located a school and playground on a prominent site in this central area (Block 10), to conclude the entry axis from Station Square.[34]

Across Ascan Avenue, Olmsted laid out tree-lined streets that flowed in longer, gently curving segments. Thus, a subtle transition is created as one moves south through the Gardens, leaving the business and commercial center on Station Square, with its connection to the larger metropolis, passing blocks of attached housing groups, and continuing on to quiet residential streets lined with single-family homes and their gardens. Beyond Union Turnpike, the boundary to the south, the rustic woodlands of Forest Park conclude this passage from the urban to the pastoral.

Because of Forest Hills Gardens' fortunate proximity to this public park, Olmsted thought it unnecessary to provide large open spaces

Inn and Greenway Terraces, view from Village Green. From Forest Hills Gardens, *1913. Courtesy Rockefeller Archive Center.*

within the tract itself. Further, he had long held that small, neighborhood parks contributed to a community's sense of identity and cohesiveness. Ideally, he suggested, a neighborhood park or playground should be within a quarter-mile walking distance of every home. Each of these spaces should have a unique design and offer recreation facilities appropriate for its particular location.[35]

Olmsted reserved two small common areas in the eastern section of Forest Hills Gardens to the left of Greenway North. Hawthorne Park (Block 27), covering an area of about an acre and a half, offers a shady expanse of lawn for strolling and sitting. The smaller Olivia Park (Block 42), named in honor of Olivia Sage, sits in a natural hollow and has been used as an amphitheater for community festivals and theatricals. The centrally located school ground was also designed to welcome residents. Olmsted's plan indicates a play area for younger children near the school building, with swings, a sandbox, and benches. Another pleasant gathering space would be the tea garden planned for the Forest Hills Gardens Inn, which would be open to residents as well as hotel guests.

Olmsted planned six blocks (numbers 3, 16, 21, 23, 30, and 33) with interior parks accessible through rear garden gates or by a private pedestrian lane, intended for the exclusive use of that block's homeowners. In two instances these private spaces were sizable, almost as large as the areas set aside for Olivia and Hawthorne Parks. In a novel arrangement, these lot holders would form a corporation to administer their

Olivia Park. From Why We Have Chosen Forest Hills Gardens for Our Home.

Station Square complex nearing completion. Courtesy Fairsted.

joint interest on the interior land, with shares in this corporation transferring with the building lots.[36] Olmsted envisioned a number of potential uses for the private enclaves. Residents might decide to turn part of the space into tennis courts or use it for other forms of active recreation. Or they might want to keep it a quiet refuge from general pedestrian traffic, a safe play space for small children. They might even use it for a communal garden. "There are many people," Olmsted imagined, "who want to try their hand at a garden—more of a garden than is possible on the ordinary house plot—but who either are unable to buy the necessary area or feel too uncertain of their gardening success to risk the additional investment in land." A communal plot would allow residents to test their green thumbs, "and to increase or decrease this space or finally give it up, just as their experience may dictate." Ever practical, Olmsted even envisioned lot holders leasing garden plots to residents of other blocks, applying the rental fees toward their own maintenance costs. Further, he designed these nonstandard blocks so that an extra street could be opened through the middle of the block, creating additional building lots, in the event that future residents lost interest in keeping up the private park. Much to Olmsted's disappointment, the interior parks did not prove popular and it was difficult to interest residents in their upkeep.[37]

While the aesthetic sensibility of the architecture at Forest Hills Gardens was old-world, Atterbury's construction techniques and materials were modern, chosen for economy and durability to demonstrate that attractive, low-cost housing was possible in the suburbs. "Buildings of tasteful design, constructed of brick, cement or other permanent material, even though of somewhat greater initial cost," de Forest explained, would be more economical in the long run. Durable and fireproof, they would result in "lesser repair bills than the repulsive, cheaply built structures which are too often the type of New York's outlying districts."[38]

Atterbury had been studying ways to standardize and simplify homebuilding since 1902. He experimented with prefabricated concrete sections, hoping to replace the myriad of handmade elements used in traditional house construction with a smaller number of machine-made parts. In 1907, with support from the Sage Foundation, he began a series of studies to determine the largest standard-size foundation, wall, and floor sections that could be fabricated in precast, hollow core concrete. The Forest Hills Gardens project gave him the opportunity to test on a large scale both the technical and aesthetic possibilities of prefabricated concrete construction.

Atterbury worked with the Carnegie Steel Company, adapting their technology to the fabrication of modular concrete building units. Soon he was able to produce and handle much larger concrete slabs than had previously been possible. By the end of October 1910 a concrete block factory was in operation on the grounds of Forest Hills Gardens (where the Grosvenor Square Apartments stand today), manufacturing standard-size house components in steel molds. An electric crane lifted slabs weighing up to three tons onto flatbed cars, which were drawn by mules along railroad tracks to building sites. There another derrick, which could move along these same tracks, lifted the slabs into position. Exterior walls were constructed from slabs a full story in height which were about six feet wide and eleven inches thick. Interior walls were made with thinner slabs. Gables, beams, lintels, porch supports, and other smaller elements were also formed in molds. Atterbury invented "Nailcrete," a type of concrete into which nails could be driven as easily as into wood. Wooden planks could be nailed directly onto Nailcrete floor slabs. Outer walls were waterproofed and coated with concrete stucco; interior walls were painted.

The Atterbury system had the potential for cutting construction costs

Forest Hills Gardens Station. From Forest Hills Gardens, *1913. Courtesy Rockefeller Archive Center.*

in several ways. Because building components were produced in the factory, weather was less of a consideration. Each slab was handled only three times from its production until it was put into place, so that houses could be built more quickly by fewer workers. Exterior joints were held to a minimum: vertical joints beneath or above windows and doors and one horizontal joint at floor level. Much of the scaffolding and temporary supports required by conventional construction was eliminated. By building houses in groups, it was possible to work efficiently on several houses at once, prefiguring the post–World War II assembly-line production of houses made famous at Levittown. In the first building test at Forest Hills Gardens, workers with no prior experience in this construction method put up completed concrete shells ready for finishing (plumbing, electricity, and painting) for three small houses in six weeks' time—which would translate to a possible production rate of one house every two weeks. By the time the second group of four thirteen-foot houses was built, construction time was down to five weeks, or a rate of one house every nine days.[39]

Atterbury revealed the artistic potential of concrete in his work at Forest Hills Gardens, exploiting its ability to be molded, colored, and textured. This cold, hard medium came to life with the addition of

Concrete grille over entrance, Burns Street, 2001. Photograph by Carol Betsch.

crushed roof tiles, bright pebbles, and bits of quartz and mica that lent color and sparkle. From covered wooden molds emerged cast concrete balconies, railings, grilles, pierced chimney tops, signage panels, light-poles, and even the delicate flèche of the Inn tower. Atterbury was able to simulate half-timbering by inserting stucco-covered terra-cotta blocks and brick-veneer panels into hollow sections of precast concrete. Atterbury and Olmsted experimented with different colors and textural effects for sidewalks and curbs on-site, where they had workers scrub the finished concrete surfaces with wire brushes and apply acid washes to reveal the aggregate.[40]

WITH THE IMPORTANT ENTRANCE section of the community reaching completion, Forest Hills Gardens was unveiled to the public with statements from each of the principals involved. De Forest laid out the Sage Foundation's intentions:

> [T]here is nothing charitable in the providing of a comfortable residential place for present flat dwellers. The town is to be run on the same business principles as any other suburban locality so far as the purchase of land is concerned, but the owner and dweller will reap

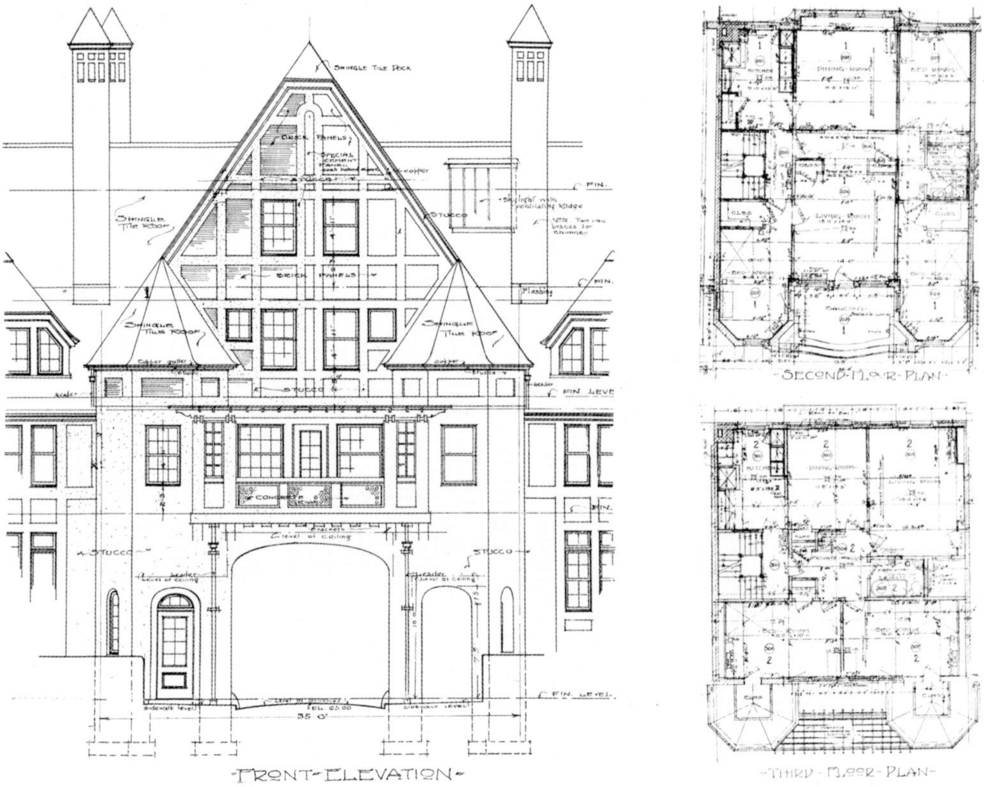

Front elevation of archway unit, Group VI. From Architecture, *August 1916. Courtesy Rockefeller Archive Center.*

the advantages of living in a cheerful community laid out to afford equal benefits to all.

Mrs. Russell Sage and the Trustees of the foundation have been profoundly impressed with the need of better and more attractive facilities in the suburbs for persons of modest means, those who could put $25 a month and upward in the purchase of a home. They believe that homes can be supplied similar to those in the garden cities of England, with greenery and flowers around them, accessible playgrounds and recreation facilities, and at no appreciably greater cost than is now paid for the same roof-room in the city. . . . If these expectations can be realized at Forest Hills Gardens, the Sage Foundation will provide healthful and attractive homes to many people. It will demonstrate that more tasteful surroundings and open spaces pay in suburban development, and thereby encourage imitation. It will encourage economical methods of marketing land.[41]

Archway unit, Group VI. LALH photograph.

De Forest had asked Olmsted, Atterbury, Bouton, and Harmon to prepare their own accounts elaborating on the distinctive features of the development. These comments were widely circulated over the next eighteen months with essentially the same text appearing in a variety of publications, including the influential progressive journal *The Survey* (itself funded by the Sage Foundation). In response to broad public interest in the project, these pieces were collected several months later into an illustrated booklet titled *Forest Hills Gardens: The Suburban Land Development of the Russell Sage Foundation*.[42]

In this publication de Forest repeated the fact that Forest Hills Gardens was not intended for "the laboring man, whose wages are small." Land costs were too high to permit this. Forest Hills Gardens was both an experimental business investment and a philanthropic endeavor. It was not a charity, and, as de Forest stated, "It will not be managed as a charity. Whoever deals with it, whether as tenant or purchasers, will be expected to pay fair value for everything received."[43]

Grosvenor Atterbury's comments in his essay "The Architectural Work" amplified de Forest's remarks, pointing out that the Sage Foundation could not control either the value of the property or "transit conditions, both as regards time and cost, [which] constitute an even more powerful factor in determining the type of prospective tenant or purchaser, and consequently both the size and quality of the dwellings that should be erected." A proper consideration of economic conditions, Atterbury continued, "demands that the buildings now erected shall be of such character that they will continue to be appropriate when, as so inevitably and so quickly happens in the vicinity of large American cities, the land shall have become too valuable" to justify keeping the initial housing stock. The usual result is great economic waste, Atterbury said, with "valuable buildings being torn down merely because it pays better to throw away the cost which they represent than to sacrifice the greater earning power of the land which they occupy."[44] Forest Hills Gardens, in contrast, would feature quality construction, built to endure.

General manager Edward Bouton echoed the hope that the Forest Hills Gardens project would demonstrate that it was possible to realize a profit on a quality suburb, intelligently planned according to modern principles. "The chief difference between the development at Forest Hills Gardens and any other land development so far undertaken in America," Bouton claimed, "is that of design or 'town planning'. . . . With the project in the hands of such well known men as Messrs. Atter-

Sign at Forest Hills Gardens Station. Courtesy Fairsted.

bury and Olmsted," he concluded, "a new, distinctive, and, it is hoped, educational work" would result.[45]

Sage Foundation Homes Company (SFHC), the entity created by the board to build and market the project, committed $1.25 million for land improvements (including grading and paving of streets, sidewalks, water supply, sewers, electricity, and plantings) and for constructing the first ten building groups. All this was to be completed in advance of offering lots for sale. The SFHC planned to establish the tone and character of Forest Hills Gardens by completing not only those "features which make little show above ground but are fundamental to the permanence of a healthy and attractive residence district," but also by erecting a large number of dwellings "in order to set a standard and control more surely the architectural character of the future town."[46]

THE DIFFERENCE BETWEEN Forest Hills Gardens and more conventional residential suburbs was apparent from the start. "The visitor is deeply impressed with the thoroughness with which things are done here," marveled one of the first reporters to journey out to the site. From tree planting to street grading to the stucco mixture for the exteriors of the dwellings, everything was guided by a master plan.[47]

5

"The English Type"

ARCHITECTURAL AND LANDSCAPE DESIGN

Olmsted and Atterbury collaborated closely throughout the first year of construction as both men considered Forest Hills Gardens to be among their most significant projects. The opportunity to design every aspect of a community—and to have it built exactly as planned—was rare. Olmsted's work at Forest Hills Gardens was occurring at the height of his confidence in this "new thing," the comprehensive plan. In his 1910 speech as first president of the National Conference on City Planning, Olmsted lauded the new scientific approach to planning that controlled all "diverse elements of the physical city."[1] At Forest Hills Gardens he had the opportunity to apply these holistic principles of comprehensive planning to a suburban site. For Atterbury, who had a long-standing interest in model housing, Forest Hills Gardens offered a testing ground for new construction techniques. But for all their interest in planning methods and building technology, both Atterbury and Olmsted kept artistry at the core of their work at Forest Hills Gardens. Together they created an architectural and landscape design inspired by the Arts and Crafts movement, described by the press as following "the English type."

Atterbury's designs incorporated an eclectic mix of architectural styles and features—arched entryways, Tudor half-timbering, complex rooflines and prominent chimneys, second-story overhangs—evoking associations with medieval European university and cathedral towns and country villages of feudal England.[2] These stylistic elements were not

Detail of Station Square. From The Survey, *January 1911.*

Storefronts, Station Square. From Forest Hills Gardens, *1913. Courtesy Rockefeller Archive Center.*

unusual; Atterbury and other architects frequently used them in designs for country estates. More striking was Atterbury's vibrant use of color, texture, and material. A warm reddish-brown terra-cotta tile, for example, covers most of the roofs in Forest Hills Gardens and provides a unifying, signature element for it. To complement this dominant color, the architect used lammie, tapestry bricks from different factories, which varied in hue and texture. (Atterbury also incorporated this over-burnt brick, usually considered a useless by-product, to interesting effect in some of his Long Island estate designs.)[3] To accent the warm tones of the buildings, Atterbury chose a rich peacock blue for features such as lampposts, wooden fences, gates, pergolas, and wrought-iron signs.[4] The subtle variety in materials gave the village an instant patina and helped create the illusion that it had evolved over a period of years.

Atterbury's masterly handling of architectural massing and site design resulted in buildings that were compatible with their immediate surroundings and neighborhoods that served the overall plan. His designs also demonstrated methods of achieving higher density of population per acre without overcrowding, one of the main principles of the English garden city movement and used by Parker and Unwin at Letchworth and Hampstead Garden Suburb. Atterbury's first ten building groups varied widely in type and plan, including row houses, detached

Detail of brickwork. LALH photograph.

Sign for Greenway Terrace, 2001. LALH photograph.

and semidetached houses grouped around a courtyard, and small attached units grouped under a single roof.

Building Group I included the prominent Station Square complex and the nine-story tower of the Forest Hills Inn, which became the town landmark. This 150-room hotel (room and board for $14 to $18 a week) functioned as the community's social center in its early years, with a restaurant, billiard room, and squash and tennis courts available for use by both community residents and hotel guests. The Inn also offered a number of "non-housekeeping" apartments, rental units designed for young single men and women who would be commuting to work in the city. No common rooms or kitchens were provided for these tenants, who could avail themselves of the Inn's amenities.[5] On either side of the Inn, linked to it by pedestrian bridges at the second-story level, were three- and four-story mixed-use buildings that comprised apartments, shops, and offices.

Just beyond Station Square, parallel to the north and south Greenways, Atterbury placed blocks of attached and semidetached houses (Group VI A and B), reminiscent of English terraced, or row, houses. A common roofline gives the appearance of a single dwelling, while distinctive arched doorways define individual entries. A unique feature of this group is the two-family house tucked into the arch spanning Arch Road. Turrets, wall and gateway copings, brushed concrete grilles and half-timber work, and decorative terra-cotta and brick panels distinguish these stylish units, sizable homes of 8 to 10 rooms.

Group II, in contrast, consists of fourteen small (4-room), attached units clustered around a semicircular drive. Located near the railroad tracks, they offered some of the least expensive housing in Forest Hills Gardens.[6] The mass of the building's large roof is broken up by dormer windows, conical towers topping rounded bays, and slender precast concrete chimneys. The facades are simple, punctuated with entry porches.

Atterbury's ability to create buildings that read well both as a single mass and as individual segments is also shown in Group III, a long narrow row of attached single family houses of 7 to 9 rooms. Here the front doors in the center of the group are recessed behind low arches along a covered loggia, while the two end units have side entries perpendicular to the street. Palladian windows, jerkin-headed roof dormers, and a rhythmic symmetrical facade enliven this group.

Ten more housing groups designed by Atterbury and other architects invited by the foundation to contribute designs echo the plans and

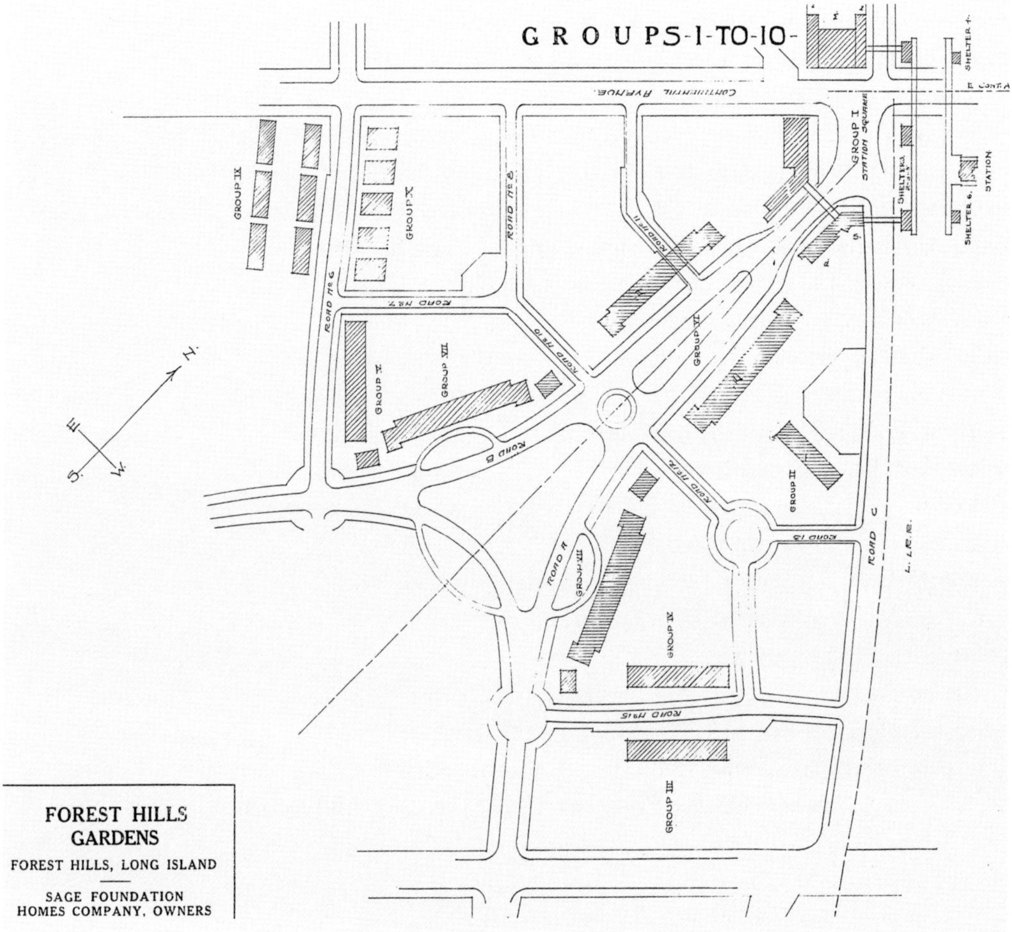

Location of first ten building groups. Courtesy Fairsted.

massing of these first designs.[7] Constructed between 1910 and 1912, their features were simpler, although covered porches, dormer roofs, prominent chimneys, and well-crafted brick and concrete facades attest to Atterbury's persistent attention to detail. The architect created a particularly interesting plan for a housing group (XII) sited on the point of the triangle made by the intersection of Markwood Road and Greenway North. It consists of two large (10 rooms and 3 baths) semi-detached houses in the central block, flanked by two smaller (7 rooms and 1 bath) detached houses, one with an entrance on Markwood, the other on Greenway. This group creates a focal point for the long vista up Greenway North, as well as a clever way for the buildings to "turn the corner," while placing attractive facades on both streets and creating a shared central courtyard. Atterbury provided four garages to the rear of the complex.[8]

Atterbury's buildings exhibited "a harmony only conceivable where there is a fundamental architectural principle" underlying the whole, wrote Edward Hale Brush in *The Craftsman*.[9] Similarly, Olmsted's landscape plan harmoniously interwove public and private areas so that common spaces flowed up to individual lawns and gardens, and private grounds melded into the larger landscape. Just as his father had, Olmsted emphasized the importance of having a clear, dominant idea guide every landscape design and subordinating the parts and details to it. "Whatever may be done for the sake of color, enrichment or decoration," he held, "must be controlled by regard for the composition of these masses and open spaces or confusion will result."[10] To maintain this degree of control, the Olmsted firm generally declined to prepare plans unless the client agreed to supervision and follow-up by their office. "We are not gardeners," Olmsted Brothers told prospective clients. But the firm was prepared "to direct such gardeners or contractors as may be employed as to the proper interpretation to put upon our plans exactly as architects do in the case of buildings." The firm also informed clients that they were "not dealers in plants," and took no commissions on purchases. If the client wished, however, Olmsted Brothers would place horticultural or-

Apartments, Station Square. From Forest Hills Gardens, *1913. Courtesy Rockefeller Archive Center.*

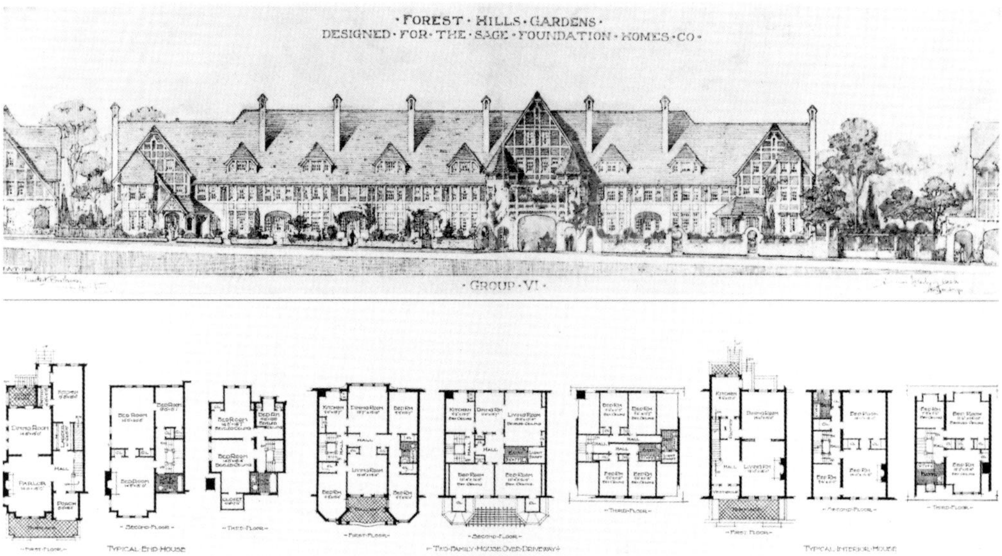

Plan and elevation, Group VI A. From Architecture, *August 1916. Courtesy Rockefeller Archive Center.*

ders with reputable suppliers on their behalf and pass along any price advantage the firm could command. On private commissions, Olmsted Brothers would send a representative of the firm to spend "at least a short time on the grounds" to ensure that the landscape plan was "satisfactorily executed," charging from $100 to $1,000 for this service depending on the size of the property.[11]

On large projects such as a suburban development, Olmsted Brothers anticipated a long-term relationship with the client. In some cases an assistant was sent to take up residence on-site for varying periods of time, while one of the Olmsteds continued in an oversight role on a yearly retainer or some other salary arrangement as the plan was executed. At Forest Hills Gardens, Olmsted Brothers recommended personnel to fill key positions on the SFHC payroll, including chief engineer C. B. Fancy and superintendent of construction Harold C. Lyons. An Olmsted employee headed up the construction office until most of the street and building work had been finished and all planting plans for streets and parks completed. The department was then divided into two sections, one focusing on engineering work, the other on horticultural matters. The Olmsted firm supervised the resident gardening staff, at one time numbering fourteen, for years, while the Sage Foundation remained in control of the project. As the community developed, Olmsted

Arched entrances, Greenway Terrace. From Forest Hills Gardens, *1912.*
Courtesy Rockefeller Archive Center.

Housing Group II. From Architecture, *August 1916.*
Courtesy Rockefeller Archive Center.

Above: Front elevation, Housing Group II. From Architecture, *August 1916. Courtesy Rockefeller Archive Center.*
Below: Front elevation, Housing Group III. From Architecture, *August 1916. Courtesy Rockefeller Archive Center.*

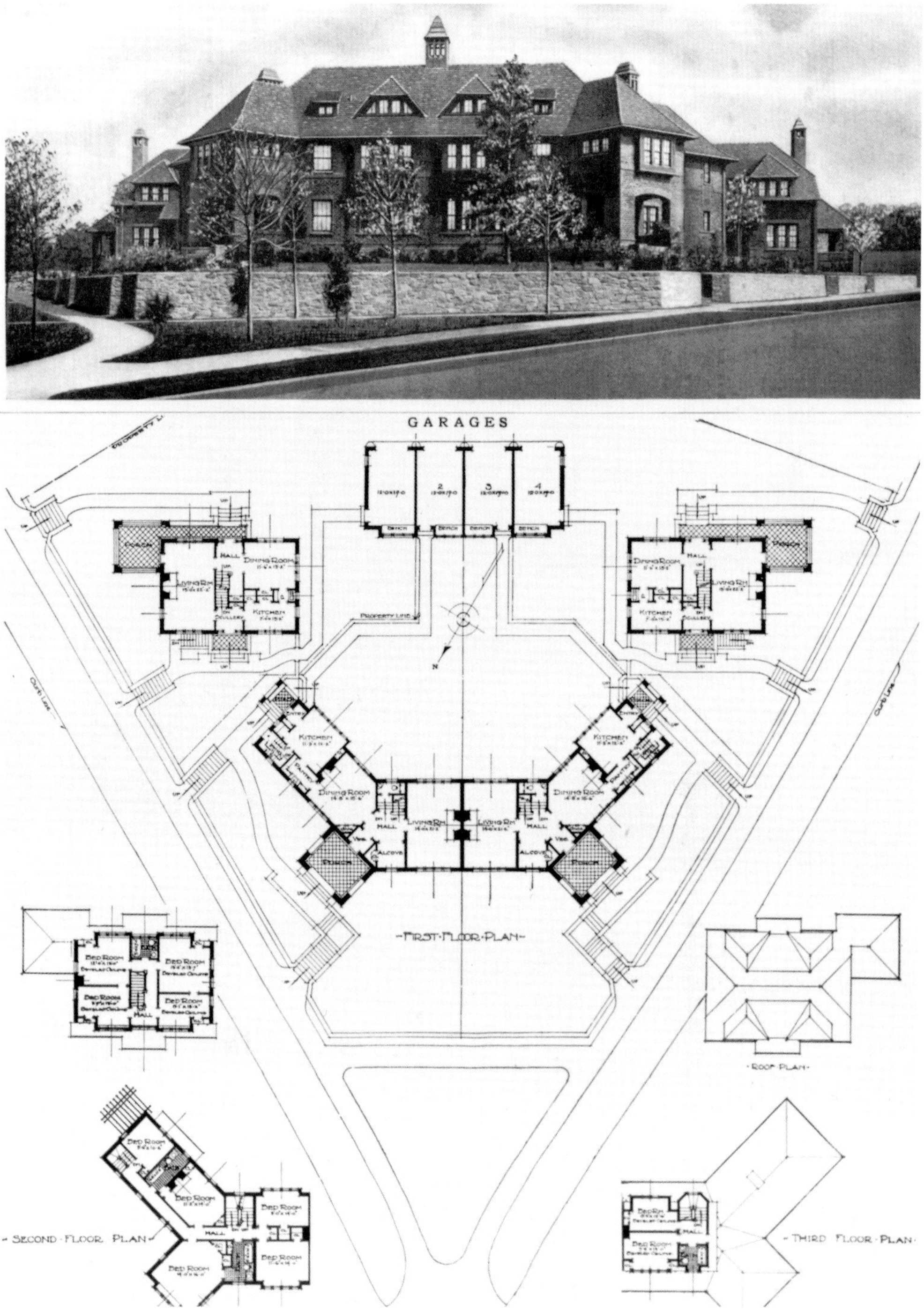

Plan, Housing Group XII. From Forest Hills Gardens, *1913.*
Courtesy Rockefeller Archive Center.

Melding of public and private landscape. Courtesy Frances Loeb Library, Graduate School of Design, Harvard University.

Station Square fountain, ca. 1914. Courtesy Frances Loeb Library, Graduate School of Design, Harvard University.

Brothers continued to make suggestions and critiqued landscape plans when asked to do so by the management company. The firm also provided landscape and planting plans to individual homeowners.[12]

At Forest Hills Gardens Olmsted created a landscape palette to complement Atterbury's Arts and Crafts architectural vocabulary. Just as the architect used details of brick, wood, stone, and concrete to create varied, textured compositions, Olmsted used trees, shrubs, and flowers to achieve similarly patterned effects in the landscape.[13] Forest Hills Gardens presented Olmsted quite a different challenge from the one he had met in Baltimore at Roland Park (where he continued to advise Bouton

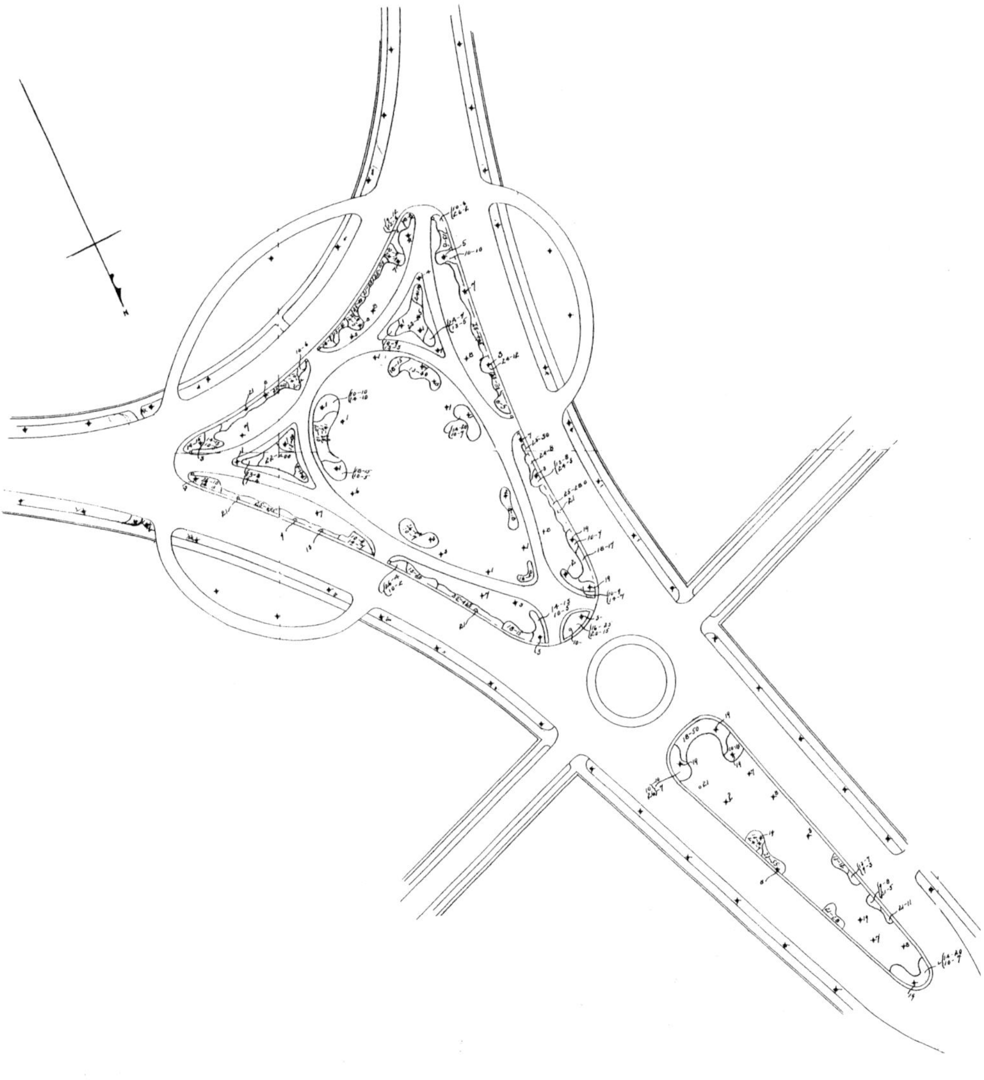

Planting study for Village Green. Courtesy Fairsted.

Greenways North and South. From Forest Hills Gardens, *1913. Courtesy Rockefeller Archive Center.*

Street with young plantings. From Architecture, *August 1916. Courtesy Rockefeller Archive Center.*

Village Green, 2001. Photograph by Carol Betsch.

during this intense planning period for the Gardens).[14] Rather than Roland Park's dramatic landscape of woodlands and steep ravines, at the Gardens he was faced with a flat, undistinguished expanse of farmland. As a result, the scenic effects there are more subtle than those at Roland Park, but the intent was similar: to integrate architecture, streets, and public spaces in a gardenlike setting. Greater emphasis was given to common areas at Forest Hills Gardens since, unlike the Baltimore suburb, the comprehensive plan provided for a formal entrance into the community, a public green, and several small parks.

The Green, the central public space, was designed as a simple composition of lawn and chestnut trees, providing a contrast to the brick-paved hardscape of Station Square. A plan drawn by the Olmsted firm in 1916 for the circle at the head of the Green added a ring of flowers, grass borders, and hedge-backed benches.[15] That same year the Green acquired a flagpole; a bronze and granite war memorial designed by A. A. Weinmann was dedicated in 1920. Olmsted designed Olivia and Hawthorne Parks with seasonal delights of color, texture, and scent in mind. Yellow jasmine, white-flowering deutzia, Indian currant, and arching evergreens marked the entrances to secluded Olivia Park. A number of existing trees were preserved for shade within. The park's delicate spring display of dogwood, cherry, jasmine, spiraea, and forsythia was followed by the snowballs, Indian currant, and honeysuckle of summer. Hawthorne Park was planned as a cool oasis of evergreens, large shade trees, and flowering shrubs with benches around its perimeter. The center of the park was graded so that it could be flooded for winter skating.[16]

Olmsted prepared plans for each block indicating the general location and orientation of houses. He considered each structure in relation to the overall plan and to its own lot. The narrowness of neighborhood streets made it possible to plant areas along the curbs and still have generous front garden plots. In carving out streets and building lots care was taken to preserve as many existing trees as possible, and hundreds of new trees were planted as well. Indeed, quipped one early visitor, trees were as sacred to the residents of Forest Hills Gardens as they were in China, "where they are worshipped."[17] Early visitors to Forest Hills Gardens found the street and yard plantings to be quite incomparable in terms of the profusion and the look of maturity which the landscape had so rapidly achieved. Through the use of relatively large trees and the generous

Left: Pan bird pool in Olivia Park. Courtesy Rockefeller Archive Center.
Right: Construction drawing for Pan figure and stone pool.
Courtesy Fairsted.

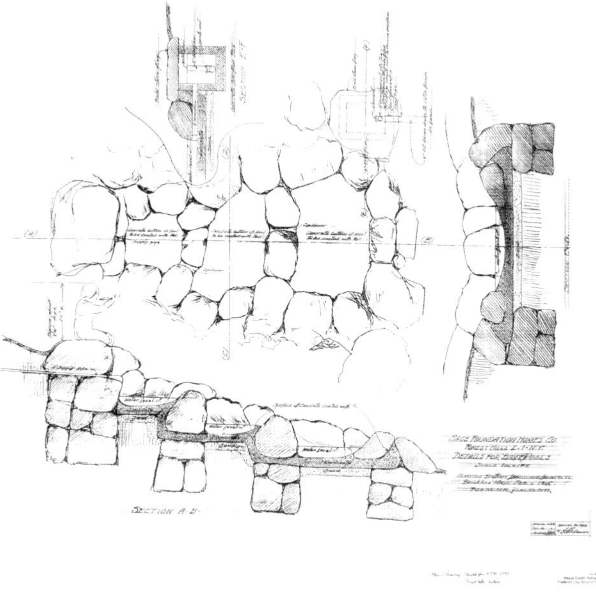

planting of fast-growing shrubs and flowers, Olmsted successfully minimized the visual effects of constant new building, "a condition which, in the typical speculative subdivision," a contemporary critic observed, usually results "in a scene of widespread devastation, slow to return to normal."[18]

Olmsted wanted each block or neighborhood of Forest Hills Gardens to have a distinguishing vista or special decorative effect. He asked Louis S. Adams, an Olmsted office associate assigned to the Gardens job, to make watercolor sketches of different plant combinations so that he could judge the color effects of alternative planting schemes.[19] Major through-streets were lined with American elms and other large-growing trees, while local streets were planted with species that would provide color throughout the year. One street might be all magnolias, another all dogwood for spring display. Slocum Crescent was planted with hawthorn, varnish-trees, and Japanese lilacs for spring and summer bloom,

Ivy Close, 2001. Photograph by Carol Betsch.

Fairway Close, 2001. Photograph by Carol Betsch.

and Norway maples for fall foliage. Tulip trees, beech, and sassafras abounded. At least seventy-five varieties of shrubs and forty different vines were used throughout the Gardens. Climbing roses, flowering vines such as clematis, and ivy grew on fences and walls, softening and "aging" the architecture.[20]

Each of the interior block parks, for which Olmsted had such high aspirations, was given a unique character. Distinctive plantings marked the entries to the private hideaways of Ivy and Fairway Close. The walls and posts at the front and rear entrances to Ivy Close were planted with trailing English and Boston ivy. Junipers, Japanese holly, and yews were used as evergreen accents, while white and purple lilacs provided delicate spring displays. For the private park in Block 16, a triangular space with a large open lawn, Olmsted selected trees and shrubs that would produce changing displays of colorful foliage, berries, and flowers. Japanese barberry, oaks, crabapples, hawthorns, and Japanese hollies showed off fruit and foliage for autumn and winter interest. Magnolias, dogwoods, and tulip magnolias flowered in spring and summer. These enclosed "secret gardens" were ideal locations for fragrant plants, and here Olmsted

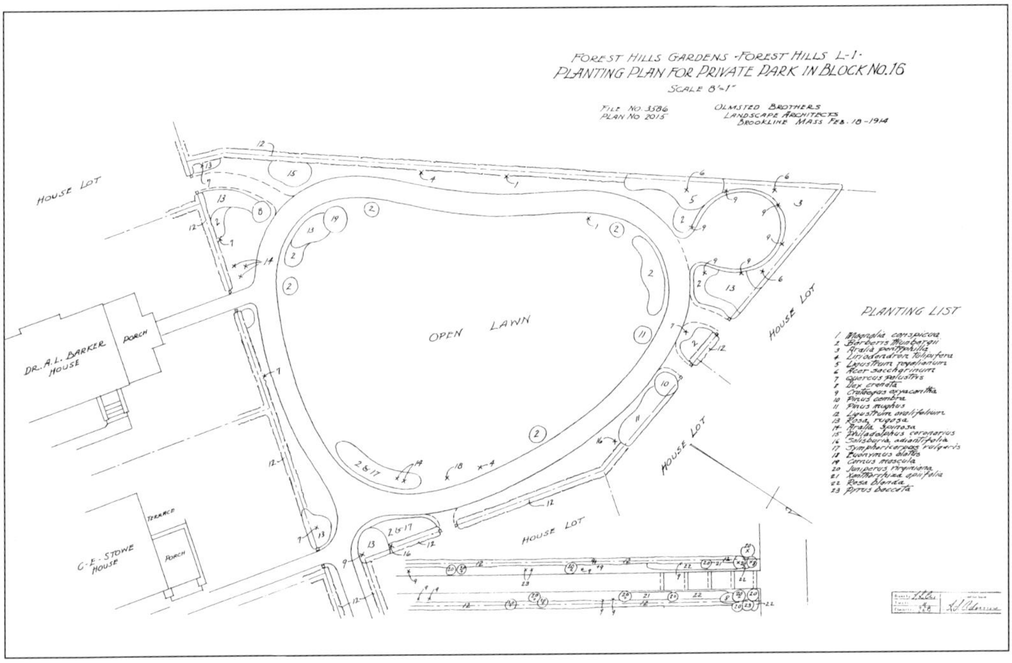

Planting plan for private park, Block 16. Courtesy Fairsted.

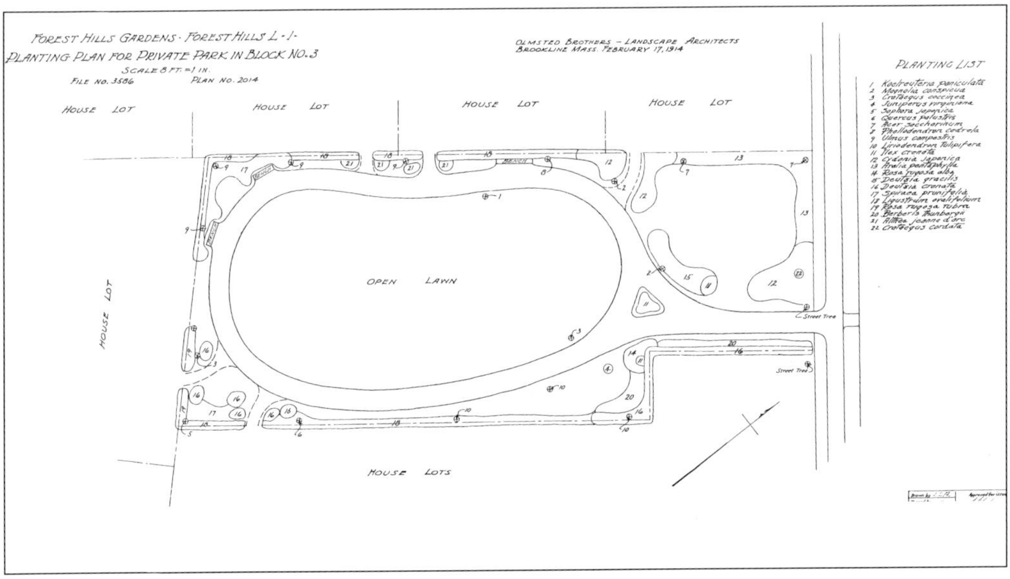

Planting plan for private park, Block 3. Courtesy Fairsted.

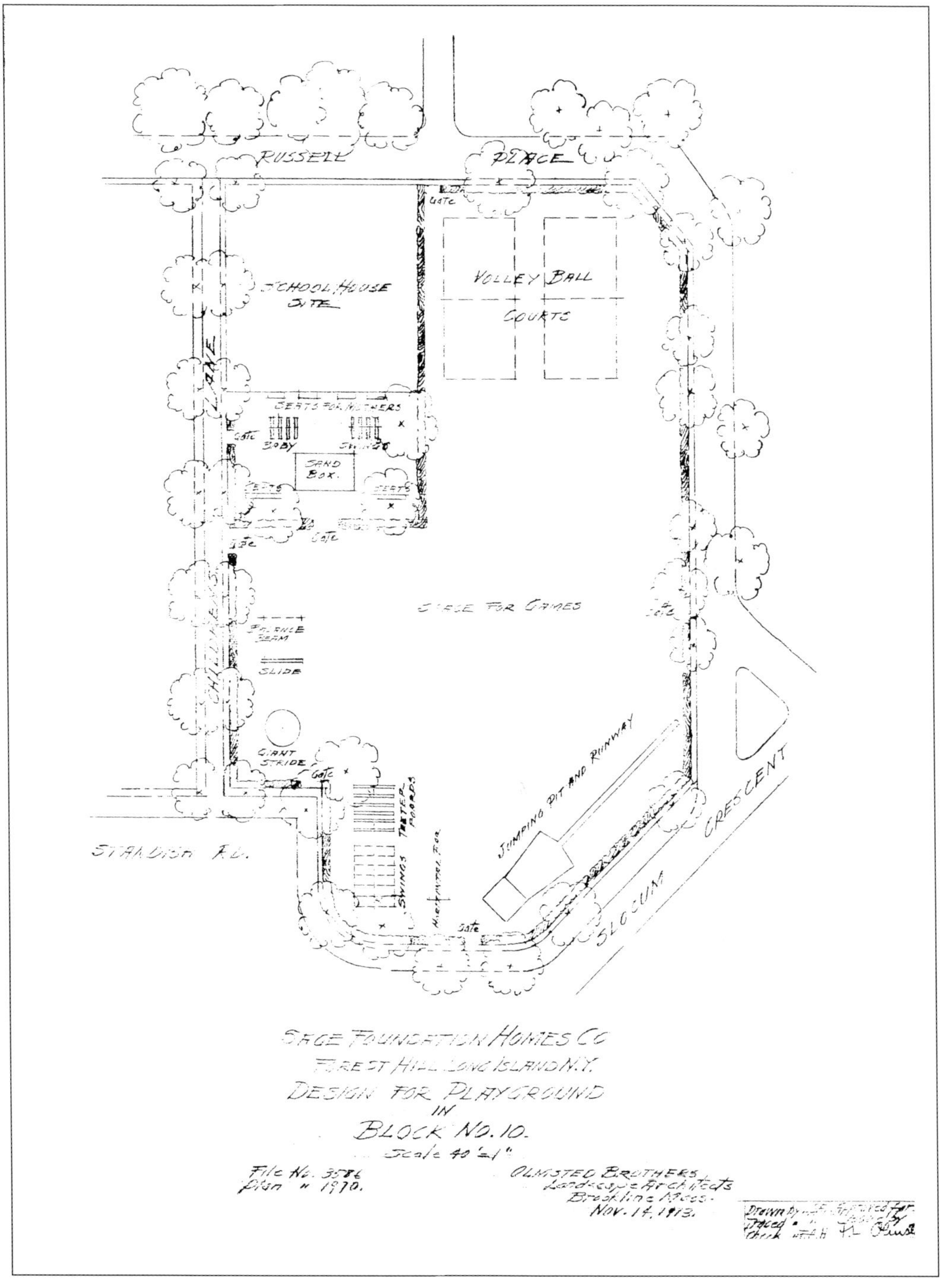

Design for playground, Block 10. Courtesy Fairsted.

House I-F-51. December, 1914. Courtesy Fairsted.

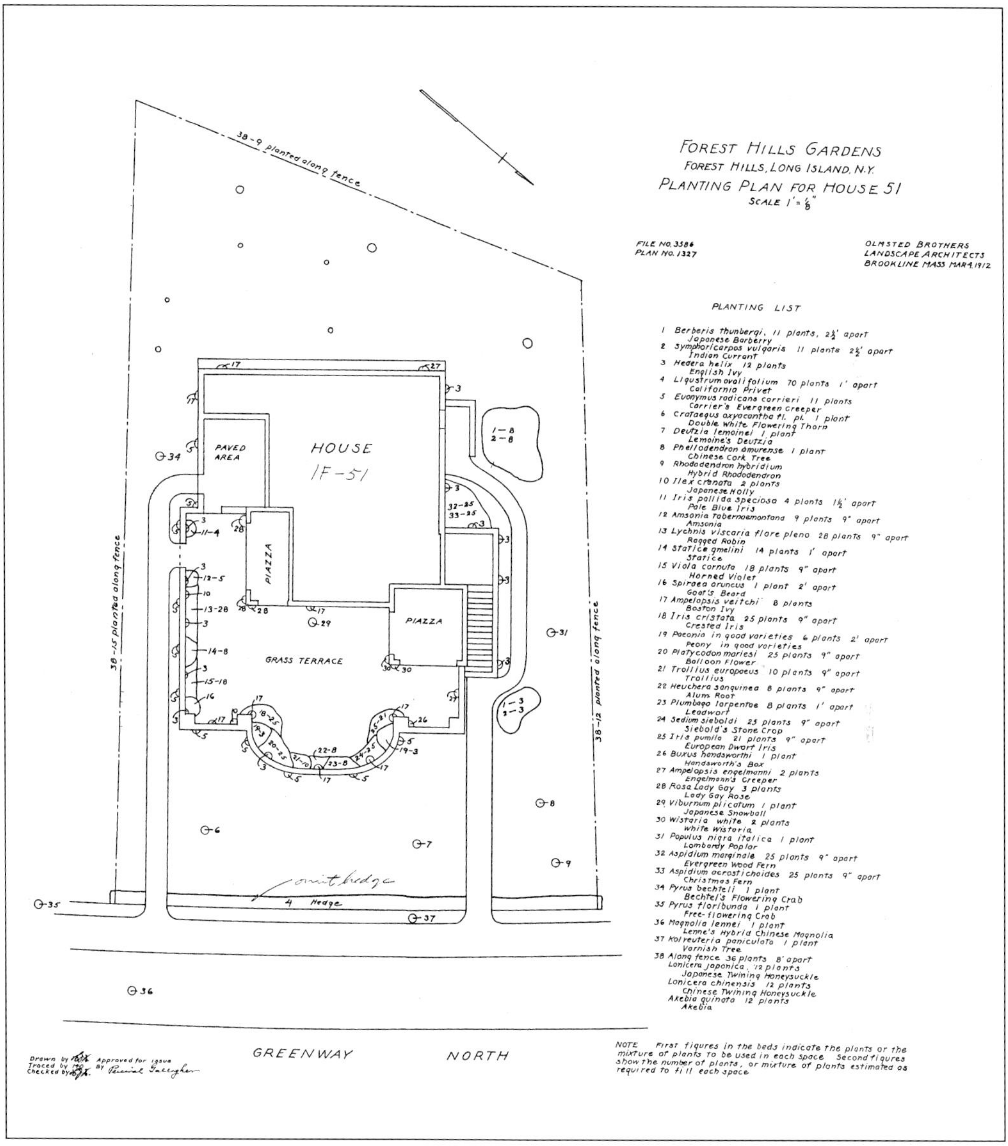

Planting plan for House I-F-51. Courtesy Fairsted.

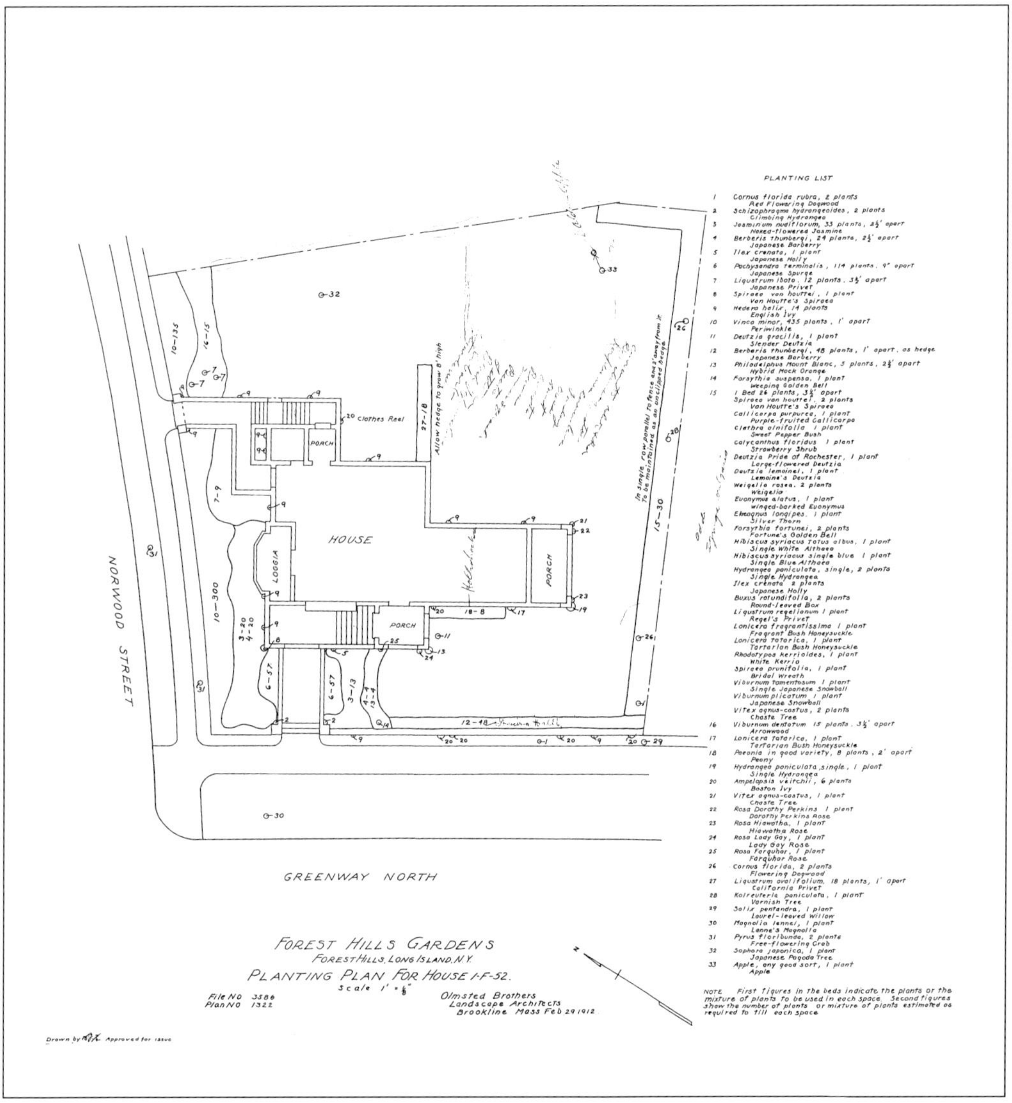

Planting plan for House I-F-52. Courtesy Fairsted.

included honeysuckle, roses, and mock orange.[21] Devil's walking stick and burning bush added interesting shapes and color. Block 3 also featured an open oval lawn highlighted with a golden raintree and a thornapple, with privet and rose hedges around the perimeter.

The Olmsted firm prepared landscape plans for a number of private residences in Forest Hills Gardens.[22] A single-family home designed by Atterbury and his associate John A. Tompkins on Greenway North (designated I-F-51) was a three-story structure with a prominent tiled roof and a second-story covered porch overlooking the front garden. Here the Olmsted firm framed a grassy terrace with a low wall covered with ivies and evergreen creepers. A large perennial bed in the center of this space was densely planted in shades of yellow, blue, and purple. Iris, peonies, blue bells, trollius, coral bells, and fall-blooming sedum would provide near continuous display. White wisteria was planted to grow up to the second-story loggia, and fragrant Lady Gay roses were selected for the garden below the side porch. The plan preserved existing trees in the backyard on a shady expanse of green lawn.

Atterbury and Tomkins also designed the house (designated I-F-52) on a corner lot on Slocum Crescent, where the plan included generous outdoor sitting spaces, connecting the house to the garden in characteristic Arts and Crafts fashion. White, pink, purple, and yellow predominate in the Olmsted firm's design for this garden. The long linear bed on the right side of the house, parallel to the fence, specified a single row of twenty-six different plants, planted three-and-a-half inches apart, "to be maintained as an unclipped hedge." This bed included white hibiscus, fall-blooming white hydrangea, honeysuckle, lavender, bridal wreath, snowball viburnum, and other fragrant and airy specimens. In the rear garden a Japanese pagoda tree and an apple tree provided pockets of shade. Penciled onto the plan in the area to the right of backyard between a privet hedge and fence are lists of vegetables; perhaps after viewing the plan, the owner requested a kitchen garden for his household.

SAGE FOUNDATION EXECUTIVE director John Glenn, himself one of the pioneering residents of the Gardens, wrote to Olmsted in 1913 to congratulate him on "the planting and the continuous succession of flowers," which were "a constant delight." Glenn captured Olmsted's achievement at Forest Hills Gardens when he wrote: "You have succeeded in bringing nature and art into harmony in a charming way."[23]

6

"Normal and Usual Social Conditions"

MARKETING AND MANAGEMENT

THE SFHC REALTY COMMITTEE set 1 June 1911 as the date Forest Hills Gardens would open for public sale. Earlier in the year, the Realty Committee had met at the Century Club to go over the terms and conditions of sale and the general marketing plan. The SFHC intended to sell building lots in series: the company would begin construction on a block when all of its lots were sold. The Realty Committee, under Harmon's guidance, recommended that potential buyers be offered extremely liberal terms of sale in order to get Forest Hills Gardens off to a fast start. They believed that many suburban development projects had foundered because of the slow rate at which property was marketed, with the result that interest charges and high administrative expenses cut into profits.

Accordingly, the initial terms required as little as 2 percent of the purchase price to be paid up front in those cases "where the purchaser proves, upon investigation" to be an exceptionally good risk. The buyer had ten years to pay off the balance. (Interest was set at 4.5 percent.) The SFHC reassured potential buyers that they would be protected in the event of future financial difficulties and even death. If a lot owner could not keep up his monthly payments, the company would give him an interest in other lots on the property which it would sell for his benefit. If a lot owner died, the company would return all money paid to date to his heirs or transfer title to the property to them "free from further payment."[1]

The SFHC also offered favorable terms for purchasing company-built

SFHC construction vehicle. Courtesy Forest Hills Gardens Corporation.

houses. These residences, priced from $5,900 to $15,000, were offered for 10 percent cash down on the price of the lot and the house, with the company securing a first mortgage for up to 50 percent of the price on the buyer's behalf. The company would prepare architectural and landscape plans based on the client's preferences at no charge to the first hundred lot purchasers who wished to build homes of their own design. The company also offered to build up to one hundred of these houses for the cost of construction plus a fixed fee of 10 percent.[2]

In October 1910 a committee consisting of Atterbury, Harmon, and Bouton had been formed to consider and "report on the proper building restrictions to be adopted in the sale of the company's land." Olmsted was asked to advise the group, and he wrote the report that was considered by the SFHC Development Committee in January.[3] Thus while the restrictive covenants for Forest Hills Gardens did not originate with his firm, Olmsted played a role in shaping them.

Olmsted was familiar with the use of deed restrictions in planned communities, a concept which at that time already had a long history in the United States. In fact, such restrictions had been in common use in Olmsted's own hometown of Brookline, since the early 1840s. Moreover, he was well acquainted with the two suburban developments credited with augmenting such controls: his father's Riverside, Illinois, and Roland Park, where he and his brother John had been working for more than a decade.

Olmsted's informal review of the use of restrictive covenants (looking in particular at subdivisions designed by the Olmsted firm) suggested that Riverside, with its modest building restrictions, was the direct forerunner of the modern restricted subdivision in the United States. Although Olmsted Sr. did not believe that developers could "control the form of the houses which men shall build," he did favor "a few simple precautions" that would militate against the construction of "ugly and inappropriate houses." A Riverside lot owner, for example, was required to observe a thirty-foot setback for houses and to "maintain one or two living trees between his house and his highway-line" in an unfenced front yard. Some of the most scenic land on the property, 700 of the community's 1,600 acres, was appropriated for public grounds where residents could come together "for recreating and enjoying . . . on common ground, and under common shade."[4]

Promotional pamphlet. Courtesy Fairsted.

Edward Bouton had pioneered in the practice of using deed restrictions as an aggressive marketing tool at Roland Park, incorporating land-use restrictions within each individual property deed.[5] Thus, deed restrictions and a maintenance tax were already in effect when Olmsted Brothers was engaged to design additional plats there. The Olmsteds recommended further restrictions to Bouton at Roland Park and were possibly the source of the idea of self-perpetuating covenants, with renewal automatic unless a stated percentage of property owners voted to revoke or amend. The Olmsteds also suggested that the maintenance fund be administered by representatives of the property owners, thus supporting the principle of community self-government.[6] Bouton stressed to potential buyers that such covenants guaranteed the value of their property, since all future development would have to be of equal quality. Restrictions at Roland Park limited lot owners to building single-family houses, established standard lot setbacks, specified a minimum value for houses, barred "nuisance uses" such as private stables, and instituted an annual maintenance assessment.

Deed restrictions became a way of signaling to potential buyers that they would be surrounded by like-minded neighbors. Although the initial covenants for Roland Park did not include racial restrictions, such language was later inserted and also used in Bouton's adjacent development, Guilford, after 1910. Bouton promoted these two properties as providing "A Thousand Acres of Restricted Land." Occupation "by any negro or person of negro extraction," except domestic servants, was prohibited. As in most upper-class neighborhoods of this period (and continuing well into the twentieth century), a tacit "gentleman's agreement" also effectively prevented Jewish buyers from moving into these restricted communities.[7]

On 22 June 1911 the Sage Foundation Homes Company filed a plat map and a Declaration of Restrictions for Forest Hills Gardens that would remain in effect until 1 January 1950. These restrictive covenants, to be written into every sales contract, controlled, first, the kinds of land use permitted on the lots, and second, the location and design of structures built on the lots. They limited commercial activity (no "noxious, dangerous or offensive thing, trade or business" allowed) to the lots facing Station Square, specifying that the bulk of the property sold at Forest Hills Gardens could be used for private residences only. Houses could not be occupied by more than two families. Private garages of one story and private stables were permitted only on specified lots. Houses were to be set back twenty-five feet from any front street, and open space was required on both sides of the building. Other building regulations concerned porches, steps, bays, and house width. A minimum cost of construction was written into each deed, varying according to lot size and location.[8]

Such regulations were fairly common by the first decade of the twentieth century. More novel was the required prior approval of building plans, something the Olmsteds had also recommended at Roland Park. Aesthetic as well as structural issues were included in the approval process, and building materials and color schemes were subject to review. Atterbury suggested the creation of an architectural review department, to be headed by him, which would vet all plans whether those of the SFHC or of private architects, prepare building specifications, and be available to consult with and offer advice to lot owners before building.[9]

As had been the case at Roland Park, property owners at Forest Hills Gardens would be assessed an annual maintenance charge, originally set at $.002 per square foot. Owners whose property abutted plots intended for private parks or private lanes were assessed an additional fee. The fund, administered by the SFHC, was to be used to maintain streets, parks and public spaces, sewers, lighting, and "any other things necessary or desirable . . . to keep the property neat and in good order."[10]

Although authority to enforce the restrictions and to collect the maintenance fees was vested in the SFHC, foundation director John Glenn assured potential residents that Forest Hills Gardens was in no sense intended to be a company town. It was the SFHC's wish that the management of the property become "as democratic as possible": all lot owners would be able to express their views. The SFHC had no intention of exercising "paternal control." It would operate in the common interest to ensure that no individual property owner built an "unsightly" house or established "nuisances," but it did not intend "to control their actions beyond seeing that the general atmosphere of beauty and order is preserved."[11] The corporation formed to maintain the community initially would be wholly owned by the SFHC, which would be the largest property owner (until a majority of lots were sold) during the early years of development. Eventually, the residents would assume full control of the suburb's administration.[12]

The restrictive covenants for Forest Hills Gardens contain no explicit economic, social, or racial restrictions; however, the developers did have such considerations in mind. They judged that the "interests of all property owners at Forest Hills Gardens would best be advanced and preserved if a certain amount of care were taken to avoid the forced association of persons not likely to have harmonious relations with each other."[13] The same kind of unspoken agreement to sell only to "desirable residents" which Bouton had instituted at Roland Park was put into practice at Forest Hills Gardens. Bouton told de Forest that the Sage Foundation had to decide "whether the community is to be Jewish or Gentile. It cannot," he counseled, "be both and be satisfactory." He disingenuously couched his argument in economic terms, suggesting that the question was purely a "commercial" consideration "without prejudice either against or in favor of Jews." In a draft statement prepared for the foundation titled "On the question of the sale of property at Forest Hills Gardens to Hebrews," Bouton suggested that the company declare that there would be "no discrimination whatever against or in favor of any race or religion, except so far as may of necessity be involved in considerations vitally affecting the success of the development, the value of the experiment and the interests of the greater number of persons likely to reside there." The purpose of the Sage Foundation's experiment, Bouton's proposed statement cautioned, was to prove that it was economically feasible to build a better kind of suburban community. To protect both the "validity of the experiment" and the foundation's investment, therefore, it was "necessary that the methods adopted in the sale of the property shall be those sanctioned by the business experience of other land companies." The experiment had to be conducted "under normal and usual social conditions, such as would enable ready comparison to be made with similar developments," he declared. There was no point in denying the fact, "however regrettable," that "the Hebrew and the Gentile do not come together in a natural way as social friends and neighbors."[14] Commitment to progressive planning did not guarantee a corresponding progressive social conscience.

EARLY IN 1911, as the first phase of development was completed and the company prepared to open for sales, a key change in personnel took place. Edward Bouton had found it increasingly difficult to spend time in New York because of his continuing responsibilities at Roland Park. John Glenn wrote to Robert de Forest, who was vacationing at Georgia's Jekyll Island Club, of his concern that "Bouton is getting over-tired from running two places at once." Glenn felt that they needed a full-time general manager on site now that the project was

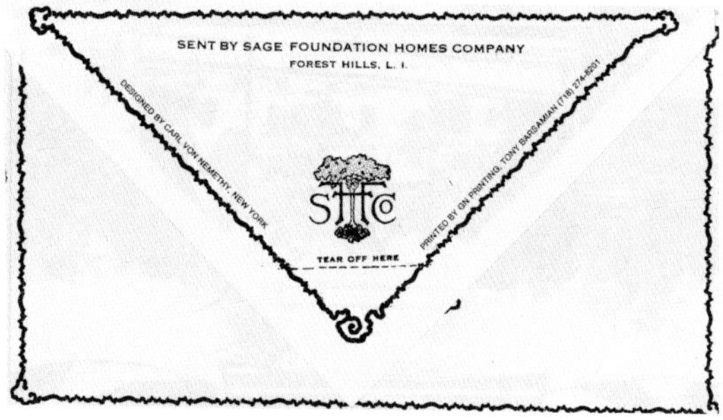

Promotional mailer. Courtesy Forest Hills Gardens Corporation.

entering the critical marketing phase. He recommended John M. Demarest, an executive in a Brooklyn real estate firm, for the job. Glenn suggested that Demarest operate "under Bouton's direction for the time being, working the whole responsibility on him by degrees, gradually but as rapidly as possible." Bouton would retain his position as a vice president of the SFHC.[15]

Olmsted's role in the project was changing as well. At the age of forty-one, Olmsted married Sarah Sharples, the sister of one of his Harvard friends, on 30 March 1911, and left for a month's honeymoon. By this time he had fulfilled his primary responsibilities for Forest Hills Gardens, and his city planning work for Pittsburgh and Rochester, his park planning for Chicago, and his duties in Washington as one of the founding members of the Fine Arts Commission were occupying increasing amounts of his time. In May, Olmsted suggested to the Sage Foundation that since the design work for the Gardens was virtually complete and his presence was no longer routinely needed, his compensation be reduced to $100 a month.[16]

Because of the publicity the project had received since its inception, more than three thousand inquiries were received before Forest Hills Gardens was officially open for sales. The SFHC decided not to advertise the property in the newspapers. Rather, in June it printed a prospectus for potential buyers titled *Forest Hills Gardens: Preliminary Information for Buyers*.[17] By 19 July, 172 lots had been bought by 72 purchasers. At the end of the month John Glenn reported to Olivia Sage on "how encouragingly things are going at Forest Hills. The result is surprising in view of the fact that we have done no general advertising. A large number of the purchasers have come thro' the recommendations of previous purchasers who were pleased with the property. Our first row of houses . . . were sold by the time their roofs were on. . . . I feel confident that the ultimate results will be satisfying and will show that you have created a beneficial object lesson that will be widely useful."[18]

General manager Demarest was not as sanguine. He reported in September that sales to date totaled $479,265, with 153 purchasers buying 364 lots. It was necessary, he felt, to pick up the pace, and he recommended "that an immediate and active advertising campaign . . . on conservative but aggressive lines" be launched in the New York press.[19] The SFHC ran advertisements for six weeks. Forest Hills Gardens was not a speculative venture, the ads emphasized, but rather an opportunity for investment. "The property is not cheap, as compared with other less carefully planned suburban developments"; it was the intent of the Sage Foundation to realize a "reasonable profit." In return, the potential buyer was offered the chance to purchase property in a development where improvements and infrastructure were already in place and could be seen, and where high quality of construction and maintenance of property values would be assured by building and other restrictions.[20] "Forest Hills Gardens IS NOT a low cost development," the developers felt it necessary to emphasize yet again. However, it was an economical venture "because improvements are permanent, cost of repairs and maintenance is reduced to a minimum, and money invested in the Gardens yields the greatest return in comfort, beauty, pleasure and satisfaction." Here was a community developing according to "a definite plan for the whole." Permanent improvements such as streets and underground infrastructure had been constructed according to the latest scientific principles. All the buildings had been designed to har-

Softening effect of plants in mature landscape. Courtesy Frances Loeb Library, Graduate School of Design, Harvard University.

monize with one another in both material and design, and the landscape and planting scheme for the entire property was designed by an expert. Restrictions were in place to guarantee that the "homes of today will be protected and in time become more attractive and more valuable."[21]

In April 1912, de Forest informed Olivia Sage that the Gardens had reached a milestone marking $1 million in sales. But the project was not close to showing any return on investment. A revised sales pamphlet issued the following year increased the minimum cash down payment from 2 to 5 percent and instituted charges for house plans and specifications provided by the company to lot owners.[22]

Although the Sage Foundation's hope of demonstrating that it was possible to build a model suburb and return a reasonable profit had not been realized, the first residents of Forest Hills Gardens suffered no such disappointments. They delighted in their physical surroundings and in the social and community activities that were originating from the talents and interests of these new neighbors. In the summer of 1913 Forest Hills Gardens held its first major celebration—a Fourth of July fete in Station Square. The community that Olmsted and Atterbury had created on paper just a few years earlier had come to life.

7

"A Village of Rare Charm"

WHY WE CHOSE FOREST HILLS GARDENS

LESS THAN TWO YEARS AFTER the property opened for sale, promotional material proclaimed that the "pioneering days are over at the Gardens." Unlike the typical suburban development, which exhibited a raw, unfinished appearance in its early years, Forest Hills Gardens already displayed the "well-seasoned look" that usually only comes with time.[1] The Sage Foundation's investment in hiring landscape and building architects "whom no . . . suburban boom companies would consider themselves justified in employing" had paid off, an early critic observed. Forest Hills Gardens, he wrote, demonstrated "the general truth of civic development that 'beauty pays.'"[2]

A steady stream of journalists and reporters traveled to Forest Hills Gardens eager to get a look at this highly touted model town. The public had heard much about the Sage Foundation's motives and plans for Forest Hills Gardens; now they wanted to know, as the reporter Louis Graves frankly put it, whether the Sage Foundation had managed to "deliver the goods."[3] Descriptions of the Gardens appeared in periodicals ranging from professional journals like *American Architect* to trade publications such as *Construction News* and *Cement Era* to popular magazines including *The Craftsman* and *American Homes and Gardens*. These initial assessments went beyond mere praise or description; the first visitors seemed transfixed by the sight that met them when they alighted from the Long Island Rail Road cars bringing them from the city. Forest Hills Gardens presented a vision of suburban living "the like

From cover of Why We Have Chosen Forest Hills Gardens for Our Home.

of which is not to be found at all in America," Graves wrote in *Building Progress*. "It smashes all the convention of commonplace suburban building. . . . So surprised is the newcomer at first view that the whole outlay seems a trifle bizarre." Graves provided a colorful account of the trip by rail to the new suburb:

> When you have barely settled down to reading your magazine, when the golden-haired heroine is just on the dint of climbing down a rope ladder from the topmost window of a lofty tower—the conductor . . . emits a jumble of sounds that are supposed to represent "Forest Hills Gardens!" Where upon you jump from your seat, rush out upon the station platform, and what do you see? Nothing less than that same medieval tower from which the heroine was preparing to descend to eager lover.
>
> Can this be just fifteen minutes from Broadway? you ask yourself? . . . No, it cannot. It is somewhere near the Rhine, and it's not new at all, because you have been transferred back a few centuries like Mark Twain's Connecticut Yankee.

Grave's effusive rhetoric captures the strong visual impression that Forest Hills Gardens made on its first sightseers. Atterbury's striking buildings set in Olmsted's graceful landscape of tree-lined streets, well-tended gardens, and shaded parks did seem to transport people to another time, another place. To some it brought to mind Swiss lake towns or medieval German hamlets. Others saw the old English villages of "Thomas Hardy country. . . . Only here, along with something of the aspect of the Middle Ages, there is combined the comfort of the twentieth century . . . scarcely seventeen miles from the Great White Way!"[4]

Critics familiar with town planning developments abroad saw beyond the aesthetics of Forest Hills Gardens to the more significant issues of planning and community development. Mary Eastwood Knevels drew on her knowledge of English garden cities in her perceptive assessment of what the designers of Forest Hills Gardens had accomplished. "Here," she emphasized, "community benefit is placed before everything else. . . . The practical application of the principle of collective planning makes the 'Gardens' truly unique among American towns."[5]

Contemporary accounts were not uniformly laudatory, however. Some critics thought that Forest Hills Gardens looked like a stage set for an operetta and that "jolly villagers should be approaching under the arch, left centre, singing the opening chorus."[6] Some labeled it a model town, which was to many American minds synonymous with "company town," enterprises that were viewed negatively by the early 1900s because of their founders' paternalistic attempts to control both the look of the community and the life of its inhabitants. And because it was sponsored by a philanthropic foundation, Forest Hills Gardens was often mistaken for a charitable or even welfare community.

Atterbury addressed the model town issue in several journal articles. "It is unfortunate," he wrote, "that the somewhat misleading word 'model' must be applied to such an eminently practical scheme as this development of the Russell Sage Foundation, for the reason that there is a kind of subtle odium which attaches to 'model' things of almost any kind, even when they are neither charitable nor philanthropic—a slightly sanctimonious atmosphere that is debilitating rather than stimulative of success." Atterbury feared that calling Forest Hills Gardens a model community would condemn the enterprise to the fate that had befallen once popular City Beautiful efforts, now belittled as mere cosmetic, frivolous exercises. He tried to address the "honestly felt" criticism that Forest Hills Gardens was "'the plaything of a wealthy widow,' destined to . . . be more enduring but less heroic than Brook Farm, more wisely conceived and more practical than the Helicon Hall of Upton Sinclair, and more carefully planned than the city of Pullman, but like all of them—foredoomed." Forest Hills Gardens, Atterbury emphasized, was a "demonstration in town planning and home building, and not in city administration." Whether self-governing and cooperative ventures would "respond to and grow under the influences and opportunities of the environment which we are endeavoring to create . . . can be answered only in the final outcome."[7]

Olmsted also tried to counter the persistent misconceptions. In a letter to the English planner Thomas Adams, he explained that when the Sage Foundation trustees undertook the enterprise, they "did not expect or attempt to do anything revolutionary or epoch-making." Their hope was "to contribute something toward advancing the 'state of the art'" in suburban planning. In itself, Forest Hills Gardens was "a mere drop in the bucket": its greatest contribution would be to demonstrate that comprehensive planning was an economically viable option for a private developer.[8] Olmsted also addressed the charge that it was inappropriate for a philanthropic institution to develop housing for the middle class. The Sage Foundation, he argued, having made a considerable investment in the land purchase, could not fairly be criticized "for recognizing market conditions and supplying . . . homes of a kind to meet the purses and wishes of those who could afford to buy in that locality." Unlike Letchworth or Hampstead Garden Suburb, he noted, which started with the idea of achieving "certain more or less beneficent results and then the money was raised," the situation at Forest Hills Gardens was the reverse: "the enterprise started with certain funds to be invested in a profitable but incidentally beneficent manner." If Forest Hills Gardens hoped to influence the more typical developer, it must demonstrate commercial success.[9]

Some early reviews perpetuated the notion that Forest Hills Gardens was intended to be a working-class community, but most analysts of the new suburb correctly characterized it as a neighborhood for the middle class. Edward Hale Brush, writing in *The Craftsman*, the journal published by Gustav Stickley that helped popularize the Arts and Crafts movement in the United States, underscored the significance of this "first garden city in America." Forest Hills Gardens was "not going to be a town where a low-paid mechanic or day laborer can afford to live," he reported (and "in view of the ill-advised and unauthorized announcement that it was to be a workingmen's colony there may be some regret or disappointment at this"). However, it was equally important to demonstrate that a suburban community could be provided for "those of moderate means seeking the peace and comfort of a model village . . . without great expense and in charming homes . . . within easy commuting distance of New York."[10]

Tea Garden cascade. From Forest Hills Gardens, *1913. Courtesy Rockefeller Archive Center.*

This idea that good housing was needed for people at all income levels was given scholarly support by Professor Scott E. W. Bedford, chair of the Department of Municipal Sociology at the University of Chicago, an institution where much of the intellectual framework for Progressivism was developed. "There is no more important problem than Housing," Bedford stated, "not only of the working classes, but *all classes*. . . . I regard as the most important effort at proper housing in America the one conducted by the Russell Sage Foundation at Forest Hills Gardens, Long Island. . . . The harmony of architecture, the winding streets, the tasteful street furniture, the railroad entrance to the town, the use of flowers and vines, the quiet taste and dignity, would certainly impress, and have an influence in solving the housing problem."[11]

THE CREATORS OF Forest Hills Gardens knew that its first residents would be critical to the success or failure of the project. "Assuming the possibility of creating a model town," quipped Grosvenor Atterbury, "where can you find the citizens with which to people it?"[12] In a more serious vein, the SFHC considered how to attract "suitable residents" whom they defined as those who would enjoy participating in and contributing to the experiment in suburban living. Once the development opened for sale, however, the marketing materials for Forest Hills Gardens were similar to those used to promote higher-end suburban developments at the time. Early advertisements stated that "social" as well as financial references would be required, which the company would investigate before approving a potential buyer's application. "The high standard demanded for the character of the purchaser at Forest Hills Gardens" would ensure "congenial neighbors and varied opportunities for social interaction." Since Forest Hills Gardens was not a social experiment, but rather an economic one, the SFHC, as the developer, focused on attracting qualified buyers who could afford the price of a lot and a suitable house. In return, the company promised to safeguard the buyer's investment by administering the building restrictions and other covenants that accompanied the title to their property, thus guaranteeing "that the homes of today will be protected and in time become more attractive and more valuable."[13]

During the first two years of sales, the SFHC kept statistics on the occupations of buyers. These records suggest that the "pioneer residents" of Forest Hills Gardens represented a fairly broad cross section, vocationally, of middle-income society. Clerks and salesmen constituted the largest category of residents (55), followed by merchants and managers (51), teachers and educators (41), architects, artists, engravers, and interior decorators (33), engineers (25), and doctors, lawyers, and dentists (22). Other early residents included social workers, secretaries, a butcher, a plumber, and a masseuse. Most of the new suburbanites moved to the Gardens from New York City or from Brooklyn and commuted to Manhattan during the work week.[14]

Within two years of its opening, 1,290 lots had been sold and 141 owner-occupied houses built at Forest Hills Gardens. By September 1914, a total of 228 houses had been completed or were under construction. Twenty-nine neighborhood streets had one or more houses lining them. Forty trains a day were running between the city and the Forest Hills Gardens Station, and the postal service delivered twice a day. The population reached 720 by 1915: 556 adults (including 134 live-in help) and 164 children under the age of seventeen.[15]

THE FOUNDING RESIDENTS of Forest Hills Gardens seemed to appreciate that they were part of a unique experience, and a kind of group ethos quickly took effect. Residents were proud of their planned town: "Other communities grow in a haphazard fashion," the first issue of the *Forest Hills Gardens Bulletin* observed in the fall of 1915. "It is our pride that our town has had, from the beginning, a cohesion, an element of unity which like our ruddy roofs ties us together in growth and amity."[16] That same year Will Phillip Hooper, a New York writer and illustrator, wrote to over fifty of his Forest Hills Gardens neighbors soliciting statements about why they had chosen to live in the new community. A collection of the responses he received was published in a pamphlet titled *Why We Have Chosen Forest Hills Gardens for Our Home*, designed and produced by his fellow community resident Frederic W. Goudy, one of the premier designers of typefaces in the United States and founder of the renowned Village Press. From 1913 to 1923, Goudy and his wife and design associate, Bertha, operated the press from the lower level of their Forest Hills Gardens home on Deepdene Road, producing graphically acclaimed books, magazines, and posters. Printed on creamy handmade paper, the cover of the *Why* booklet featured a Goudy-designed title block in green and copper reminiscent of William Morris's designs for his Kelmscott Press.

The SFHC provided the photographs of homes, streetscapes, and gardens which illustrated each page and paid for the printing, happy to assist with a resident-inspired publication that it could use as a marketing tool. The residents' comments highlighted the same theme that the company had emphasized in its advertisements: the value of residing in

Hooper garden. From Why *booklet.*

Bird pool in Demarest garden. From Why *booklet.*

a planned community that combined the charms of country living with convenient access to the city.[17]

Eight respondents cited the Sage Foundation's involvement as a factor in their decision to purchase property at the Gardens. The Sage imprimatur inspired confidence: buyers would be "dealing with a concern as reliable as the Government." (Other developments might "whither and die before they grew to manhood," but "the Sage millions would not fail.") Furthermore, the Sage Foundation was committed to providing fair value: "I was drawn as the needle to the magnet by the name 'Sage'; here I knew there would be a square deal." Another resident concluded, "The name Sage seemed a guarantee that promise was equivalent to performance."[18]

The earliest residents enjoyed thinking of themselves as pioneers. "To live in Forest Hills now is to be one of the creators of a town. We are Pilgrim Fathers and Mothers," wrote one. Another enjoyed the "adventure of colonizing . . . freed of its ancient hardships." Forest Hills Gardens struck a cord as being "the real thing," "the American suburbanite's apotheosis of dreams." Several respondents said that they had been attracted by the idea of living in a model community "planned right, built from the bottom up." Even at this early stage of development residents appreciated the results of united efforts: "the planner, the architect and the landscape gardener have created a village of rare charm," declared one woman. A resident "Bohemian-American Tenor" praised the town as "one great garden of artistic uniformity where the people, the homes, the flowers and the song birds and the artist" realize their "ideal dwelling place."

For many of the new homeowners the "reasonable restrictions" that accompanied their property deed were a positive selling point, an assurance that property values would be maintained. At Forest Hills Gardens you need not worry that "a pseudo-Swiss chalet-bungalow [would appear] on one side of you, while a retired bar-keep on the other side puts up a Swedish-Renaissance cottage with a Greco-Roman pergola and a catch-as-catch-can roof." Residents could also be confident of having "satisfactory neighbors," who could be "congenial . . . friends with mutual tastes." As one resident proclaimed, "the company's restrictions have given us a community of delightful homes and neighbors."

Some of the comments supported the Sage Foundation's contention that all classes of city dwellers, not just the very poor, were in need of better housing alternatives. These new suburbanites appreciated the foundation's "liberal policy" that enabled middle-class people to purchase. "Rent paying and living like impersonal sardines stifled us and the clatter of the city wearied us," wrote one resident; they were happy to escape the "brick walls and germ laden dust of the city." Clarence Perry, head of the Sage Foundation's recreation department and an influential planning theorist in the 1920s, described the "quietness, . . . freedom from the janitor, and relief from subway and elevated" that Garden residents were seeking. Ruby Ross Goodnow, an interior decorator, who as Ruby Ross Wood would define "the tasteful house" for generations of aspiring suburbanites until her death at midcentury, wrote of the "many amusing and substantial" pleasures that the Gardens offered, including "a restful absence of hideous placards and fly-specked shops, a comfortable permanence."

Finally, the first residents valued their new home as a place in which they could enjoy at once "the advantages of the city and the freedom of the country." They appreciated the "proximity to New York and the excellent train service," which allowed them to commute to the city for work or entertainment, while their children "could grow up breathing pure air" and "play in safety." Goudy summed up the experience of living in the Gardens: "the desire to live on a road with individual characteristics, with wayside greens and flowers, to have unrestricted views of distant country, trees with birds to sing in them, and space for our own flowers and garden, fresh air and a home—Forest Hills Gardens seemed to offer all these. After living here eighteen months we find even more than these—congenial neighbors and friends with mutual tastes."

IN THE FALL OF 1915 the Sage Foundation Homes Company began to publish the *Forest Hills Gardens Bulletin*, which it distributed to residents each month. The *Bulletin* was to be the town crier of the Gardens, said SFHC general manager John Demarest: its purpose was "to interpret the community . . . and to create an atmosphere of neighborly feeling."[19] It was also a way to perpetuate the founding spirit of the community.

Residents formed a variety of social groups and began traditions that future generations would continue to nurture. In the spring of 1913 a committee of residents approached the SFHC about establishing a community social center. The company spent $18,000 to move an old farmhouse to the corner of Metropolitan and Ascan Roads and fitted out the center with a tennis court, a baseball field, and an indoor bowling alley. Over one hundred families joined in the first year. In October 1915 the baseball diamond was the site of a colorful contest: the mens' baseball team, dressed in women's clothes, challenged the women's team (dress "unannounced"). The women won, eight to four.[20] The Inn was the setting for Saturday evening dances and popular concerts on Sundays. The West Side Tennis Club provided another option for socializing and rec-

Village Green lined with cars during U.S. Open. From Why *booklet.*

reation. In 1913 the SFHC had purchased a 32-acre plot from the Cord Meyer Company with the intention of offering some of the land to the venerable New York athletic club, which had been looking to relocate in the suburbs. The SFHC believed that the presence of the tennis club would not only add social cachet to the new community but would also protect Forest Hills Gardens on its western boundary from the incursion of unsuitable development.[21]

Entrance to tennis courts. From Forest Hills Gardens, *1913. Courtesy Rockefeller Archive Center.*

Outdoor activities were very popular. Bird watching was practically a religion, and the Forest Hills Gardens Audubon Society flourished. Grosvenor Atterbury crafted birdhouses designed to attract different species, and the *Bulletin* faithfully reported sightings. Gardening was also a favored activity. The Women's Club offered lectures on the topic, and pictures of private gardens were featured in the *Bulletin*. By 1916 a cooperative playground had been organized, providing supervised games for children. Tennis courts for residents, located along Continental Avenue, were flooded in winter for skating parties, where residents occasionally enjoyed "the graceful, fancy skating" of Miss Frida Whitaker, a Garden resident who performed such demonstrations at the Waldorf-Astoria hotel in the city.[22]

With an unusually high percentage of artistic and creative occupa-

Contemporary replica of Atterbury's birdhouse, 2001. LALH photograph.

Dancing in Olivia Park. Courtesy Rockefeller Archive Center.

tions represented among residents, it is not surprising that a theater group was one of the first to be organized. Early performances of the Garden Players often took place outdoors in Olivia Park and the Inn Tea Garden. Members held play readings in one another's homes and successfully competed against other amateur theatrical troupes in New York City's Little Theatre Tournament.

Garden residents also pursued intellectual interests. The Women's Club studied a variety of topics including American art and child care. With a view toward better understanding the circumstances of World War I, the club sponsored a series of six lectures titled "The Making of Modern Europe" given by a resident who was professor of history at Columbia University. When the United States entered the war, club women formed a chapter of the National Surgical Dressing Committee, which rolled bandages. To raise money for surgical material, they sponsored a *bal masque* at the Forest Hills Inn.

Other organized activities for women reflected the interest of many of the first residents in the progressive agenda. The Women's Church Guild formed a club to study the problems of immigration, visiting Ellis Island, settlement houses, and milk stations in tenement areas on Manhattan's Lower East Side. The Women's Club made a contribution

Church-in-the-Gardens. Courtesy Rockefeller Archive Center.

to establish a dental clinic in the tenement district. The Mothers' Club brought the kindergarten movement (education of pre–school age children) to the Gardens, and a Forest Hills Suffrage Club was established. The Health Committee worked to battle the ubiquitous flies and mosquitoes that plagued outdoor activities.[23]

The Men's Club pursued its own ambitious intellectual program, including lectures on building construction and the (albeit brief) history of the Gardens. Resident Lyman Beecher Stowe (grandson of Harriet) gave a talk on Booker T. Washington and southern education. Fellow Gardenite and artist Boardman Robinson spoke of his experiences in revolutionary Russia, illustrating the dispatches of the journalist John Reed.

In 1915, as a gift to the growing community, Olivia Sage paid for the construction of the Church-in-the-Gardens, designed by Grosvenor Atterbury. Before they had a permanent home, the congregation had worshiped in a storefront provided by the SFHC and in a portable chapel.[24] Other community institutions also had made their start in temporary homes during these first years. A portable school opened in December 1910 with two classrooms for seventy-five pupils; a second opened in

May 1914. In April 1912 the Forest Hills branch of the Queens Borough Library was established in the Inn.[25]

The most notable community activities were the celebrations and civic observances held in the public spaces and parks that Olmsted had designed. Residents prized these spaces as the defining elements of the community. As Lucy Allen Smart, the editor of the *Bulletin*, expressed it: "Station Square and the Green . . . help to make effective the community spirit which is here. The architecture of the Square and the landscape gardening of the Green are strong factors in the centralization of the community life."[26] At Christmas time, for example, the communal Christmas tree and Yule log lit up Station Square, and residents flocked to holiday parties at the Inn. Carolers led by torchbearers accompanied Santa, who paraded in his sleigh through the community's curving neighborhood streets, stopping to leave a small gift at every house with a candle in the window, signaling that a child lived within.

Fourth of July was the occasion for major celebration at the Gardens. It is understandable that the commemoration of American independence took on added meaning during the years of World War I, but Forest Hills Gardens' first residents also seemed to feel a special connection to the founding fathers honored on that day. They believed that their planned community was the embodiment of "that old village spirit which made the strength and ideal of our forefathers." "Forest

View toward Inn, across Village Green, 1914. Courtesy Fairsted.

Fouth of July games in Station Square. Courtesy Rockefeller Archive Center.

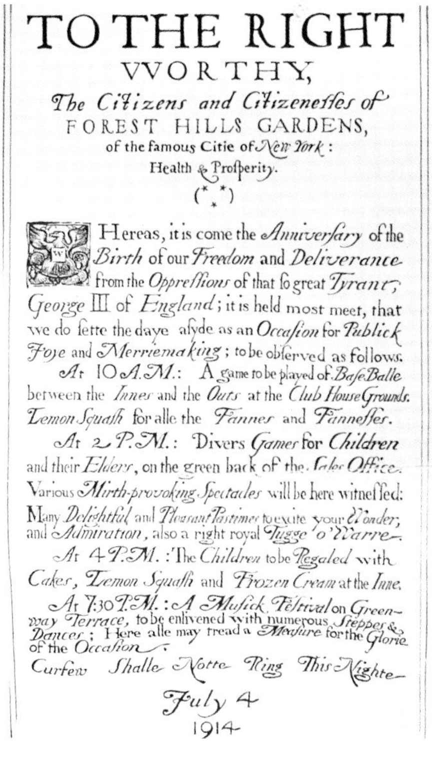

TO THE RIGHT
VVORTHY,

The Citizens and Citizeneſſes of
FOREST HILLS GARDENS,
of the famous Citie of *New York* :
Health & Proſperity.
(*,*)

WHereas, it is come the *Anniverſary* of the *Birth* of our *Freedom* and *Deliverance* from the *Oppreſſions* of that ſo great *Tyrant*, *George* III of *England*; it is held most meet, that we do ſette the daye aſyde as an *Occaſion* for *Publick Joye* and *Merriemaking*; to be obſerved as follows.

At 10 *A.M.*: A game to be played of *Baſe Balle* between the *Innes* and the *Outs* at the *Club House Grounds*. *Lemon Squaſh* for alle the *Fannes* and *Fanneſſes*.

At 2 *P.M.*: Divers *Games* for *Children* and their *Elders*, on the green back of the *Sales Office*. Various *Mirth-provoking Spectacles* will be here witneſſed: Many *Delightful* and *Pleasant Pastimes* to excite your *Wonder*, and *Admiration*, also a right royal *Tugge o' Warre*.

At 4 *P.M.* : The *Children* to be *Regaled* with *Cakes*, *Lemon Squaſh* and *Frozen Cream* at the *Inne*.

At 7:30 *P.M.* : *A Muſick Feſtival* on *Greenway Terrace*, to be enlivened with numerous *Steppes* & *Dances*; Here alle may tread a *Meaſure* for the *Glorie* of the *Occaſion*.

Curfew Shalle Notte Ring This Nighte

July 4
1914

Fourth of July Proclamation.
Courtesy Rockefeller Archive Center.

Fourth of July decorations, Greenway Terrace. Courtesy Rockefeller Archive Center.

Fife and drum corps, Fourth of July.
Courtesy Rockefeller Archive Center.

SFHC management and others in costume.
Courtesy Rockefeller Archive Center.

Hills Gardens," they proclaimed, "will help to make the nation great by illustrating the greatness possible to a small village. There is liberty in the curves of our streets and union in these red roofs that give back one smile the color of the common sun."[27]

After the success of the first community Independence Day celebration in 1914, a standing Fourth of July Day Committee was formed to organize increasingly elaborate festivities. Each year Goudy's Village Press produced beautiful hand-lettered Independence Day proclamations and programs detailing the day's activities. Colorful posters were designed by resident artists such as Herman Rountree and Annie Hooper. The 1915 celebration featured the unveiling of the fountain in Station Square, followed by games for children and adults. There was a tilting contest for the men and a competition among the women to see who could drive a nail the straightest. In Olivia Park, Irmgard, baroness von Rottenthal, performed five interpretive dances in the spirit of Isadora Duncan. That evening there was dancing of quite a different sort to the music of the Seventh Regiment Band in a Station Square illuminated by Japanese lanterns. Spotlights were shone on portraits of Presidents Wilson and Washington. Some residents donned period costumes. SFHC construction manager Charles Scammell and his wife came as General and Mrs. Washington, and general manager Demarest and Mrs. Demarest portrayed Uncle Sam and Mrs. Columbia.[28]

On Independence Day 1916 the official Forest Hills Gardens flag, featuring the letters F and H entwined in a branching and securely rooted tree, was unveiled and raised. Also on that date the first in a series of symbolic dramas was presented in Olivia Park. In *The Happy Stranger: A Forest Hills Allegory*, "a bevy of attractive young women" personified "the material and spiritual features of this community, setting forth the pilgrimage of city men and women to this paradise of God's out-of-doors" where one's "Burden of woes becomes a mass of Roses."[29] Later that afternoon children gathered in the Tea Garden for a tea party and games and viewed the costume parade in Station Square, which had a circus theme. That evening a crowd of 5,000 gathered for dancing in Station Square, wending their way home at 1:00 A.M. to the strains of "Home Sweet Home." Patriotic fervor was at its height at the 1917 Independence Day observance, when former president Theodore Roosevelt gave his "100% American" address in Station Square.

The pioneer residents of Forest Hills Gardens were not alone in devoting so much time and energy to holiday pageants. The historian

David Glassberg has pointed out that during the Progressive Era people displayed a near mania for such displays. In his words, historical pageantry was "a public ritual of communal self-discovery."[30] These productions were considered "democratic art" by community leaders, a means of transmitting American values and ideals to the masses and developing civic pride and solidarity. Educators and social workers promoted public pageants as an opportunity for education and productive play, and as an alternative to popular pastimes such as frequenting saloons, attending burlesque shows, and viewing the usual holiday parades that seemed increasingly to degenerate into near riots in many cities. Indeed the Sage Foundation had been supporting pageant productions through its funding of the Playground Association, founded in 1906, for just these reasons. The foundation also underwrote a national "Safe and Sane July Fourth" campaign, encouraging public fireworks displays, for several years.

THE FIRST DECADE of development in Forest Hills Gardens had been a remarkable one. By September 1921 the number of houses completed or under construction had passed the four hundred mark. The war, however, had its effect on business. Rising labor and material costs and wartime rationing and shortages depressed sales. In his annual summing up, Demarest regretted "to have to report that the year 1921 was the poorest in the history of the company's business." Land sales totaled only $56,635, and house sales had fallen to $182,809.[31] As the proportion of the land owned by the SFHC decreased, the foundation's trustees began to think about the future of the maturing garden community.

In June of 1921, Olmsted and Atterbury drafted a statement outlining the issues they thought the trustees needed to discuss. Now that about 75 percent of the original tract had been sold and approximately half of this part of the property had been developed, how, they asked, "is the company to dispose of any obligations which may rest upon it in respect to continuing physical maintenance . . . in such a way as to maintain the standards which it has set?" They worried that there could be serious problems over "the methods and the financial means for administering the restrictions in regard to that remaining half" when the SFHC completed land sales.[32]

Olmsted and Atterbury, who had made periodic visits to the Gardens, had noted a gradual lowering of what Olmsted admitted were

A later residence at Forest Hills Gardens. Albert P. Armour residence, designed 1925 by Douglass Fitch. Courtesy Library of Congress, Prints and Photographs Division, Gottscho-Schleisner Collection, LC-G612-T-46369 DLC.

"vaguely defined artistic standards," as well as "noticeable breaches of specific restrictions" included in the land covenants. Although this was not an uncommon phenomenon in higher-end planned developments, Olmsted observed (for the latecomers "always tend on the average to overbuild their lots more than the first comers"), "to drift into lowering of standards without notice to the early purchasers," he believed, "would be utterly unfair."[33]

Equally troubling to Olmsted was his impression that many of the more recent lot owners had not hired designers who were competent to achieve the high quality characteristic of the Gardens. He suggested that buyers be given a list of approved architects who would work out plans in consultation with Atterbury. Unsatisfactory plans would be rejected by the company without comment unless the owner paid to have Atterbury revise them. Similarly, Olmsted believed that owners should be required to submit acceptable landscape plans before house plans were approved. If owners did work with an approved landscape designer, they would still have to pay for a review of the plan by Olmsted

Brothers to verify its compliance with Forest Hills Gardens standards.[34]

In a letter to foundation trustees in which he addressed Olmsted and Atterbury's concerns, John Demarest acknowledged that the SFHC's position in the maturing community was changing, and now, as was inevitable, the relationship was less personal. He agreed that the company should be looking toward the time when a group of residents would assume responsibility for administering restrictions and maintenance charges. Residents should be educated about these responsibilities, he believed, and the Gardens' Community Council was a good first step. This representative group, formed in 1919, was already voicing the community's concerns regarding the public schools, transportation, taxes, and other civic matters, and it had taken over the planning of the seasonal celebrations that had become an important part of community life. Looking back over the early years of development, Demarest concluded, he was gratified to see how very well the protective covenants had worked out, but in his opinion it was not yet time for the SFHC to relinquish its control.[35]

Interior, Albert P. Armour residence. Courtesy Library of Congress, Prints and Photographs Division, Gottscho-Schleisner Collection, LC-G612-T-46403 DLC.

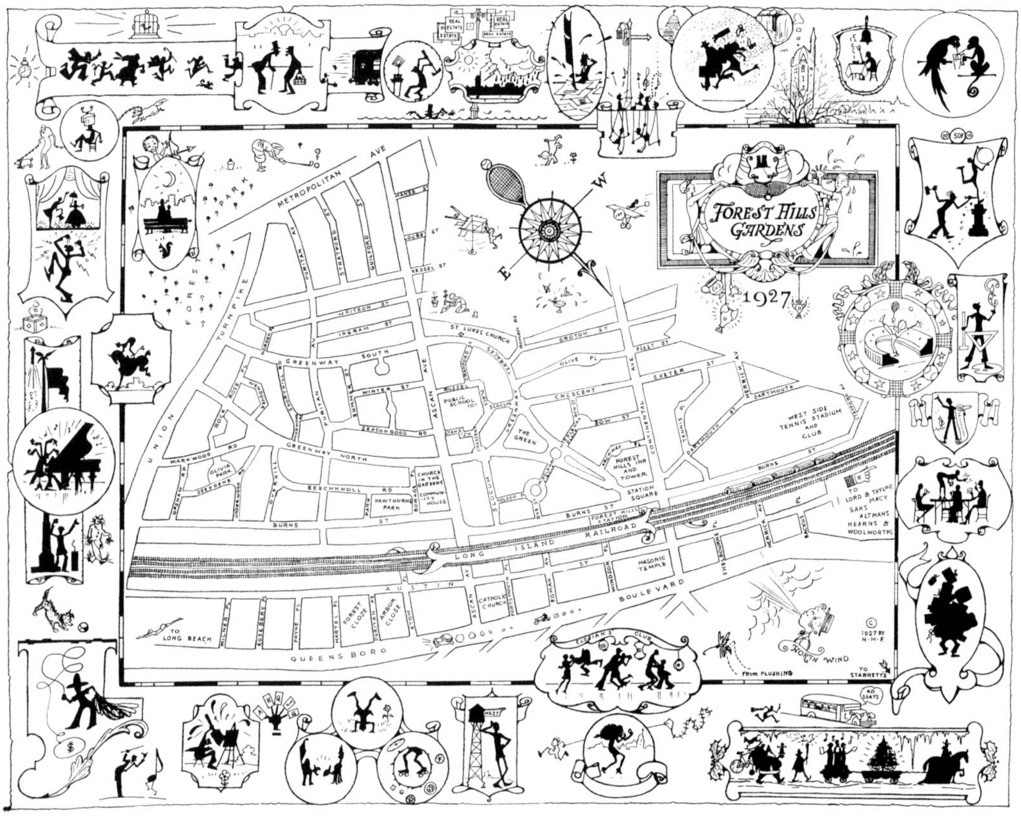

Map of Forest Hills Gardens, 1927. Courtesy Forest Hills Gardens Corporation.

The Sage Foundation trustees, however, did not agree with either their chief designers or their general manager. It seemed to them that the time had come to get out of the real estate business. The foundation's purpose in developing the model garden community had been "to provide more healthful and attractive homes for many people and to demonstrate that careful city planning, convenient thoroughfares, quiet domestic local streets and ample public spaces would make a satisfactory suburban development and encourage imitation."[36] This the Sage Foundation had successfully done. The one aim not yet accomplished, largely because of the effect of World War I, was to realize a profit, but the trustees believed that the foundation's continued participation until the final lots were sold would not appreciably change the financial picture.[37]

The state of the foundation's own finances also played a part in its decision to conclude participation in Forest Hills Gardens. The foundation had experienced several years of declining income, reaching a low point in 1917. Forest Hills Gardens represented its largest outlay of capital. By selling its interest, even at a loss of about $350,000, the trustees could restore funds to principal. This transaction, along with an additional legacy from Olivia Sage received at her death, helped return financial health to the foundation. In addition, the trustees were formulating a new mission for the next decade: to obtain a better understanding of how to achieve results in the field of social work and how to make research findings more useful to practitioners.[38]

The trustees decided that Demarest was the person most likely to maintain the character of Forest Hills Gardens in the spirit in which it had been created. Accordingly, in May 1922 the Russell Sage Foundation sold all of its stock in the Sage Foundation Homes Company for $1,920,000 to a syndicate organized by Demarest and a majority of lot owners.[39] "The Foundation is of the opinion," read the statement accompanying the announcement of the transfer, "that its chief purposes in organizing and developing Forest Hills Gardens have been accomplished." In December the property owners established the Gardens Corporation (later the Forest Hills Gardens Corporation) to act as their common agency "to promote and to sustain in Forest Hills Gardens in all suitable ways the living and aesthetic conditions for which the Gardens was founded."[40] On 1 January 1923, the SFHC conveyed ownership of streets, common lands, and sewers to the Gardens Corporation, which also assumed responsibility for administering the town's maintenance fund and supervising new construction.

THE SAGE FOUNDATION had accomplished its goal of creating a town whose combination of physical plan, architectural design, landscape treatment, and progressive real estate policy was unique in early twentieth-century suburbia. But would a mature Forest Hills Gardens governed by residents themselves be able to preserve its special quality? As they looked to the future, the first residents wondered whether their own efforts would be enough to safeguard that harmonious ensemble of architecture and landscape which made Forest Hills Gardens a place apart. But they meant to try: "As there are fewer and fewer bare spaces and more and more houses, we lose the appearance of the country, and it will be necessary to make an effort to keep the village atmosphere. . . . We must cherish everything that keeps our community life distinctive from the big city."[41]

8

The Legacy of Forest Hills Gardens

Our best architects have abandoned the suburbs to the ordinary practitioner and to the speculative builder. And the discipline of town planning at the suburban scale has been allowed to die.—Robert A. M. Stern (1978)

The seekers after their hearts' desire—a perfect place to live and enjoy life—too often meet the same experience. Seeking the places most attractive by nature, piling into them thousands after thousands without constructive forethought… their very numbers begin to distill the poison that blights the paradise they seek.—Frederick Law Olmsted Jr. (1922)

FOREST HILLS GARDENS has been scrutinized, analyzed, and evaluated almost from the day the first spade of earth was turned. It has been both praised and criticized, but there has been general agreement that Forest Hills Gardens is a notable milestone in the history of the American suburb, serving as an example for two generations of planners and developers in the pre–World War II era. The architect and historian Robert A. M. Stern stated, "Its unique combination of city planning and architecture . . . made Forest Hills Gardens the preeminent expression of the suburban ideal . . . and the most important suburb built in New York, the only one to assume international importance."[1] Now the debate over what constitutes "the good suburb" has once again come to the fore of the planning agenda. Early and mid-century suburbs are showing their age and experiencing many of the same concerns typically associated with urban areas: loss of population, deteriorating infrastructure and housing stock, rise in crime, decline in employment opportunities, and shortages of affordable housing. Suburbs that have developed over the last thirty years farther and farther from central cities have created their own set of problems: sprawl, overcrowding, traffic congestion, lack of recreational and commercial venues within walking distance of homes, and environmental and conservation concerns.

A lively discussion on how to revitalize older suburban communities and guide new development has been prominently displayed in the press and popular "shelter" and lifestyle magazines, as well as in the scholarly literature of planning, landscape architecture, and urban history. In understanding that suburbs, too, have a history, we are rediscovering the planning principles that went into building good ones. Suburbs will continue to grow. The question for citizens, politicians, and planners is the same one that Olmsted framed at the beginning of the twentieth century when professional planning in the United States was in its infancy: How do we shape and control that growth? Nearly half the country's population now resides in the suburbs.[2] But just as the boom in urban development in the early 1900s brought with it a myriad of physical, aesthetic, and social problems, the mass suburbanization of the United States since the 1950s is also a Pandora's box. Although a house in the suburbs is still venerated as the American Dream, the proliferation of market-driven, largely uncontrolled, low-density residential and commercial development which has realized that dream has created a nightmare of suburban sprawl, sterile streetscapes, architectural mediocrity, dependence on the automobile, neglect of the public domain, and environmental degradation—the list can seem interminable. So, like Carol Kennicott in Gopher Prairie and like the pioneering residents of Forest Hills Gardens, many Americans are once again asking if there is not a better way to build communities.

DID FOREST HILLS GARDENS achieve its goals of creating a model for more intelligent and effective suburban planning and design? Robert de Forest considered this question in 1922, as ownership of the community passed from the Sage Foundation to the residents' association under the management of John Demarest. If judged purely as a business proposition, the answer would have to be no, de Forest admitted. In fact, the foundation lost $360,800 on its investment.[3] But in terms of "planning, restrictions, maintenance charge, basis of sales, investigations of prospective purchasers," he claimed, "it has been...

Greenway Terrace, 2001. LALH photograph.

Burns Street, 2001. Photograph by Carol Betsch.

entirely successful and has accomplished what the Sage Foundation intended."[4] Frederick Law Olmsted agreed. The Sage Foundation went into the field of suburban real estate development, he recalled, with the hope that they would further the state of the art.[5] That they had assuredly done. Sage trustee John Glenn summarized the accomplishment: Forest Hills Gardens had demonstrated "the aesthetic and the practical values of a carefully planned real estate development, at a period when such planning was almost unique. . . . The many imitators and the fame of the Gardens themselves are eloquent testimony," he wrote, to the project's success.[6]

One of the earliest, most balanced, and still germane analyses of Forest Hills Gardens came from the planning theorist and community activist Clarence Perry, who, with his physician wife, was among the first fifty families to move into the suburb, remaining until his death some thirty years later. In the 1920s, Perry was developing his concept of the neighborhood as the primary unit of planning to create what he termed modest residential communities. Struck by the fact that he lived in a reasonable approximation of the kind of model development he sought to promote, Perry often used the plan of Forest Hills Gardens to illustrate a new type of residential community, one that acknowledges the larger urban context while creating its own distinctive identity.

Perry identified six elements that defined the planned neighborhood unit: size, boundaries, open spaces, institutional sites, local commercial area, and internal street system. With a population of about five thousand, Forest Hills Gardens was the right size to support an elementary school, the focal institution in Perry's neighborhood scheme. The suburb had well-defined boundaries on two sides, the railroad on the east and Forest Park to the south, but the western and northern perimeters (following the original property lines at time of purchase) were less distinct and less satisfactory by Perry's estimation. Perry praised Olmsted's road system for facilitating internal circulation and contributing to the ambience of the community. He approved of the centrally located green, the prominent site for the school just beyond, and the small community parks and interior block retreats. The shops in Station Square met his requirement for a local business district to serve residents. Finally, Perry emphasized that Forest Hills Gardens was noteworthy because its physical plan, distinctive architecture and landscape, and other special features engendered local pride and united residents in efforts to perfect and preserve them. The layout of Forest Hills Gardens and its developers' efforts to attract prospective purchasers who would make "congenial members of the colony," Perry said, had facilitated the formation of groups that contributed to a rich communal life from the outset.[7] Perry commended the many voluntary associations, the communal celebrations, and the active participation of residents in the homeowners association.

Perry also saw the shortcomings of the Forest Hills Gardens plan but concluded that these unsatisfactory features were due to either irremediable or unforeseeable conditions. They had been addressed in principle; the plan simply did not go far enough.[8] More definite and visible boundaries to the west and north and the elimination of through-roads connecting to major commuting thoroughfares would have helped to protect the community from outside traffic, Perry claimed. (It is not known whether Perry was aware that the incorporation of the two widest streets was required by terms of the land sale, but he did recognize that it had been a "concession" to the city's proposed street plan.) Even so, the exponential rise in the number of automobiles, he noted, could not have been predicted in 1909. A more significant shortcoming in Perry's view was that, while generous for its time, Olmsted had not provided enough space for play and active recreation. He also thought

Mature trees on Olivia Place, 2001. LALH photograph.

that Station Square, albeit a handsome and well-designed space, was not the most appropriate place for community celebrations and other civic activities because of its primary function as a traffic center. Forest Hills Gardens could have benefited from having a larger central green and a real community center complex located near the school. Finally, Perry found the commercial facilities in Station Square inadequate to the needs of the residents, although he acknowledged that a variety of shops was nearby.

How much of Perry's critique remains valid today? A review of recent issues of the *Forest Hills Gardens News*, published by the Forest Hills Gardens Corporation, highlights what management and residents consider to be both the advantages and disadvantages of life in the Gardens today. Commuter through-traffic is still seen as a problem, but the fact that Forest Hills Gardens is served so efficiently by public transportation is probably more appreciated by today's inhabitants than it was by the original residents. And the Gardens remains a remarkably pleasant place for the pedestrian (to a visitor used to the traffic common to most city and suburban streets, it seems remarkably quiet). Community maintenance is a major theme in the newsletters. Projects to upgrade sidewalks, reseed parks, and plant trees have led the list of recent undertakings. Upkeep was one of the key elements of the original concept for Forest Hills Gardens and has certainly been largely responsible for the development's enduring value. The Gardens Corporation has reminded residents that it is "first a maintenance organization. That means we should be *maintaining* our streets, sidewalks, sewers and parks. Unfortunately, we suffered a lack of funds for a number of years and must now address repairs and 'catch-up' in addition to 'upkeep.'"[9] Today it does seem that maintenance efforts have not been able to keep pace: private lawns are immaculate, but the Green and the two small parks look less manicured despite their major refurbishment about five years ago. Several newsletters mention lawsuits that had been filed by people claiming injury while walking on neighborhood streets and sidewalks, although a major repaving project has been under way since 1995. Forest Hills Gardens is not immune to the problem of crime, particularly against property. In 1998 the community hired a private security patrol to augment the efforts of the New York City Police Department.

Lack of compliance with and "even total contempt" for the architectural guidelines for new construction and renovation is a significant problem, according to the residents association. By explaining the origins and history of Forest Hills Gardens in the newsletters and the reprinting of historical maps, photographs, and other original material, the Corporation has attempted to instill in newer residents a feeling of connection to their community. Underscoring the integral role of architectural and other deed restrictions in maintaining the suburb's beauty and value, the Architecture Committee issued new legal procedures to handle noncompliance, which has become more of an issue as homeowners renovate and add onto homes that in some cases are over a half century old. The committee called on residents to assist them in maintaining "Atterbury's ideals, whether through addressing routine issues such as window replacement and paint color or through attempting to save houses that have stood for generations in quiet dialog with their neighbors from being remade into temples to their owner's economic success."[10]

But the newsletters record as well the enduring pleasures of living at Forest Hills Gardens and the residents' sense of connection with its past. The annual Children's Day on Flagpole Green is a continuing tradition, as are Christmas Eve festivities. The love of trees endures; 150 new ones were planted over a three-year period beginning in 1998. The train station has been restored and the adjacent railroad property replanted. The local Boy Scouts recently made replicas of the purple martin birdhouse designed by Grosvenor Atterbury and installed them around the Gardens. Many community groups still gather to play or do work on behalf of their community as the Gardens' pioneers did. Despite the predictions of some early critics, Forest Hills Gardens was not a mere stage set, frozen in time and not quite of the real world. It was and is a living community.[11]

HOW PERVASIVE DID THE GARDEN city ideal become in this country? Although the English and European experiments in building garden communities were widely publicized in the early 1900s in the United States and written about well into the 1920s and 1930s, the garden city concept never really took hold here.[12] Ebenezer Howard's economic and social theories would not be transplanted onto American soil. What did take root were Parker and Unwins's planning principles, including site-sensitive design and a method of achieving higher population density by carving out large residential blocks and grouping housing units together. Nevertheless, the single-family detached house remained the American ideal.

The developments built in the 1910s and 1920s that came closest to the garden city idea were industrial housing projects sponsored by

Letchworth banner, designed ca. 1909 by Edmund Hunter.

manufacturing companies and the federal government's projects to build housing for munitions and shipyard workers during World War I. In 1913 the Kohler company began building a model community adjacent to its plumbing manufacturing works in Kohler, Wisconsin, planned by Werner Hegemann and Elbert Peets, with the Olmsted firm as landscape architects. Similar projects were begun during the same period, including Goodyear Heights, Ohio, designed by Warren Manning, for the Goodyear Tire Company; Eclipse Park near Beloit, Wisconsin, designed by the firm of George B. Post and Sons, for a manufacturer of industrial machinery, Fairbanks, Morse, and Co.; and Kincaid, Illinois, designed largely by O. C. Simonds, for the Peabody Coal Company. More conventional elite suburbs such as Shaker Heights, Ohio, developed by the Van Sweringen brothers beginning in 1916, drew on aspects of Forest Hills Gardens, including such features as connection to public transportation; unified design of streets, lots, houses, and landscape; a main square of shops; and the provision of architectural guidelines, standards, and restrictions.

As the United States entered World War I, the federal government for the first time entered the community-building business. Olmsted accepted an appointment as manager of the Town Planning Division of the United States Housing Corporation, a federal program for constructing housing for war workers, which, although drastically curtailed at the war's end, produced some important model planned communities such as Yorkship Village near Camden, New Jersey, and several housing projects around Bridgeport, Connecticut. Under Olmsted's leadership, each project was directed by a design team headed by a town planner.[13]

The 1920s were a time of even more radical experiments in suburban development. In 1924 a group of New York businessmen and housing reformers created the City Housing Corporation, a limited dividend company that would finance the building of model homes and communities. Its most notable experiment was begun four years later at Radburn, New Jersey, heralded as "a garden city for the motor age." Designed by Clarence Stein and Henry Wright, Radburn's plan attempted to accommodate the automobile without giving it priority over all other concerns. Using the "superblock" as the organizing unit, Stein and Wright created a hierarchical street system, with a main beltway encircling the superblocks and diverting traffic around the community. Vehicular and pedestrian traffic were kept separate, and all community facilities were accessible to residents on foot by using linked paths and pedestrian over- and underpasses. Houses were oriented toward interior common parkland, emphasizing that this was a garden community, while cul-de-sacs and service roads permitted vehicular access for residents and necessary services.

During the 1930s, the federal government made a foray into town planning with its New Deal Greenbelt program. The program envisioned creating self-sufficient new communities throughout the country which would provide housing for workers employed in nearby cities, although only three were built. The towns would be encircled by "greenbelts" of agricultural land, with land-use plans designed to preserve the rural landscape. In this way, the concept addressed the problems of town and country simultaneously, just as Ebenezer Howard had with his garden city. The Greenbelt program marked the culmination of a fertile period of experimentation in suburban development.

Post–World War II prosperity spurred on the suburbanization of America. Government housing, financial, and tax policies made it easier to get a mortgage on a new home in the suburbs than to rent or renovate in the old center cities. Cheap land and local government subsidizing of utility rates in new communities, combined with federal support

Levittown, Long Island, New York, 1958. Courtesy Library of Congress, Prints and Photographs Division, Gottscho-Schleisner Collection, LC-G613-72794.

of highways, led to a proliferation of single-family housing developments that consumed vast amounts of former farmland and open space. Zoning regulations and market forces, rather than multidisciplinary planning, drove design. The new suburbs gave primacy to the car, which became essential for doing the simplest errand and getting to work, school, or play. Sidewalks disappeared. Formulaic houses turned out with cookie-cutter efficiency lined curving streets that lead nowhere. Houses were pushed back from the street, distant from communal life, and garages dominated the front facades. Strip malls replaced village greens and town centers as gathering places.

These suburbs of the 1940s and 1950s have been mocked and caricatured, although there is no question that they provided millions of Americans a good place to live. They answered the American dream of a house, a picket fence, and a backyard. The original Levittown, on Long Island, for example, the prototypical postwar suburb, was built as a real town with a small commercial center, a village green, and sites for schools and churches. But most of the suburban developments that followed in the wake of Levittown's remarkable success did not include these important features. Rather, they were just bedroom communities, endless isolated pockets of residences, sprawling farther and farther away from city centers. Whether their developers' intent was to create a real community or just to build a collection of houses, these residential enclaves extended across the country devouring open land and turning some regions into a continuous suburb, branching off along an endless commercial strip. We have learned that sprawl does not age gracefully. It has given us what has been been described as "the geography of nowhere."[14]

In the 1960s the issues of urban regeneration and renewal once again came to the fore. Like Ebenezer Howard and the Olmsteds many years earlier, policymakers acknowledged that the fates of cities and suburbs were intrinsically bound, that growth and renewal had to be considered on a regional basis. Both the federal government and the private sector backed promising ventures in community building. Businessmen Robert Simon and James Rouse developed Reston, Virginia, and Columbia, Maryland, respectively, visionary new communities that harked back to the model of comprehensive planning created at Forest Hills Gardens. The Urban Growth and New Community Development Act of 1970 made federally guaranteed loans available to public and private developers of new towns, and included experiments in building the "new town in town" to revitalize decaying inner city neighborhoods. But these efforts were hindered by the depressed housing and labor markets of the 1970s; the government program was phased out by mid-decade without one inner city new town to show for its efforts. Reston and Columbia have matured into vibrant, attractive communities, although more slowly and at greater cost than anticipated.[15]

It was not until the early 1980s that planners, architects, environmentalists, and social commentators showed a renewed interest in the subject of community planning. The development of Seaside, Florida, an eighty-acre planned community with a master plan by Andres Duany and Elizabeth Plater-Zyberk, was marked by a publicity blitz similar to the one that had accompanied the birth of Forest Hills Gardens. Promoted as "the new town, the old ways," Seaside was the first experiment in what Duany and Plater-Zyberk termed Traditional Neighborhood Development, which looked to small-town America as a model. Postwar suburbs, they said, had ignored or forgotten what made traditional towns such pleasing places in which to live. The typical suburb of the 1950s, they held, was less a community "than an agglomeration of houses, shops, and offices connected to one another by cars, not by the fabric of human life."[16] Our older cities and many small towns, by contrast, were neighborhoods of distinct identity and character. Duany and Plater-Zyberk observed that such places have become so rare in this country that towns with charm and tradition such as Charleston, South Carolina; Savannah, Georgia; Princeton, New Jersey; Marblehead, Massachusetts; and Alexandria, Virginia, have become tourist attractions.

SINCE THE DEVELOPMENT of Seaside, hundreds of neotraditional communities, based on the methodologies and practices that have come to be known as the new urbanism, have sprung up across the country.[17] The most visible of these is Celebration, Florida, the Walt Disney Company's well-publicized plunge into the town planning and community-building business. Drawing up the master plan in the early 1990s, Celebration's creators promised that it would be a culmination of and improvement on all previous community planning and design. It would demonstrate a system for developing communities, pledged Disney chairman Michael Eisner, that would have people fifty years hence proclaiming "Thank God for Celebration." Even the venerable

Celebration, Florida, 2000. Photograph by Charles D. Warren.

architectural historian Vincent Scully bestowed his blessing on Celebration, avowing that it marked "the return of community."[18]

With 4,900 acres available, this $2.5 billion project was an experiment on a grand scale. The master plan, produced with input from several architects and planners and finalized by Robert A. M. Stern and Jacquelin T. Robertson, incorporated the familiar features of traditional town planning to create a compact community of several distinctive neighborhoods: a town center (which boasted buildings designed by celebrated architects); a network of streets designed as public spaces which, to encourage pedestrian activity, intersect with bike trails and pathways; a higher residential housing density and a greater housing mix than in the conventional suburb; and generous common open spaces. A pattern book established design and planning principles for the community, which would be governed by a set of restrictive covenants administered by a homeowners association (under the control of the Disney Company until the town was three-quarters completed). Residents would pay a monthly fee into a maintenance fund.[19]

Even before the first residents moved in, however, critics began to attack Disney's town. Like its Florida neighbor Seaside, Celebration has been damned with faint praise for its picture-perfect streetscapes. Critics have condemned both towns as exercises in social engineering; their aesthetic virtues have been dismissed variously as merely conformist, sentimental, nostalgic, and elitist. They are derided as Potemkin villages, "Stepford towns," and "themed living" stage sets—language reminiscent of some of the early criticism of Forest Hills Gardens. On the one hand pilloried for embodying "the triumph of the simulated over the real, of illusion over substance" and for fabricating "instant and . . . ersatz history," Celebration at the same time has been disparaged when it began to display the substantive problems of ordinary communities. Headlines such as "A Mickey Mouse Utopia," "Disney's New Town May Be So Perfect It's a Nightmare," "Trouble at the Happiest School on Earth," and "Town That Disney Built Is Hit by First Violent Crime" trumpeted the new community's confrontation with the realities of everyday life.[20]

However, little is written from the perspective of the residents. Recent accounts of the first years at Celebration attest to its residents' commitment to building a community and their enjoyment in being pioneers. Like their counterparts at Forest Hills Gardens, many of Celebration's first residents were attracted by the chance to participate in the development of a new town. At Celebration, said one, "there is that pioneering mentality. We aren't here to create a utopia. We're here to try to make right what went wrong with America's communities. And set a standard for solutions. We are figuring out a better way."[21]

For many if not most of the first residents, confidence in the Disney name as a guarantee of quality, value, permanence, and innovation was a major inducement to move to the new town. And, perhaps like some of the Forest Hills Gardens pioneers who professed similar faith in the Sage Foundation, some of Celebration's citizens expected perfection, believing that, as some critics held, "the controlled reality of Disney World could be transferred to a real town."[22] But like Forest Hills Gardens, Celebration became "a real town" from the moment real people moved in. Disney could not and did not prevent real life, with its attendant conflicts and problems, from happening. Like the Sage Foundation, the Disney Company found that managing a town was an undertaking to which it was not particularly well-suited. By 1997 Disney had removed the company name from billboards and literature, purporting to choose to put "less emphasis on 'Disney' and more on 'Celebration.'"[23]

THE ARCHITECT AND PLANNER Clarence Stein wrote that community planners create "a stage, a theater for the good life." The planner, according to Stein, seeks to provide a setting in which residents can live "a varied life, a convenient life, a beautiful life; where they will grow and change, and their surroundings can also change with them." Thus community planning begins not with design aesthetics but rather with an "exploration of how people will live there."[24] Suburban communities, however well planned and designed, cannot offer panaceas. At its worst a suburban community is an anonymous collection of houses with no distinctive identity or character; some seem to exist simply as fenced and guarded retreats.[25] At its best, however, a suburban community demonstrates the benefits of foresighted planning that addresses the challenging social, economic, and environmental issues facing us today.

It was this kind of comprehensive planning that distinguished the community designs of the Olmsted firm.[26] In the mid-nineteenth century, Olmsted Sr. recognized that "the misfortune of most existing suburbs" was their lack of "any general plan . . . [or] any intelligent design" to secure what should be the benefits of domestic life: the "happy

Frederick Law Olmsted Jr. *by Herman Dudley Murphy, n.d., oil on canvas. Courtesy National Academy of Design, New York (909-P).*

combination" of civilized "conveniences, comforts and luxuries, which have been heretofore gained by close congregation," and the benefits and pleasures of country life.[27] In the early twentieth century, Olmsted Jr. proved a worthy successor to his acclaimed father. He, too, recognized the rising importance of suburban satellite communities on the American landscape and the necessity for bringing the art and science of the new discipline of comprehensive planning to guide and control their development.

Like his father, Frederick Law Olmsted Jr. believed that the residential suburb was deserving of the best efforts of planners, architects, landscape architects, and other professionals working together in "a great cooperative enterprise" to create, as he would reflect in the 1920s, "the pleasantest place to live that can possibly be made."[28] Remarkably, even in the radically different world of the twenty-first century, Olmsted and Atterbury's Forest Hills Gardens remains just such a place. That

Old locust tree in private yard, 2001. Photograph by Carol Betsch.

this community, now nearing its one-hundredth anniversary, remains visually distinctive, has changed so little, and continues to suit new generations of residents, is perhaps the truest testament to the talent and foresight of its creators and the quality and flexibility of its original plan and design.

During the 1920s, Olmsted articulated what he saw as the primary lessons from Forest Hills Gardens, when he was in the midst of designing two larger suburban enclaves, Mountain Lake in Lake Wales, Florida, and Palos Verdes Estates, a coastal community on the Palos Verdes peninsula west of Los Angeles. Although these were two very different kinds of communities, in dramatically different landscape settings, Olmsted affirmed that the essential characteristics that had made Forest Hills Gardens a model were equally applicable and important in his East and West Coast resort community projects.

Olmsted recognized the necessity of having a single vision to guide

Greenway Terrace, attached houses, 2001. Photograph by Carol Betsch.

such a project, one that leads to a unified design of buildings, streets, and landscape. It is the comprehensive master plan, he maintained, that is key to ensuring "harmonious, beautiful and convenient residential communities."[29] These complex undertakings required a team of consultants and designers "with the broadest and most thorough artistic and technical training" (the sort of collegial effort Olmsted particularly enjoyed).[30] However, he emphasized, "experience . . . has taught the fundamental importance of having everything—design, construction, planting, purchasing, maintenance, operations, publicity, sales and all business relations—head up to a single general manager who will have all the strings in his hands all the time."[31]

The conventional speculative suburb begins with the house, focusing on its plan, style, and amenities. Public spaces, shops, churches, and schools are often afterthoughts. At Forest Hills Gardens, in contrast, the Sage Foundation was committed to completing an infrastructure of the highest quality—paving, sidewalks, streetlights, sewage, electricity, and landscape design—before it began the marketing phase of the development. In addition, the foundation itself designed and constructed the important buildings at the entrance on Station Square, a variety of attached and semidetached housing groups, and many single-family homes. Such an investment was critical to establishing a comprehensive aesthetic, to setting standards of craftsmanship, to controlling the architectural character, and to accentuating the importance of the public spaces within the community.

Forest Hills Gardens was proving, Olmsted believed, that planning and a long-term commitment to management and maintenance were crucial. Olmsted steadfastly held that a developer must exercise "a very firm and just yet flexible control over the land which it sells, by means of restrictions in the deed." Experience had shown that if deed restrictions are "judiciously framed and discreetly enforced, a very effective control is possible, without creating any difficulty in making sales, indeed with a decided increase in selling price to non-speculative investors."[32]

Finally, Olmsted argued that "marketing policies must control design and production" if a development project was to be an artistic and financial success.[33] Forest Hills Gardens was conceived as a business proposition because its creators knew that they could best influence others to emulate their model if it was financially successful. Bad timing was in large part the reason for the Sage Foundation's inability to show a profit before it sold its interest in the community: the shortage of labor and materials during World War I and the subsequent increases in the cost of both significantly inflated the costs of construction. But the continuing strength of the community in today's real estate market has vindicated Robert de Forest's belief that "there is money to be had in taste."

FOREST HILLS GARDENS is at once modern and classic, seemingly timeless. The tribute penned by a visitor in the late 1920s rings true today: "It would be scarcely possible even for a person strolling through Forest Hills to remain unstirred by the loveliness of its houses and streets, by the beauty of its trees, by the striking tidiness and neatness of its general appearance. These things are ineffable. They do not always lend themselves to a mere utterance in words, however graceful. But the atmosphere is palpable. One feels it. And one is grateful for it."[34]

NOTES

Introduction

1. Robert de Forest, "Forest Hills Gardens," *Survey*, 25 January 1911, 569.

2. Louis Graves, "A 'Model Village' Underway," *Building Progress* 2 (January 1912): 19.

3. Olmsted, Vaux, & Co., "Preliminary Report upon the Proposed Suburban Village at Riverside, Near Chicago, by Olmsted, Vaux, & Co., Landscape Architects," reprinted in *The Papers of Frederick Law Olmsted*, vol. 6, *The Years of Olmsted, Vaux, & Co., 1865–1874*, ed. David Schuyler and Jane Turner Censer (Baltimore: Johns Hopkins University Press, 1992), 275.

4. Frederick Law Olmsted Jr. and Harland Page Kelsey, "The Smoke Nuisance," *American Civic Association*, Department of Nuisances, series 2, no. 1 (March 1908): 803.

1. "A Garden City for America"

1. *New York Tribune*, 1 December 1910; *New York Sun*, 25 November 1910; Portland *Eastern Argus*, 25 November 1910; Seattle *Times*, 27 November 1910, Forest Hills Gardens Collection, Russell Sage Foundation Records, Rockefeller Archives Center, North Tarrytown, N.Y. (hereafter cited as RSF), series 3, box 18, folder 150. The clippings are dated but do not have page numbers.

2. *Atlanta Constitution*, 26 November 1910, ibid.

3. Bournville (begun 1888), near Birmingham, was built by George Cadbury for workers in his chocolate factory. William Lever constructed Port Sunlight (begun 1894), near Liverpool, for his soap factory employees.

4. *Grand Rapids Press*, 26 December 1910; Washington, D.C., *Times*, 30 November 1910, RSF, series 3, box 18, folder 150.

5. *Seattle Times*, 27 November 1910; *Pueblo Chieftain*, 26 November 1910, ibid.

6. *Cleveland Plain Dealer*, 2 December 1910; Saginaw *Herald*, 27 November 1910, ibid.

7. "The Russell Sage Foundation, 1907–1947: An Historical Introduction," in *The Russell Sage Foundation: Social Research and Social Action in America, 1907–1947*, ed. David Hammack (Frederick, Md.: UPA Academic Editions, 1988), 1.

8. The ten areas de Forest suggested as worthy of support were building tenements in the city and small suburban houses on a business basis for the working class; lodging houses for women; "neighborhood charity buildings" in New York City; retail stores for the poorer classes that would limit profits; affordable insurance for the poor; tuberculosis sanatoria; convalescent homes; support of children's playgrounds; industrial education; and an exhibition hall in New York. John Glenn, Lillian Brandt, and F. Emerson Andrews, *Russell Sage Foundation, 1901–1946*, 2 vols. (New York: Russell Sage Foundation, 1947), 1:7.

9. Ibid.

10. John Glenn to Louise Ware, 25 March 1925, RSF, series 3, box 19, folder 157.

11. Robert W. de Forest, "Forest Hills Gardens: What It Is, Why It Is, and What It Is Not," in *Forest Hills Gardens: The Suburban Land Development of the Russell Sage Foundation*, pamphlet no. 1 (1911): 9. (On the pamphlet, see chapter 4, note 42.)

12. Robert de Forest to Frederick Law Olmsted Jr., 7 December 1908, Olmsted Associates Records, Manuscript Division, Library of Congress, Washington, D.C. (hereafter cited as OA), series B, no. 3586.

13. "The Sage Foundation at Forest Hills," and Samuel Howe, "Forest Hills Gardens," *American Architect* 102 (30 October 1912): 159, 153.

14. Editorial note prefacing Frederick Law Olmsted, "A Suburban Town Built on Business Principles," *New Boston* 1 (January 1911): 395.

15. Atterbury was the architect of Wawapek Farm, Robert de Forest's Cold Spring Harbor, Long Island, estate. Olmsted redesigned the old gardens at Nethermuir, his brother Henry's estate, also in Cold Spring Harbor. See Robert MacKay, Anthony Baker, and Carol A. Traynor, *Long Island Country Houses and Their Architects, 1860–1940* (New York: Society for the Preservation of Long Island Antiquities in association with W. W. Norton, 1997), 51–55 and 318–19.

16. Frederick Law Olmsted, "City Planning. An Introductory Address," in *Proceedings of the Second National Conference on City Planning and the Problems of Congestion* (1910), 15–16.

17. Frederick Law Olmsted, *Pittsburgh. Main Thoroughfares and the Down Town District. A Report by Frederick Law Olmsted* (Pittsburgh: Civic Commission, 1911), 1.

18. On Olmsted's city planning reports, see Susan L. Klaus, "'Efficiency, Economy, Beauty': The City Planning Reports of Frederick Law Olmsted, Jr., 1905–1915," *Journal of the American Planning Association* 57 (Autumn 1991): 456–70. Olmsted's report for Newport, Rhode Island, was published in 1913.

2. All in the Family

1. At his fiftieth college reunion Frederick Law Olmsted Jr. was hailed as the "worthy son of a father whose work was likened . . . to that of Phidias in Greece." Harvard College Class of 1894, *Fiftieth Anniversary Report* (Norwood, Mass.: Plimpton Press, 1944), 406.

2. The reasons for and timing of this act remain an enigma. Olmsted Sr.'s own father died in 1873. Perhaps this loss, coupled with the growing confidence that he finally had a healthy son of his own, kindled his desire to have the name Frederick Law Olmsted live on into the next generation. Laura Wood Roper, whose *FLO: A Biography of Frederick Law Olmsted* (1973; Baltimore: Johns Hopkins University Press, 1983) remains the standard biography and who had the cooperation of Olmsted Jr. in preparing her book, dates the name change to about age four, presumably on the recollection of Olmsted himself (338). Melvin Kalfus, in his psychological study, *Frederick Law Olmsted: The Passion of a Public Artist* (New York: New York University Press, 1990), cites letters written by Olmsted Sr. as late as 1876 that still refer to the child as Henry, which would place the name change around the age of seven (81). Olmsted Jr. did not seem concerned with analyzing the psychological aspects of having his name changed. According to his daughter, he "always said that this didn't affect him too much, since he was always known at that time, familiarly, as Boy, but one wonders." Charlotte Olmsted Kursh, "The Middle Kingdom," unpublished manuscript, undated, 63, quoted by permission. The most recent biography, Witold Rybczynski, *A Clearing in the Distance* (New York: Scribner, 1999), does not comment on the name change.

3. Olmsted Sr. quoted in Mariana Van Rensselaer, "Frederick Law Olmsted," *Century Magazine* 46 (October 1893): 864.

4. On the Olmsted office in Brookline, see Cynthia Zaitzevsky, *Frederick Law Olmsted and the Boston Park System* (Cambridge: Belknap Press of Harvard University Press, 1982), 127–35, and Susan L. Klaus, "All in the Family: The Olmsted Office and the Business of Landscape Architecture," *Landscape Journal* 16 (Spring 1997): 80–93. In 1979 the Brookline property, known as Fairsted, was acquired by the National Park Service, which operates it as the Frederick Law Olmsted National Historic Site.

5. Frederick Law Olmsted Jr. notes prepared 20 April 1902 for the *Harvard Alumni Bulletin*, OA, series B, no. 2919. Olmsted Sr. to Olmsted Jr., Frederick Law Olmsted Papers, Manuscript Division, Library of Congress, Washington, D.C. (hereafter cited as OP), 5 September 1890.

6. Olmsted Sr. to Olmsted Jr., 1 August 1894, OP.

7. Olmsted Sr. to Olmsted Jr., 29 July 1895, OP. For the Biltmore period, see also Susan L. Klaus, "'Such inheritance as I can give you': The Apprenticeship of Frederick Law Olmsted, Jr.," *Journal of the New England Garden History Society* 3 (1993): 1–7.

8. Olmsted Sr. to Olmsted Jr., n.d. [1895], OP. One of their shared "weaknesses" was color blindness. Both Olmsteds had a "subnormal sensitiveness to red." See Olmsted Jr. to Laura Wood Roper, 10 October 1948, OA, series B, no. 2964. Olmsted does not indicate that either of them found this a problem in working. Aware of their condition, the Olmsteds no doubt depended on their assistants to compensate for it. As Zaitzevsky notes in her charac-

terization of the office under Olmsted Sr., "his partners, apprentices and draftsmen apparently functioned very smoothly as a design team and were able to work from his written and verbal instructions and simple sketches." *Frederick Law Olmsted and the Boston Park System*, 97.

9. Olmsted Sr. to Olmsted Jr., n.d. [1895], OP.

10. Olmsted Jr. to Olmsted Sr., 1 January 1895, OA, series H, letterbook 3.

11. Olmsted Jr. to Olmsted Sr., 31 January 1895, OP.

12. Olmsted Jr. to Laura Wood Roper, 10 October 1948.

13. George Vanderbilt had invited John Singer Sargent to the estate to paint the triumvirate responsible for great work—Vanderbilt, Olmsted Sr., and architect Richard Morris Hunt. Struck by the resemblance between father and son, Sargent asked Olmsted to pose in the clothes his father had left behind, while he completed the portrait of Olmsted Sr. that still hangs in the great house. Roper, *FLO*, 467. Arthur Shurcliff, who trained in the Olmsted office, described the resemblance: "When I first met F. L. Olmsted, Jr., in 1896, I saw at once his striking resemblance to his father, . . . the same presence, build and shape of the head and hands. The voice was the same and the deliberate effort to choose the right word to express a carefully considered idea." "The Recollections of Arthur Shurcliff," unpublished manuscript, 1952, 12, Shurcliff Collection, Frances Loeb Library, Harvard Graduate School of Design, Cambridge, Mass., box 8a.

14. Olmsted Jr. to Roper, 10 October 1948. Olmsted took over Eliot's position as landscape architect for the Boston municipal park system. He also worked on plans for parks, parkways, and other improvements for his hometown, Brookline. He made three or four visits a year to Biltmore, as the huge project continued to occupy the firm's time into the first decade of the twentieth century. When John died in 1920, Rick decided to continue the practice as Olmsted Brothers, "both for sentimental and for business reasons, believing that the many changes in the name of the Olmsted firm in the past were rather unfortunate." Olmsted to Arthur C. Comey, 25 March 1920, OA, series B, no. 20. The name was retained by the firm's (nonfamily) partners for several years after Olmsted's own death in 1957. In 1961 the partners began to practice under the name Olmsted Associates.

15. Office business took Olmsted Jr. up and down the eastern seaboard and as far afield as Montreal and Detroit. In 1899 his appointment diary shows that he spent a full three months over the course of the year traveling, and that pace only intensified as his career progressed. Indeed, in that era of time-consuming travel by rail or steamer, the principals of the firm were continually on the road. Plans for a private client with a modest property usually involved only a single site visit by one of the Olmsteds themselves, with follow-up left to an associate. Larger, usually public, projects could require multiple visits by a principal, the detailing of an assistant to live on-site for varying periods of time, or both.

16. John Taylor Boyd, "The Work of the Olmsted Brothers, Part II," *Architectural Record* 44 (November–December 1918): 503.

17. When he was approached about establishing a professional organization in 1899, Olmsted initially objected to the idea as premature, given the paucity of trained practitioners. Nevertheless both brothers were among the eleven founding members, and each served

two terms as president: John served as first president of the ASLA from 1899 to 1901, and again in 1904–1905; Rick served as president from 1908 to 1909 and again from 1919 to 1923.

Harvard president Charles Eliot, father of the firm's first nonfamily member partner, asked Olmsted Jr. to create the curriculum. Olmsted Jr. to Charles Eliot, 16 August 1898, OA, series H4. Olmsted's notes for the course indicate that he began with a historical review of the gardens and landscapes of the ancient world and the Renaissance, then moved on to English landscape history and its influence in the American colonies. Fifteen lectures were allocated to contemporary landscape treatment of private estates in the United States and abroad; the first year of instruction culminated with fourteen lectures on streets, parks, and public spaces in Washington, New York, and Boston. Olmsted became the Charles Eliot Professor of Landscape Architecture, a post he held until 1915. By 1906, however, the volume of his practice forced him to reduce his personal involvement in teaching. He continued to advise advanced students and to lecture on occasion at Harvard through 1917.

18. U.S. Congress, *The Improvement of the Park System of the District of Columbia*, ed. Charles Moore, Senate Report No. 166, 57th Congress, 1st sess. (Washington, D.C.: Government Printing Office, 1902), 12.

19. Many people assumed that the "Olmsted" of the McMillan Commission was Olmsted Sr. Contemporary accounts often neglected to add "Jr." after Rick Olmsted's name, compounding the confusion. Olmsted himself stopped using the designation Jr. within a few years of his father's death in 1903. Although the work of the two is easily distinguishable by date, errors in attribution persist.

20. The McMillan plan focused on the monumental core of the city, with little mention of residential areas. For Olmsted's role on the McMillan Commission, see Susan L. Klaus, "'Intelligent and Comprehensive Planning of a Common Sense Kind': Frederick Law Olmsted Jr.'s Contributions to Comprehensive Planning, 1900–1916" (master's thesis, George Washington University, 1988). Olmsted's major contribution to the report was a three-pronged approach that provided recreational and scenic areas both in the historic core and in developing residential areas by reserving spaces within the city for neighborhood parks and playgrounds; by preserving and developing existing scenic areas; and by connecting the parks and open spaces with a network of scenic parkways. His proposal has been hailed as the only part of the McMillan plan that addressed the human problems of city living. See Fredrick Gutheim, "Capital Planning," review of *Monumental Washington* by John W. Reps, *Landscape* 17 (Spring 1986): 28.

21. Although the standard history of American city planning remains Mel Scott, *American City Planning since 1890* (Berkeley: University of California Press, 1971), the literature on planning history has expanded rapidly over the past decades. A useful overview of the field is Mary Corbin Sies and Christopher Silver, "The History of Planning History," in *Planning in the Twentieth-Century American City*, ed. Sies and Silver (Baltimore: John Hopkins University Press, 1996), 1–34. See also Eugenie Ladner Birch, "Advancing the Art and Science of Planning: Planners and Their Organizations," *Journal of the American Planning Association* 46 (January 1980): 22–49; Blaine Brownell, "Urban Planning, the Planning Profession, and the Motor Vehicle in Early Twentieth-Century America," and Gordon Cherry, "Aspects of Twentieth-Century Planning," both in *Shaping an Urban World*, ed. Cherry

(London: St. Martin's Press, 1980), 59–77 and 1–21, respectively; and Donald A. Krueckenberg, ed., *Introduction to Planning History in the United States* (New Brunswick, N.J.: Center for Urban Policy Research, 1983).

22. On Olmsted Sr.'s urban philosophy, see Thomas Bender, *Toward an Urban Vision: Ideas and Institutions in Nineteenth-Century America* (Lexington: University Press of Kentucky, 1975); David Schuyler, *The New Urban Landscape: The Redefinition of Urban Form in Nineteenth-Century America* (Baltimore: Johns Hopkins University Press, 1986); and S. B. Sutton, *Civilizing American Cities: A Selection of Frederick Law Olmsted's Writings on City Landscape* (Cambridge: MIT Press, 1971).

23. On the City Beautiful phase of city planning, see Jon Peterson, "The City Beautiful Movement: Forgotten Origins and Lost Meanings," *Journal of Urban History* 2 (August 1976): 415–34; Mario Manieri-Elia, "Toward an 'Imperial City': Daniel H. Burnham and the City Beautiful Movement," *The American City: From the Civil War to the New Deal,* ed. Giorgio Ciucci, Francesco Dal Co, Mario Manieri-Elia, and Manfredo Tafuri (Cambridge: MIT Press, 1983); William H. Wilson, "The Ideology, Aesthetics, and Politics of the City Beautiful Movement," in *The Rise of Modern Urban Planning, 1800–1914*, ed. Anthony Sutcliffe (London: Monsell, 1980), 165–98; and idem, *The City Beautiful Movement* (Baltimore: Johns Hopkins University Press, 1989). For the relationship between progressivism and city planning, see Roy Lubove, "The Twentieth-Century City: The Progressive as Municipal Reformer," *Mid-America* 41 (October 1959): 195–209; Francesco Dal Co, "From Parks to the Region: Progressive Ideology and the Reform of the American City," in Ciucci et al., *The American City*, 143–292; and William H. Wilson, "Moles and Skylarks," in Krueckenberg, *Introduction to Planning History*, 88–121. On the relationship between physical order and social control, see Paul Boyer, *Urban Masses and Moral Order in America, 1820–1920* (Cambridge: Harvard University Press, 1978).

24. Charles Mulford Robinson, *Modern Civic Art or the City Made Beautiful* (New York: G. P. Putnam, 1903), 10.

25. In addition to preparing comprehensive planning reports for several cities between 1905 and 1915, as mentioned in chapter 1, Olmsted headed the National Conference on City Planning from 1910 to 1919 and served as first president of the American City Planning Institute (later the American Institute of City Planners), established in 1917. For a comparison of the senior and junior Olmsteds as planners, see Jon A. Peterson, "Frederick Law Olmsted Sr. and Frederick Law Olmsted Jr.: The Visionary and the Professional," in Sies and Silver, *Planning the Twentieth-Century American City*, 37–54.

26. Olmsted to Robert de Forest, 20 December 1908, OA, series B, no. 3586. An article written on his return, "Through American Spectacles. An expert's view of English 'Garden City' schemes," *Garden Cities and Town Planning* 4 (May 1909): 198–200, discusses his visit to Letchworth, the garden city thirty-five miles from London that was inspired by the theories of the English visionary and social critic Ebenezer Howard. Olmsted does not mention Hampstead Garden Suburb, a smaller commuter suburb on the outskirts of London; however, de Forest's letter of 4 January 1909 to Olmsted notes that the Sage Foundation had "fairly complete data" on both. This trip was Olmsted's fourth European study tour. His vacations were invariably busman's holidays, opportunities for "looking at the landscapes of this interesting world, and seeing what people are doing to them and what

they do to people." Olmsted quoted in Harvard College Class of 1894, *Fiftieth Anniversary Report*, 407. Olmsted continually found the "store of memories of such things, actually seen, and judged to with a critical eye" an invaluable resource in this work. Olmsted to C. A. Elder, 27 December 1911, OA, series B, no. 5491. Design elements and construction details once seen might provide inspiration years later, becoming "useful perhaps in totally different recombinations." And equally important, he wryly observed, was the opportunity to discern "some of the things *not* to do." Olmsted to Robert de Forest, 20 January 1909, OA, series B, no. 3586.

3. *"A Suburban Town Built on Business Principles"*

1. Robert de Forest to Olmsted, 7 December 1908, OA, series B, no. 3586.

2. Olmsted to Robert de Forest, 20 December 1908, OA, series B, no. 3586.

3. Frederick Law Olmsted, "The Scope and Results of City Planning Abroad," in U.S. Congress, *City Planning. Hearing before the Committee on the District of Columbia*, 61st Cong., 2d sess., Senate Document no. 422 (Washington D.C.: Government Printing Office, 1910), 66–67.

4. For the English garden city movement, see Stanley Buder, *Visionaries and Planners: The Garden City Movement and the Modern Community* (New York: Oxford University Press, 1990); Frank Jackson, *Sir Raymond Unwin: Architect, Planner, and Visionary* (London: A. Zwemmer, 1985); Peter Hall, *Cities of Tomorrow: An Intellectual History of Urban Planning and Design in the Twentieth Century* (London: Basil Blackwell, 1988); Walter Creese, *The Search for Environment: The Garden City, Before and After*, expanded ed. (Baltimore: Johns Hopkins University Press, 1992); and Stephen V. Ward, *The Garden City: Past, Present, and Future* (London: E & F N Spons, 1992). The architects, planners, and theorists of the English garden city movement were, of course, also drawing on the example of Victorian model industrial towns, including Saltaire (1851–72), developed for Sir Titus Salt's spinning and loom workers; Port Sunlight (1888–1910), sponsored by Lord Leverholme and named for his Sunlight soap; and Bournville (1894–1914), built alongside the Cadbury chocolate works but open to non-employee residents as well. See Jack Reynolds, *Saltaire: An Introduction to the Village of Sir Titus Salt* (Bradford, Eng.: Bradford Art Galleries and Museums, 1985); Edward Hubbard and Michael Shippobottom, *A Guide to Port Sunlight Village* (Liverpool: Liverpool University Press, 1988); and Michael Durman and Michael Harrison, *Bournville, 1895–1914: The Model Village and Its Cottages* (Birmingham: University of Central England, 1995).

5. F. J. Obsorn, preface to Ebenezer Howard, *Garden Cities of Tomorrow*, paper ed. (Cambridge: MIT Press, 1966), 9.

6. Osborn distinguishes among the three terms. "Garden city," as Howard defined it, is a self-sufficient urban settlement built on property that is publicly owned or held in trust for the community, designed for both living and working, restricted as to size of population, and encircled by a greenbelt of agricultural land. A "garden suburb" is what would today be termed a "bedroom community," a residential development close to an urban area with a "well-planned open lay-out." "Garden village" generally referred to a planned housing

estate in a rural area adjacent to a factory. Ibid., 26–27. Parker and Unwin designed all three types of communities: the model garden village New Earswick (initial plan 1902), the first garden city, Letchworth (initial plan 1904), and Hampstead Garden Suburb (initial plan 1906).

7. Parker and Unwin's plans underwent extensive revisions during the years of construction, and in some cases other architects were brought in (notably Edwin Lutyens at Hampstead Garden Suburb). Execution also was compromised because of economic conditions. See Mervyn Miller, *Letchworth: The First Garden City* (Chichester, Sussex: Phillimore, 1988), and Mervyn Miller and A. Stuart Gray, *Hampstead Garden Suburb* (Chichester, Sussex: Phillimore, 1992). Parker and Unwin's work was widely covered in popular magazines such *House and Garden*, *Scribner's*, and *The Craftsman*, as well as in professional journals. Unwin's 1909 *Town Planning in Practice* was also well known; Olmsted referred to it in his 1910 address to the National Conference on City Planning. (The two met when Unwin attended the conference the following year.)

8. Raymond Unwin and Barry Parker, *The Art of Building a Home* (London: Green, 1901), 93.

9. In the United States, the nineteenth-century political economist Henry George proposed addressing the inequalities of "socially generated" wealth—that is, increases in the value of land that were the unearned product of labor and capital—with a single property tax. This could "in George's view, remove the incentive to speculate and keep land off the market, erase inequalities caused by property ownership, and make unnecessary any tax on productive factors or products." See Matthew Edel, Elliot D. Sclar, and Daniel Luria, *Shaky Palaces: Homeownership and Social Mobility in Boston's Suburbanization* (New York: Columbia University Press, 1984), 269. Organized labor took up the single tax cause, and there was some support for it among capitalists at the end of the century, when it was linked with municipal reform and attacks on monopolies (further, it was seen as less of a threat to business and wealth than an income tax).

10. For de Forest, see *Dictionary of American Biography*, suppl. 1 (1944): 236–37; also *New York Times*, 18 November 1922; *New York Sun and Globe*, 11 January 1928; and his obituary in *New York Times*, 7 May 1931, RSF, series 3, box 3, folder 19, and box 4, folder 31; Winifred Howe, *A History of the Metropolitan Museum of Art*, 2 vols. (New York: Columbia University Press, 1946), 2:14–16; and Calvin Tompkins, *Merchants and Masterpieces: The Story of the Metropolitan Museum of Art* (New York: Henry Holt, 1989), 188.

11. The American Wing became the repository of Olivia Sage's gift of 434 pieces of American furniture and decorative arts. Howe, *History*, 1:35.

12. Robert de Forest quoted in Robert de Forest and Lawrence Veiller, "The Tenement House Problem" in *The Tenement House Problem, Including the Report of the New York State Tenement Housing Commission of 1900*, 2 vols., ed. de Forest and Veiller (New York: Macmillan, 1903), 1:3. The commission revised the building code to outlaw "dumbbell flats," an arrangement in which the rooms of an apartment were lined up from the front of the building to the rear, so that the majority of them had no direct sunlight or fresh air.

13. In one of the many paradoxes inherent in progressivism, this eagerness to contribute one's time coincided with the rise of professionalism. It was increasingly believed that re-

lief of poverty required an investigation of its underlying social and economic roots, a task more suited to trained professionals than well-intentioned volunteers. See Don S. Kirschner, *Paradox of Professionalism: Reform and Public Service in Urban America, 1900–1940* (New York: Greenwood Press, 1986). On the interest among those of de Forest's class and generation in the problems of the city, see Thomas Bender, *Toward an Urban Vision: Ideas and Institutions in Nineteenth-Century America* (Baltimore: Johns Hopkins University Press, 1975).

14. Mrs. Philip N. Moore, "Women's Interest in Civic Welfare," *American City* 1 (September 1909): 44. Although women were active in areas that addressed social issues throughout the early 1900s, it would be decades before they were present in significant numbers in the professions of planning, architecture, and landscape architecture, as the gap between professional and engaged amateur widened. On the role of women in the City Beautiful movement and the Progressive Era, see Dolores Hayden, *The Grand Domestic Revolution* (Cambridge: MIT Press, 1981); Susan Marie Wirka, "The City Social Movement: Progressive Women Reformers and Early Social Planners," in *Planning the Twentieth-Century American City*, ed. Mary Corbin Sies and Christopher Silver (Baltimore: Johns Hopkins University Press, 1996), 55–75; Eugenie Ladner Birch, "Woman-Made America: The Case of Early Public Housing Policy," and her "From Civic Worker to City Planner: Women and Planning, 1890–1980," in *The American Planner*, ed. Donald A. Krueckenberg (New York: Methuen, 1983), 149–75 and 396–427; and Dorothy May Anderson, *Women, Design, and the Cambridge School* (West Layfayette, Ind.: PDA Publishers, 1980).

15. Olmsted himself was interested in the university settlement house movement. While at Harvard he joined Dr. Edward Everett Hale's Tolstoi Club, the precursor to Hale House, one of the first college-associated settlement houses.

16. On the social settlement movement, see Allen E. Davis, *Spearheads for Reform: The Social Settlement and the Progressive Movement, 1890–1910* (New York: Oxford University Press, 1967).

17. For a discussion of Olivia Sage's views on philanthropy and its context of late nineteenth-century Protestant humanitarianism, see Ruth Crocker, "From Widow's Mite to Widow's Might: The Philanthropy of Margaret Olivia Sage," *American Presbyterians* 74, no. 4 (Winter 1996): 253–64. I am grateful to the author, who is working on a biography of Olivia Sage, for making this article available. For more on Olivia Sage, see RSF, series 3, box 1, folder 1, and Irvin G. Wyllis, "Margaret Olivia Slocum Sage," in *Notable American Women, 1607–1950: A Biographical Dictionary*, ed. Edward T. James (Cambridge: Belknap Press of Harvard University Press, 1971), 222–23.

18. "Russell Sage," in *Dictionary of American Biography* (1935), 8:292–93. See also RSF, series 3, box 1, folder 9.

19. John Glenn, Lillian Brandt, and F. Emerson Andrews, *Russell Sage Foundation, 1907–1946*, 2 vols. (New York: Russell Sage Foundation, 1947), 1:3.

20. Ibid., 1:8.

21. Quoted in David Hammock, ed., *The Russell Sage Foundation: Social Research and Social Action in America, 1907–1947* (Frederick, Md.: UPA Academic Editions, 1988), 2–3.

22. Glenn et al., *Foundation*, 1:5. After World War I the foundation moved away from direct support for social action to advancing basic research in the social sciences and to strengthening professional practice. See Eric Wanner's foreword and David C. Hammack, "A Center of Intelligence for the Charity Organization Movement," in *Social Science in the Making: Essays on the Russell Sage Foundation, 1907–1922*, ed. Hammack and Stanton Wheeler (New York: Russell Sage Foundation, 1994), 1–33.

23. Robert de Forest, "In Memoriam: Margaret Olivia Sage, Philanthropist," *Survey*, 9 November 1918, 151.

24. Glenn et al., *Foundation*, 1:20. In addition to de Forest and Olivia Sage, other trustees were John Glenn, head of the Charity Organization Society of Baltimore; Cleveland H. Dodge, associated with the Red Cross, YMCA, and the American Museum of Natural History; Robert C. Ogden, associated with the Rockefeller Foundation, the General Education Board, and the Peabody Fund, all committed to improving education in the South for both races; Daniel Coit Gilman, president of The Johns Hopkins University; Alfred T. White, president of the Brooklyn Bureau of Charities and developer of privately subsidized low-income housing; Gertrude S. (Mrs. William B.) Rice, a founder of the Charity Organization Society; Helen M. Gould, a philanthropist and friend of Olivia Sage and, at thirty-nine, the youngest member; and Louise Lee Schuyler of Bellevue Hospital nursing school.

25. De Forest, "In Memoriam," 151. Grosvenor Atterbury designed the foundation's original headquarters, a nine-story Italianate Renaissance building near Gramercy Park, in 1912. It is interesting that three women are connected to model communities: Henrietta Barnett and Hampstead Garden Suburb; Olivia Sage and Forest Hills Gardens; and Mary Emery and Mariemont, a suburb of Cincinnati. Their involvement, however, seems more coincidental than a significant issue of gender or moment in women's history. Two (Sage and Emery) were elderly women who inherited their husband's fortune and were guided by male advisers to large-scale projects unlike anything they had sponsored before. Only Henrietta Barnett's involvement with Hampstead Garden Suburb can be seen as connected to her previous experience. At the time, she had been working alongside her husband, Canon Barnett, founder of the East End settlement house Toynbee Hall, for more than twenty-five years, and had gained a great deal of experience as a speaker and writer advocating reform of working conditions. Thus she was more of a public figure and activist than the other two women. She worked to raise funds and obtain political approval, made notes on Unwin's initial sketch plan, and later battled with Lutyens on the nature of the town center; yet even with her active interest, it was the professionals who left their mark on Hampstead Garden Suburb. Olivia Sage served as nominal president of the Sage Foundation board until her death, but the organization was always run by a professional staff. Ruth Crocker maintains that the foundation "seems out of character with [her] life to date, which had been marked by a strong commitment to numerous religious organizations, for the foundation was to be secular and was to be run by social-science experts" ("From Widow's Mite," 259). Mary Emery inherited $20 million at the death of her husband, who had been involved in, among other business interests, real estate development. Like Olivia Sage, she depended on the advice of her family's business manager, Charles J. Livingston, for her philanthropy. She was seventy in 1913, when land acquisition for what became Mariemont was begun, and nearly eighty when John Nolen was hired to draw up the master plan in 1920.

26. Combining social action and social research, the Sage Foundation was at the forefront of the major initiatives of the Progressive Era in the years preceding World War I. Sage Foundation funds helped underwrite the First National Conference on City Planning and the Problems of Congestion and the creation of the National Housing Association, whose mission was to focus more specifically on housing standards and practices. The foundation supported the influential *Survey: A Journal of Commitment to Philanthropy* and several other important Progressive Era publications. It also funded the first review of the legal basis for city planning in this country, *Carrying Out the City Plan: The Practical Application of American Law in the Execution of City Plans* (1914), written by Flavel Shurtleff under Olmsted's supervision and to which Olmsted contributed a foreword. The foundation continued to play a major role in housing and planning policy for the New York metropolitan region through the 1920s.

27. Glenn et al., *Foundation*, app. A, 668.

28. "Mrs. Russell Sage in Jamaica Project," *New York Times*, 7 March 1909. This initial purchase, about three miles south of Forest Hills Gardens, was never developed by the Sage Foundation. It was sold in January 1917.

29. David Ward and Olivier Zunz, "Between Rationalism and Pluralism: Creating the Modern City," in *The Landscape of Modernity: Essays on New York City*, ed. Ward and Zunz (New York: Russell Sage Foundation, 1992), 3.

30. "The Cord Meyer Company Put Elmhurst on the Map," *Forest Hills–Kew Gardens Post*, 26 September 1935, RSF, series 3, box 20, folder 158. The Cord Meyer property was on the site of an old Dutch settlement known as "Whitepot," because, according to popular legend, the land had been purchased from Native Americans for three white clay pots. In 1664 the English took over the Dutch colony of New Netherlands, giving English names to the settlements: Whitepot became New Towne (later Newtown). In 1896 Cord Meyer, a German immigrant who had made a fortune manufacturing fertilizer, began to develop property in the old village seat of Newtown. Because the area shared the name of the malodorous Newtown Creek, Meyer decided to call his proposed community "Elmhurst," evoking tree-lined streets, which as yet existed only on paper. In 1904 Meyer formed the Cord Meyer Development Company. Over the next four years the company purchased land near the Elmhurst site on both sides of Hoffman Boulevard, eventually controlling six hundred acres.

31. The park, created in 1892, was originally known as Brooklyn Park. With the borough consolidation in 1898, title passed to New York City. See Jeffrey A. Kroessler and Nina S. Rappaport, *Historic Preservation in Queens* (New York: Queensborough Preservation League, 1990).

32. The 25-by-100-foot lot had been the standard for New York since the city was laid out on a grid in 1807.

33. *Forest Hills*, promotional brochure, Cord Meyer Development Company, [1908?], Queens Borough Public Library, Long Island Division (hereafter cited as QPL), Forest Hills Gardens vertical files. Houses would range in cost from $4,000 to $12,000, on terms of 10 percent down and the rest in monthly installments. By contrast, the typical Queens dwelling of the period was a three-story brick row house, with five-room apartments on

each floor renting from $18 to $20 a month. See Vincent Seyfreid, *Queens: A Pictorial History* (Norfolk, Va.: Donning Company, 1982), 50.

34. The Queensboro Bridge was completed in March 1908 and officially opened 12 June 1909. For transportation history of New York City, see Clifton Hood, *722 Miles: The Building of the Subways and How They Transformed New York* (New York: Simon and Schuster, 1993). Rapid transit in the form of elevated trains extended into Queens by 1917. The subway under Queens Boulevard reached Roosevelt Avenue in 1933.

35. Rosalind H. Amador, "Recollections: Farmland, Daisy Fields in 1908 That Was the Forest Hills of Today," *Forest Hills–Kew Gardens Post*, 4 May 1941, QPL, FHG vertical files.

36. Hendrickson quoted in Hood, *722 Miles*, 171.

37. Computed using the Bureau of Labor Statistics Consumer Price Index. The price was certainly an inducement to sell, but Meyer may also have been worried about increasing competition from other speculative developers. His own Forest Hills project had taken off slowly: a visitor to the Cord Meyer Development Company's Forest Hills property around that time would have found just eight "pseudo English brick and timber type houses," and one street sign. "Forest Hills Gardens: Curving Street and Cobblestones," *Newsday*, 27 May 1990, 7. Cord Meyer and his sons continued to develop their remaining property in Forest Hills and the adjacent Kew Gardens well into the 1920s. The company, which is still in operation under family management, states that it has no archival information on the sale to the Sage Foundation. Letter to author from George S. Meyer, 5 April 1995. Two additional land purchases were made by the Sage Foundation for Forest Hills Gardens: 25 acres (Tract II) in 1912; and 23 acres (Tract III) in 1913, which included 10 acres that the foundation sold the same year to the West Side Tennis Club, site of the U.S. Open tennis championships until the 1970s.

38. Frederick Law Olmsted, "A Suburban Town Built on Business Principles," *New Boston* 1 (January 1911): 395. The journal was launched in conjunction with an ambitious city planning and reform effort initiated by the city's business and civic leaders.

39. On the relationship between physical order and social control, see Robert H. Wiebe, *The Search for Order* (New York: Hill and Wang, 1967), and Paul Boyer, *Urban Masses and Moral Order in America, 1820–1920* (Cambridge: Harvard University Press, 1978). On city planning and progressivism, see also Roy Lubove, "The Twentieth-Century City: The Progressive as Municipal Reformer," *Mid-America* 41 (October 1959): 195–209; Francesco Dal Co, "From Parks to the Region: Progressive Ideology and the Reform of the American City," in *The American City: From the Civil War to the New Deal*, ed. Giorgio Ciucci, Francesco Dal Co, Mario Manieri-Elia, and Manfredo Tafuri (Cambridge: MIT Press, 1983); and William H. Wilson, "Moles and Skylarks," in *Introduction to Planning History in the United States*, ed. Donald A. Krueckenberg (New Brunswick, N.J.: Center for Urban Policy Research, 1983), 88–121. Daniel T. Rodgers sets American progressivism in an international context; see his *Atlantic Crossings: Social Politics in a Progressive Age* (Cambridge: Belknap Press of Harvard University Press, 1998). Rodgers concludes that "in the United States, more than elsewhere, progressive politics was nested within the surrounding capitalistic frame" (195). See also idem, "In Search of Progressivism," *Reviews in American History* (December 1982): 113–32.

40. In the United States the housing reformers soon split off from the new professional organizations interested in city planning. Planning, the conventional wisdom soon held, was a public endeavor; housing should be left to the private sector. The new planning professionals believed that only they had the scientific and technical knowledge needed to view the planning process comprehensively, to deal with the complexity of the modern city. Olmsted rapidly became disaffected with this view. By 1911 he was writing, "Personally I do not recognize the existence of professional city planners, nor do I believe that we shall ever have such a profession, because I regard the subject as too vast and complex . . . to be staked off and occupied by any group of people having a sufficiently uniform training and point of view to be properly classed as members of a single profession." Olmsted quoted in "What Is City Planning?," *New Boston* 2 (August 1911): 149.

41. Olmsted to Thomas Adams, 23 July 1912, OA, series B, no. 3586; Olmsted quoted in the *Los Angeles Times*, 23 December 1911, OA, series B, no. 5354.

42. De Forest, "Forest Hills Gardens. What It Is, Why It Is, and What It Is Not," in *Forest Hills Gardens: The Suburban Land Development of the Russell Sage Foundation*, pamphlet no. 1 (1911): 9. Olmsted observed in a letter to the English planner Thomas Adams that there was no local labor market to provide jobs for the day laborer. The cost of commuting into Manhattan was expected to be between 26 and 36 cents, making it too expensive for the average blue-collar worker. Olmsted to Adams, 23 July 1916, OA, series B, no. 3586.

43. See "An Outline of Real Estate Development in the United States," *Architectural Forum* 62 (May 1935): 431–40.

44. See Robert B. MacKay, Anthony Baker, and Carol A. Traynor, eds., *Long Island Country Houses and Their Architects, 1860–1940* (New York: Society for the Preservation of New England Antiquities in association with W. W. Norton, 1997), 49–57 and 315–30, for brief discussions of Atterbury's Long Island houses, as well as some contemporaneous projects of the Olmsted firm, which had more than one hundred commissions on Long Island between 1905 and 1925.

45. See Richard Plunz, *A History of Housing in New York City: Dwelling Types and Social Change in the American Metropolis* (New York: Columbia University Press, 1990); John F. Bauman, Roger Biles, and Kristin M. Szylvian, eds., *From Tenements to Taylor Homes: In Search of an Urban Housing Policy in Twentieth-Century America* (University Park: Pennsylvania State University Press, 2000); and Robert A. M. Stern, Gregory Gilmartin, and John Montague Massengale, *New York 1900: Metropolitan Architecture and Urbanism, 1890–1915* (New York: Rizzoli, 1983). A recent biography on Flagg is Mardges Bacon, *Ernest Flagg: Beaux-Arts Architect and Urban Reformer* (Cambridge: MIT Press, 1986). There has been no book-length study of Atterbury. Brief sketches of other architects involved in housing reform and at Forest Hills Gardens can be found in Mark Alan Hewitt, *The Architect and the American Country House, 1890–1940* (New Haven: Yale University Press, 1990). At the turn of the century, New York was at the center of housing reform in the United States. In the 1890s the City and Suburban Homes Company sponsored model tenements designed to return a 5 percent profit to investors. The company built a village (Homewood) of 127 workers' cottages in Brooklyn, in the hope that the promise of home ownership would help instill "American values" in the working class (especially recent immigrants). Flagg designed the Alfred Corning Clark Building (1896) for C&S Homes,

and model tenements in 1898, 1909, and 1911 for the Fireproof Tenement Association. Lawrence Veiller estimated that housing reformers constructed about 200 buildings between 1855 and 1905, while speculative builders erected more than 50,000. Veiller quoted in Wright, *Building the Dream*, 123.

46. For Atterbury, see Donald Dwyer, "Grosvenor Atterbury," *Dictionary of American Biography*, suppl. 6 (1960): 25–27; and Grosvenor Atterbury Papers, Rare and Manuscript Collections, Carl A. Kroch Library, Cornell University, Ithaca, N.Y, Collection no. 3762, box 1. For his interests in worker housing, see Margaret Crawford, *Building the Workingman's Paradise: The Design of the American Company Town* (New York: Verso, 1995), chap. 6.

47. Morrison H. Heckscher, "The Metropolitan Museum of Art: An Architectural History," *Metropolitan Museum of Art Bulletin* 53 (Summer 1995): 55.

48. Grosvenor Atterbury, "The Architectural Work," in *Forest Hills Gardens*, pamphlet no. 1 (1911): 18.

49. In addition to the planning history citations above, see also Jon Peterson, "The City Beautiful Movement: Forgotten Origins and Lost Meanings," *Journal of Urban History* 2 (August 1976): 415–34; Mario Manieri-Elia, "Toward an 'Imperial City': Daniel H. Burnham and the City Beautiful Movement," in Ciucci et al., *The American City*; and William W. Wilson, *The City Beautiful Movement* (Baltimore: Johns Hopkins University Press, 1989).

50. The architectural historian Richard Guy Wilson points out that the Arts and Crafts movement was expressed not in one specific style "but as a mood, an attitude, a sensibility. . . . Certain elements appear frequently—motifs derived from nature, a concern with simple form and complex detail, a glorification of medieval art and society, and the exaltation of the vernacular—but the visual forms and social concerns differed." Wilson, "'Divine Excellence': The Arts and Crafts Life in California," in *The Arts and Crafts Movement in California: Living the Good Life*, ed. Kenneth R. Trapp (New York: Oakland Museum/Abbeville, 1993), 17. Much of the latest scholarship on the Arts and Crafts movement in America has been associated with museum exhibitions; see also Wendy Kaplan, *"The Art That Is Life": The Arts and Crafts Movement in America, 1875–1922* (Boston: Boston Museum of Fine Arts/Little, Brown, 1987), and James D. Kornwolf, "The Arts and Crafts in American Houses and Gardens," in *The Ideal House: The History of Twentieth-Century American Craft, 1900–1920*, ed. Janet Kardon (New York: Harry N. Abrams, 1993).

51. "Forest Hills Gardens, Long Island," *Construction News*, 4 October 1913, 9.

4. *"The Thoroughness with Which Things Are Done Here"*

1. On the second phase of city planning, see Francesco Dal Co, "From Parks to the Region: Progressive Ideology and the Reform of the American City," in *The American City: From Civil War to New Deal*, ed. Giorgio Ciucci, Francesco Dal Co, Mario Manieri-Elia, and Manfredo Tafuri (Cambridge: MIT Press, 1983), 143–260; Mel Scott, *American City Planning since 1890* (Berkeley: University of California Press, 1971), chaps. 1–3; and Mary Corbin Sies and Christopher Silver, eds., *Planning the Twentieth-Century American City* (Baltimore: Johns Hopkins University Press, 1996), sec. 1.

2. Course prospectus quoted in *Architectural Record* 26 (November 1909): 385–86.

3. On early American town planning, see John Reps, *The Making of Urban America: A History of City Planning in the United States* (Princeton: Princeton University Press, 1965).

4. Olmsted, Vaux, & Co., "Preliminary Report upon the Proposed Suburban Village at Riverside, Near Chicago, by Olmsted, Vaux, & Co., Landscape Architects," reprinted in *The Papers of Frederick Law Olmsted*, vol. 6, *The Years of Olmsted, Vaux, & Co., 1865–1874*, ed. David Schuyler and Jane Turner Censer (Baltimore: Johns Hopkins University Press, 1992), 275. Although the Riverside plan and report were attributed to Olmsted and his partner, Calvert Vaux, the essential work was done by Olmsted while Vaux was out of the country. See David Schuyler, "Frederick Law Olmsted's Riverside," *Planning History Present* 7, no. 2 (1993): 1.

5. Olmsted, Vaux, & Co., "Preliminary Report," 276. Olmsted and Vaux appear to have devised the term "parkway" at about the same time that they were planning Riverside. They saw the need for "a series of ways designed with express reference to the pleasure with which they may be used; . . . and that these ways must be so arranged that will be conveniently accessible from every dwelling house and allow its occupants to pass from it to distant parts of the town, as, for instance, when they want to go to a park." See "Observations on the Progress of Improvements in Street Plans, with Special Reference to the Parkway Proposed to be Laid Out in Brooklyn," quoted in S. B. Sutton, *Civilizing American Cities: A Selection of Frederick Law Olmsted's Writings on City Landscape* (Cambridge: MIT Press, 1979), 42, and "Report of the Landscape Architects and Superintendents of the President of the Board of Commissioners of Prospect Park, Brooklyn" (1868), section on "The Park Way—Approaches and Connections," in *Landscape into Cityscape: Frederick Law Olmsted's Plans for a Greater New York City*, ed. Albert Fein (New York: Van Nostrand Reinhold, 1981), 131–32. It has been suggested that Ebenezer Howard may have been influenced by Riverside, since Howard was in Chicago in 1872. See Walter Creese, *The Search for Environment: The Garden City Before and After* (Baltimore: Johns Hopkins University Press, 1992), 152–53; and Frank Jackson, *Sir Raymond Unwin: Architect, Planner, and Visionary* (London: A. Zwemmer, 1985), 60–61.

6. Spiro Kostoff, *America by Design* (New York: Oxford University Press, 1878), 100. Over the past twenty years suburban history has emerged as a popular area of study, and the literature is voluminous. Some of the now classic and some newer works in this area are Sam Bass Warner, *Street Car Suburbs: The Process of Growth in Boston, 1870–1900* (Chicago: University of Chicago Press, 1978); Robert A. M. Stern, guest ed., *The Anglo-American Suburb*, Architectural Design Profile (London: Architectural Design, 1981); Kenneth T. Jackson, *Crabgrass Frontier: The Suburbanization of the United States* (New York: Oxford University Press, 1984); Henry C. Binford, *The First Suburbs: Residential Communities of the Boston Periphery, 1815–1860* (Chicago: University of Chicago Press, 1985); Robert Fishman, *Bourgeois Utopia: The Rise and Fall of Suburbia* (New York: Basic Books, 1987); Marc Allen Weiss, *The Rise of the Community Builders: The American Real Estate Industry and Urban Land Planning* (New York: Columbia University Press, 1987); Michael Ebner, *Creating Chicago's North Shore: A Suburban History* (Chicago: University of Chicago Press, 1988); John Stilgoe, *Borderland: Origins of the American Suburb, 1820–1939* (New Haven: Yale University Press, 1988); Mary Corbin Sies, "Paradise Retained: An Analysis of Persistence in

Planned, Exclusive Suburbs, 1880–1980," *Proceedings of the Third Conference in American Planning History* (Hillard, Ohio: Society of American City and Regional Planning History, 1990); James Howard Kunstler, *The Geography of Nowhere* (New York: Touchstone, 1994); Philip Langdon, *A Better Place to Live: Reshaping the American Suburb* (Amherst: University of Massachusetts Press, 1994); and Andres Duany, Elizabeth Plater-Zyberk, and Jeff Speck, *Suburban Nation: The Rise of Sprawl and the Decline of the American Dream* (New York: North Point Press, 2000).

7. Olmsted to Charles H. Chaney, 30 August 1915, OA , series B, no. 2919.

8. Minutes of the meetings of the Sage Foundation Realty Development Committee (hereafter cited as Minutes), 29 April and 7 May, 1909, RSF, series 3, box 21, folder 167. For early suburban development in Brooklyn, see "Metropolitan Neighborhoods," in *New York 1900: Metropolitan Architecture and Urbanism*, by Robert A. M. Stern, Gregory Gilmartin, and John Montague Massengale (New York: Rizzoli, 1983), 421–25. Olmsted and Atterbury were compensated $250 per month plus expenses "as designers, as consultants, and as quasi directors." Olmsted to de Forest, 17 May 1909, OA, series B, no. 5386.

9. Thomas Bender, *New York Intellect: A History of Intellectual Life in New York City, from 1750 to the Beginnings of Our Own Time* (Baltimore: Johns Hopkins University Press, 1988), 135.

10. Minutes, 20 and 27 May; 4 and 22 July; 10 June 1909, RSF, series 3, box 21, folder 167.

11. Frederick Law Olmsted, "Through American Spectacles: An Expert's View of the English Garden City Schemes," *Garden Cities and Town Planning* 4 (May 1909): 199. Olmsted to Atterbury, 15 June 1909, OA, series B, no. 3586.

12. Atterbury to Olmsted, 19 June 1909, OA, series B, no. 3586.

13. Minutes, 17 June 1909, OA, series B, no. 3586.

14. De Forest to Olmsted, 25 June 1909, RSF, series 3, box 23, folder 182.

15. Olmsted's figures took into account the $831,000 purchase price of the property plus an estimated $350,000 for general improvements (streets, sewers, etc.), $10,000 for parkland, $100,000 in interest and taxes, $50,000 for advertising, and $50,000 for administration and design. The final plan, filed with the city in April 1911, showed 2,000 standard 25-by-100-foot building lots on 44 blocks. Such lots typically accommodated a row house, two rooms deep, with a large rear yard. At Forest Hills Gardens, of course, buyers could purchase more than one lot if they wanted a larger building site.

16. Minutes, 1 July and 8 July 1909, RSF, series 3, box 21, folder 176. Rents were no longer mentioned. Forest Hills Gardens was built as and remains primarily an owner-occupied community. In 1915, when a state census was conducted, all but one of the community's 166 homes were owner occupied. See William E. Coleman, "Notes on *Why We Have Chosen Forest Hills Gardens for Our Home*," *Forest Hills Gardens,* no. 1 (1992): 34. Coleman, a historian and Forest Hills Gardens resident, provides information on residents quoted in the *Why* booklet, a collection of statements of the first Gardens residents published in 1915 (see also chapter 7, note 17). When ownership of Forest Hills Gardens passed to the Gardens Corporation on 1 January 1923, there were approximately 450 resident and 150 nonresident property owners. See *Your Gardens Corporation*, an informational booklet distrib-

uted to residents in May 1923. The Gardens Corporation does not keep statistics on residents today.

17. The original Olmsted-Atterbury plan included a 12-unit apartment building along the Continental Avenue side of Station Square. Atterbury's design for Block 12, at the head of the Green and in front of the school, called for single-family homes; however, this block remained undeveloped when the Sage Foundation sold Forest Hills Gardens in 1922. After a protracted court battle, the 95-unit Leslie Apartment (the only rental building in FHG) was constructed there in 1943, blocking the view of the school and thus obviating Olmsted's idea of terminating the axis from Station Square at a public space. Today there are eleven apartment buildings in Forest Hills Gardens, which provide 650 housing units. See Jeff Gottlieb and William E. Coleman, "The Apartment Houses of Forest Hills Gardens," *Forest Hills Gardens* 2 (1994): 39–51.

18. *Reflections on Roland Park*, pamphlet (Cross Keys, Md.: James W. Rouse and Company, n.d.), [3–4]; Olmsted to Dominquez Land Co., 6 April 1912, OA, series B, no. 5354.

19. *Reflections on Roland Park*, [14].

20. The first section of Roland Park was laid out by the Kansas City landscape architect George Kessler in 1891. Bouton contacted Olmsted Brothers in 1897. John Charles was the primary partner involved in the planning phase, 1897–98; Rick began to take an increasing role at Roland Park from 1902 on. For the development of Roland Park, see Roberta M. Moudry, "Gardens, Houses, and People: The Planning of Roland Park, Baltimore" (master's thesis, Cornell University, 1990). For the Olmsted Brothers and suburban development, see Arleyn A. Levee, "The Olmsted Brothers' Residential Communities: Preview of a Legacy," in *The Landscape Universe: Historic Designed Landscapes in Context*, ed. Charles A. Birnbaum, proceedings from a symposium held at Wave Hill, Bronx, N.Y., 23 April 1993 (Bronx, N.Y.: Catalog of Landscape Records in the United States with National Park Service Preservation Assistance Division, 1993), 199.

21. Olmsted to W. W. Parce, 10 December 1913, OA, series B, no. 3391.

22. Minutes, 29 July 1909, RSF, series 3, box 21, folder 176.

23. Olmsted to Thomas Adams, 23 July 1912, OA, series B, no. 3586.

24. Ralph Peters to Edward Bouton, 1 June 1910, OA, series B, no. 3586.

25. On the two Olmsteds as comprehensive planners, see Jon A. Peterson, "Frederick Law Olmsted, Sr. and Frederick Law Olmsted, Jr.: The Visionary and the Professional," in Sies and Silver, *Planning the Twentieth-Century American City*, 37–54.

26. Editorial, "The Sage Foundation at Forest Hills," and Samuel Howe, "Forest Hills Gardens," *American Architect* 102 (30 October 1912): 159, 153.

27. Olmsted, "Introductory Address on City Planning," *Proceedings of the Second National Conference on City Planning* (1910), 19.

28. "Draft of Statement Concerning Block 23, Forest Hills Gardens, Addressed to Prospective Purchasers," attached to a letter from John M. Demarest to John M. Glenn, 6 December 1911, RSF, series 3, box 19, folder 157. Three major roads that became boundaries of Forest Hills Gardens already existed in rudimentary form or were on the drawing boards.

Hoffman (now Queens) Boulevard ran parallel to the Long Island Rail Road tracks across from what became the entrance to the Gardens. This road, then 80 feet wide and scheduled to be enlarged to 200 feet, was to be the primary commuting route to and from Manhattan. On the western side of the Forest Hills Gardens property, Metropolitan Avenue was being developed as an extension of an existing elevated road, on which electric trains would run from Manhattan, through Queens, and on to Brooklyn. To the south, Union Turnpike, which separated the Forest Hills Gardens site from the public park to the rear of the development, also was a commuting route to Brooklyn.

29. Olmsted, "A Suburban Town Built on Business Principles," *New Boston* 1 (January 1911): 396.

30. Charles C. May, "Forest Hills Gardens from the Town Planning Viewpoint," *Architecture* 34 (August 1916): 170.

31. Olmsted, "The Landscape Work," *Forest Hills Gardens: The Suburban Land Development of the Russell Sage Foundation*, pamphlet no. 1 (1911): 13. (On the pamphlet, see note 42 below.) These local streets varied in width from 32 feet to 50 feet, with the majority 40 feet wide. With the exception of Ascan and Continental Avenues, the streets of Forest Hills Gardens are closed one day a year to nonresidents to maintain their private status.

32. Quote from May, "Forest Hills Gardens," 170.

33. Olmsted's minimal design for Station Square was soon changed. By 1915 Olmsted employee L. S. Adams reported after a site visit that "the Square has certainly lost its simplicity and charm and is very restless." The center island had been extended and the fountain was changed into a planter. Two "safety kiosks" were added to serve as a police outpost and call-in station. Large elm trees had also been added around the periphery. Adams described the atmosphere as "stuffy": "All feel that the quaint dignity of the former square has been blasted." L. S. Adams report, 23 June 1915, OA, series B, no. 3586.

With the opening in 1936 of the Forest Hills subway station at 71 Street and Continental Avenue, the LIRR reduced train service to Forest Hills Gardens, and over the years maintenance on the station lapsed. In 1990 a portion of the embankment retaining walls collapsed. A Friends of Station Square group was formed to work with the LIRR to restore the station and surrounding area, and a refurbished station opened in June 1999. Residents have also supported restoration work on the kiosks and the tower clock. See Ronald Marzlock, "The Long Island Railroad Station and Station Square," *Forest Hills Gardens* 2 (1994): 2–7, and William Coleman, "The Forest Hills Station: An Architectural Treasure," *Forest Hills Gardens News*, August 1990.

34. Public School 101 opened in a temporary building on Block 10 in May 1914. The school still operates in a building constructed in the 1920s.

35. Olmsted first made this recommendation in his 1905 report to the New York City Improvement Commission and included it in most of his subsequent city planning reports. It was this idea of a park within walking distance of every family that the planning theorist Clarence Perry popularized in the 1920s as the neighborhood unit concept. Perry worked for the Sage Foundation as head of their recreation department during the 1910s and lived in Forest Hills Gardens from 1912 until his death in 1944.

36. "Draft of Statement Concerning Block 23, Forest Hills Gardens, Addressed to Prospec-

tive Purchasers" attached to letter from John M. Demarest to John M. Glenn, 26 March 1912, RSF, series 3, box 19, folder 157. Block owners would vote each year whether to give up the lease on the interior land. If they did, the property would revert to the company, which would give each owner the opportunity to purchase the area in the rear of his own lot before offering it for public sale.

37. Olmsted, "The Landscape Work," 14–15. Olmsted wrote in 1924 that the interior parks had proved to have little value as a selling point and that "the house holders who have joint interest in such a space have seldom shown any interest or ability in cooperating to make it satisfactory and useful." Olmsted to William H. Harmon, 21 October 1924, OA, series B, no. 20. Edward Bouton had a similar experience when he introduced interior parks in his Baltimore suburb. See Bouton, "Development of Roland Park, Baltimore," *Proceedings of Homebuilders and Subdividers. Division of the National Association of Real Estate Boards. Annals of Real Estate Practice* 3 (1924): 21. Only three interior parks were actually built: Blocks 3, 30, and 33. The other reserved spaces were used for building lots, turned into a cul-de-sac, or had a road cut through, as, for example, Ivy Close in Block 23.

38. De Forest, "Forest Hills Gardens," 8.

39. At Levittown, by comparison, production of conventionally constructed houses reached a rate of sixteen per day. See Barbara A. Kelly, *Expanding the American Dream: Building and Rebuilding Levittown* (Albany: State University of New York Press, 1993). Frederick Squires, "Houses at Forest Hills Gardens—Pre-Cast Hollow Concrete Floor, Wall and Roof Units and Exposed Aggregates," *Concrete-Cement Age* 6 (February 1915): 3–8, 58–54. See also "Studies in Economic Construction," *Cement Age* 11 (December 1910): 315–25, and John Burchard, "Atterbury," in *Rational Design*, vol. 3 of *The Evolving House*, ed. Albert Farwell Bemis (Cambridge: MIT Press, 1933), 349–52. Despite some savings in labor costs, the concrete houses proved to be very expensive. This was not unexpected, however, given the high startup costs involved in building the concrete factory and working with novel methods of construction. Moreover, workers at Forest Hills Gardens were paid at New York union rates. There were also difficulties in bringing materials to the site, and there was insufficient on-site space for storing materials. In addition, frequent changes in plans during the initial phase of construction added to costs. See Minutes, 7 December 1911, OA, series B, no. 3586. About thirty concrete houses were built at Forest Hills Gardens.

40. Edward Hale Brush, "A Garden City for the Man of Moderate Means," *Craftsman* 14 (January 1911): 446; Squires, "Houses at Forest Hills Gardens," 5.

41. "Sage Model Town Named," *New York Times*, 25 November 1910.

42. The Sage Foundation booklet *Forest Hills Gardens: The Suburban Land Development of the Russell Sage Foundation*, pamphlet no. 1, was first issued in February 1911 and reprinted November 1911 and December 1912. The twenty-page pamphlet contained the initial press release statements under the following titles: "Forest Hill Gardens. What It Is, Why It Is, and What It Is Not," by Robert W. de Forest; "The Development of a Harmonious Neighborhood," by Alfred T. White; "The Landscape Work," by Frederick Law Olmsted; "The Architectural Work," by Grosvenor Atterbury; "Scientific Methods of Handling and Distributing Suburban Land," by William F. Harmon; and "Quality of Design" by Edward H. Bouton. A second edition, *Forest Hills Gardens: Portfolio of Pictures and Planning Diagrams*,

pamphlet no. 2, was issued in December 1913. See "Forest Hills Gardens," *Survey* 25 (7 January 1911): 561–70; "Forest Hills Gardens," *American City* 4 (4 March 1911): 135–36; Atterbury's "Forest Hills Gardens, Long Island. An Example of Collective Planning, Development, and Control," *Brickbuilder* 21 (December 1912): 317–18; Olmsted, "A Suburban Town Build on Business Principles," *New Boston* 1 (January 1911); and Olmsted quoted in "The Sage Foundation at Forest Hills," *American Architect* 102 (30 October 1912): 139–40.

43. De Forest, "Forest Hills Gardens," 8–9.

44. Atterbury, "The Architectural Work," 16–17.

45. Bouton, "Quality of Design," 21–22.

46. De Forest quoted in "Forest Hills Gardens," *Survey*, 569; Atterbury quoted in "The Architectural Work," 18. De Forest and Alfred T. White (president of the Brooklyn Bureau of Charities) and foundation executive director John Glenn made up the SFHC board; Olmsted, Atterbury, general manager Bouton, and real estate adviser Harmon constituted the SFHC Committee on Development, which had oversight of the day-to-day operations.

47. "Forest Hills Gardens, Long Island," *Construction News*, 4 October 1913, 374.

5. "The English Type"

1. Frederick Law Olmsted, "City Planning. An Introductory Address," *Proceedings of the Second National Conference on City Planning and the Problems of Congestion* (1910), 15–16.

2. Susan Holbrook Perdue, "Forest Hills Gardens: Architecture and Landscape Planning in a Model Suburb, 1908–1915" (master's thesis, University of Virginia, 1985), chap. 6, provides information on Atterbury's designs for Forest Hills Gardens.

3. Atterbury's use of lammie brick in his family home in Shinnecock Hills is thought to be the first use of this material in domestic architecture. His design for the de Forest home used red and green roof tiles. Atterbury's 1906 Bryne house at Oyster Bay exhibits rooflines and massing that prefigure his Forest Hills Gardens designs. Stucco and colored concrete aggregate, important materials at FHG, also appear in his early private work. See Robert B. MacKay, Anthony Baker, and Carol A. Traynor, eds., *Long Island Country Houses and Their Architects, 1860–1940* (New York: Society for the Preservation of New England Antiquities, 1997), 49–57.

4. The color was evidently similar to "Horizon Blue" (no. 8630) made by the Cabot paint company, which the Gardens Corporation used in their maintenance work. "Paint Approval 1936–1950," Record Group 2775, Forest Hills Gardens Corporation (hereafter cited as FHG Corp.), box 19, Rare and Manuscript Collections, Carl A. Kroch Library, Cornell University, Ithaca, N.Y. Perdue notes that Atterbury was a friend of the artist Albert Herter, for whom he designed a house on Long Island in 1898, which is described (MacKay et al., *Long Island Country Houses*, 52) as having pink stucco walls and blue-green wood trim. Herter is said to have created a blue-green color known as "Herter blue," which may have been the color used by Atterbury both for that house and in Forest Hills Gardens. See Perdue, "Forest Hills Gardens," n. 132.

5. Samuel Howe, "Forest Hills Gardens," *American Architect* 102 (30 October 1912): 155. The housekeeping complex at 10 Station Square (now called the Raleigh) was converted into an apartment house in the 1920s. The Inn became an apartment building in 1967. The Marlboro (2 Dartmouth Street) was originally designed as housekeeping apartments managed by the Inn. All of these buildings were converted to cooperative apartment houses in 1981. See Jeff Gottlieb and William E. Coleman, "The Apartments of Forest Hills Gardens," *Forest Hills Gardens* 2 (1994), 39–49.

6. The building lots closest to Station Square were the least expensive.

7. Atterbury's associates John Almy Tompkins and Stowe Phelps assisted him in designs for Forest Hills Gardens. Other architects who worked there include Lewis Colt Albro, Aymar Embury II, Wilson Eyre, Harrie T. Lindeberg, Eugene Schoen, Frederick J. Sterner, and J. T. Tubby.

8. Atterbury's innovative designs for these housing groups were a distinct contrast to the ubiquitous city row house of the period. But as appealing as the buildings were, Forest Hills Gardens' creators knew that they faced a major marketing challenge in popularizing such dwellings, given the "American dream" of a freestanding home set in a big yard. Indeed, the greater part of housing offered at Forest Hills Gardens is freestanding, with the size of houses increasing as one moves farther away from Station Square.

9. Edward Hale Brush, "A Garden City for the Man of Moderate Means," *Craftsman* 19 (January 1911): 447.

10. Frederick Law Olmsted Jr., "Report to Accompany Preliminary Plan for the Grounds of the Nordhoff High School," 6 January 1912, OA, series B, no. 5435.

11. "Circular as to Professional Methods and Charges," revised 1894, scrapbook 1, Office Memorandum, Fairsted; Olmsted Brothers to Prentiss L. Coonley, 4 March 1910, OA, series B, no. 3555.

12. Olmsted to Lee J. Ninde, 7 November 1913, OA, series B, no. 5437.

13. For a discussion of Arts and Crafts landscapes, see Diana Balmori, "The Arts and Crafts Garden," *Tiller* 1 (1983): 17–27; David Streatfield, "Arts and Crafts Gardens in California," in *The Arts and Crafts Movement in California: Living the Good Life*, ed. Kenneth Trapp (Oakland: Oakland Museum and Abbeville Press, 1993), 135–53; and Wendy Hitchmough, *Arts and Crafts Gardens* (New York: Rizzoli, 1997).

14. For the landscape design of Roland Park, see Roberta M. Moudry, "Gardens, Houses, and People: The Planning of Roland Park, Baltimore" (master's thesis, Cornell University, 1990), 118–33.

15. Olmsted to Demarest, 14 August 1912, OA, series B, no. 3586; nos. 3586-1083 and 3586-1084, "Alternative Plans for Planting the Village Green," 25 March 1910; no. 3586-2144, "Plan for Circle in Village Green," 11 May 1916, Fairsted.

16. *Forest Hills Gardens*, pamphlet no. 3 (December 1913). *News of the Gardens Corporation*, no. 9 (1938), a newsletter of the homeowners association, mentioned that since 1922 paved paths had been added in Hawthorne Park and Olivia Park had been replanted with rhododendrons, dogwoods, and honeysuckle.

17. Franklin Clarkin, "The Sage Paradise for New York," *Boston Evening Star*, 1 January 1913, RAC, series 3, box 20, folder 3.

18. Charles C. May, "Forest Hills Gardens from the Town Planning Viewpoint," *Architecture* 34 (August 1916): 171.

19. Olmsted Brothers office memorandum, 23 November 1911, OA, series B, no. 3586.

20. *Forest Hills Gardens: Preliminary Information for Buyers*, pamphlet no. 2 (July 1911), Fairsted, box 61. (On the pamphlet, see chapter 6, note 17.)

21. "Planting Plan for Private Park in Block 16," no. 3586-2015, Fairsted.

22. As yet there is no complete listing of landscape plans done by the firm for individual homeowners in Forest Hills Gardens. *The Master List to the Design Projects of the Olmsted Firm, 1857–1950*, compiled in 1987, lists only one private resident in Forest Hills Gardens. This list is currently being updated and will soon be available online. A rough count of the preliminary inventory of all plans for Forest Hills Gardens, prepared by the Frederick Law Olmsted National Historic site in the early 1990s, yielded the names of thirty-five clients for whom planting lists were prepared. Many other homeowners had grading plans done for their property. There were a number of planting plans created for company-built speculative houses, identified by a model number, but it would be difficult to determine if these plans were in fact carried out without linking the house to an owner.

23. John Glenn to Olmsted, 10 September 1913, RSF, series 3, box 23, folder 182.

6. "Normal and Usual Social Conditions"

1. "Report of the Committee on Building," 30 November 1909, OA, series B, no. 3586; Statement by John Demarest, "Sage Foundation Announces Its Easy Payment Plan," 29 August 1911, RSF, box 61, folder 157. It is difficult to make meaningful comparisons of financing with other subdivisions because of the number of variables involved in developing a property. However, J. C. Nichols was offering roughly similar terms in 1909 in his Country Club District development. A four-bedroom house selling for $7,750 required the purchaser to make a down payment of $775, with a first mortgage for 50 percent of the price offered at 5 percent interest. See Worley, *J. C. Nichols and the Shaping of Kansas City* (Columbia: University of Missouri Press, 1993), 190.

2. *Preliminary Information for Buyers,* pamphlet no. 2 (July 1911).

3. Minutes, 25 October 1910 and 3 January 1911, RSF, series 3, box 21, folder 167.

4. Olmsted, Vaux, & Co., "Preliminary Report upon the Proposed Suburban Village at Riverside, Near Chicago, by Olmsted, Vaux, & Co., Landscape Architects," reprinted in *The Papers of Frederick Law Olmsted*, vol. 6, *The Years of Olmsted, Vaux, & Co., 1865–1874*, ed. David Schuyler and Jane Turner Censer (Baltimore: Johns Hopkins University Press, 1992), 286, 288.

5. *Reflections on Roland Park,* pamphlet (Cross Keys, Md.: James W. Rouse and Company, n.d.), [3]. J. C. Nichols claimed that his Country Club District was the first to use self-

perpetuating deed restrictions; however, these were filed with a plat map in 1909. See Worley, *J. C. Nichols*, 129.

6. Roberta M. Moudry, "Gardens, Houses, and People: The Planning of Roland Park, Baltimore" (master's thesis, Cornell University, 1990), 138–39. The original restrictions at Forest Hills Gardens were to run until 1 January 1950. They have been extended periodically since then.

7. See Garrick Power, "The Covenant of Roland Park," paper presented at the Third National Conference of American Planning History, 30 November–2 December 1989, Cincinnati, Ohio, 4. Power cites a 1928 survey that recorded only thirteen Jewish families in Roland Park/Guilford. J. C. Nichols prohibited sales to blacks; in 1919, however, he declared that it was "unAmerican and undemocratic, and so unfair to exclude a man on account of his nationality, regardless of what he is himself" (Worley, 151). Nevertheless, the Country Club District continued de facto segregation until well into the 1960s. In 1917 the Supreme Court overturned local residential segregation ordinances, but it was not until 1948 that "gentlemen's agreements" and other discriminatory practices used by real estate boards and neighborhood associations were declared unlawful. Government housing policies of the 1930s and 1940s explicitly upheld existing patterns of racial segregation in areas where public housing was to be constructed. Similarly, during the 1940 and 1950s, federal programs promoting home ownership encouraged the use of restrictive covenants for the purposes of maintaining neighborhood "stability," protecting property values, and controlling racial tensions.

8. "The Forest Hills Gardens Development. Its Restrictions, and the Powers of the Membership Corporation Which Enforces Them," reprinted in *Regional Plan of New York and Its Environs*, vol. 7, *Neighborhood and Community Planning, Appendix B: The Neighborhood Unit* (New York: Committee on Regional Plan of New York and Its Environs, 1929), 132–35.

9. Ibid., 132–33. Minutes, 21 June 1911, RSF, series 3, box 20, folder 163. In a review of twenty-five randomly selected subdivisions designed by the Olmsted firm, Olmsted found that 12 percent of those planned between 1900 and 1910, 33 percent of those designed between 1911 and 1920, and 80 percent of those designed between 1921 and 1940 required prior approval of building plans. See Olmsted, "Deed Restrictions that Affect Houses in Planned Neighborhoods," *Architectural Record* 88, no. 6 (November 1940): 34.

10. "The Forest Hills Gardens Development," 135.

11. "Interview with Mr. John M. Glenn, General Director of the Russell Sage Foundation," 4 September 1911 (prepared as press release), RSF, series 3, box 20, folder 158.

12. The Roland Park Civic League is the oldest continuously active homeowners association in the country. It was founded as a voluntary association with Bouton's cooperation in 1895 and was incorporated as an independent organization in 1907. See Moudry, "Gardens, Houses, and People," 294–95.

13. Glenn, interview; Minutes, 17 February 1911, RSF, series 3, box 21, folder 167.

14. Edward Bouton to Robert de Forest, 29 May 1911, OA, series B, no. 3586.

15. John Glenn to Robert de Forest, 1 March 1911, RSF, series 3, box 19, folder 157; "John Demarest Dies Long Island City," obituary, *New York Star*, 23 July 1935, RSF, series 3, box 20, folder 158. Bouton resigned as vice president in December 1911; he remained on the Realty Development Committee until January 1913.

16. Minutes, 1 June 1911, RSF, box 2, folder 167.

17. "Report of the General Manager," 11 September 1911, OA, series B, no. 3586. *Forest Hills Gardens: The Suburban Land Development Company of the Russell Sage Foundation*, pamphlet no. 1 (1911); this pamphlet was reprinted periodically until 1919 as *Forest Hills Gardens: Preliminary Information for Buyers*.

18. Minutes, 19 July 1911, RSF, series 3, box 21, folder 167; John Glenn to Mrs. Russell Sage, 8 July 1911, RSF, series 3, box 18, folder 149.

19. "Report of the General Manager," 11 September 1911, OA, series B, no. 3586.

20. *New York Times*, 26 October 1911, RSF, series 3, box 22, folder 174.

21. In 1916 the SFHC published a compilation of these ads in a booklet titled *A Forward Movement in Suburban Development: Ten Talks about Forest Hills Gardens*.

22. Robert de Forest to Mrs. Russell Sage, 25 April 1912, RSF, series 3, box 23, folder 182; Minutes, 5 April 1913, ibid. By September 1914 a total of 1,290 lots had been sold. The SFHC had completed 140 houses and had 15 under construction; an additional 9 had been built by outside contractors. "Report of the General Manager," 10 September 1914, RSF, series 3, box 20, folder 159.

7. "A Village of Rare Charm"

1. "Forest Hills Gardens, Long Island," *Construction News*, 4 October 1913, 9.

2. Franklin Clarkin, "The Sage Paradise for New York," *Boston Evening Transcript*, 18 January 1913, RSF, box 20, folder 162.

3. Louis Graves, "A 'Model Village' Underway," *Building Progress* 2 (January 1912): this and following quotes from p. 19.

4. *Boston Evening Transcript*, 18 January 1913; Samuel Howe, "Forest Hills Gardens," *American Architect* 102 (30 October 1912): 155.

5. Mary Eastwood Knevels, "What the Suburban Dweller May Learn from a Model Town," *American Homes and Gardens* 12 (February 1915): 39–40.

6. *Boston Evening Transcript*, 18 January 1913. This characterization of town as stage set would be repeated in much of the criticism of the Walt Disney Company's town of Celebration, Florida. The similarities in the rhetoric inspired by the two developments are discussed in the next chapter.

7. Grosvenor Atterbury, "Forest Hills Gardens," *Survey* 25 (7 January 1911): 565, 563.

8. Olmsted to Thomas Adams, 30 April 1912, OA, series B, no. 3586.

9. Olmsted to Adams, 23 July 1912, OA, series B, no. 3586, and 30 April 1912.

10. Edward Hale Brush, "A Garden City for the Man of Moderate Means," *Craftsman* 14 (January 1911): 445–46.

11. Dr. Scott E. W. Bedford quoted in *Forest Hills Gardens Bulletin* (hereafter cited as *Bulletin*) 1, no. 5 (20 November 1915).

12. Atterbury, "Forest Hills Gardens," 563.

13. Sage Foundation Homes Company, *A Little Story of 21-Months' Work in Forest Hills Gardens, Long Island*, [1913], Fairsted, box 64.

14. "Characterization List by Occupation of Purchasers at Forest Hills Gardens," 1 February 1912, RSF, series 3, box 20, folder 161; "Characterization List by Occupation of Purchasers at Forest Hills Gardens," 9 January 1913, OA, series B, no. 3586.

15. "Report of a Conference held at 30 Broad Street on September 10, 1914," RSF, series 3, box 20, folder 159. Thirty-one houses were being rented, 15 were under construction by the SFHC, and 9 were being built by outside contractors, for a total of 196. Data from the New York State Census, June 1915, is summarized in *Bulletin* 1, no. 1 (25 September 1915).

16. *Bulletin* 1, no. 1 (1 July 1916).

17. In 1991 the Forest Hills Gardens Corporation printed a replica of the *Why* booklet, which was distributed with the first issue of *Forest Hills Gardens*, produced by the Corporation's History Committee, chaired by town historian William E. Coleman (two issues were published). The information on Goudy is taken from Coleman's article "Frederic Goudy and the Village Press in Forest Hills Gardens, 1913–1923," *Forest Hills Gardens*, no. 1 (April 1992): 4–9. Another article by Coleman in that issue, "Commentary on the *Why* Booklet," provides information about the respondents quoted (see pp. 30–44). All of the quotations of residents in the following paragraphs are from the *Why* booklet.

18. The Sage name impressed at least one transient visitor to the Gardens as well. F. M. Monroe, president of the Maltzyme Company of Brooklyn ("Makers of Maltzyme plain or with cod liver oil and other healthful additives," according to his letterhead) spent three months at the Forest Hills Inn in the fall of 1912. "It seems to me," he later wrote in a letter of appreciation to the management, "that the Sage Foundation is a great blessing to people of moderate means, and I, for one, am very grateful to have the privilege of enjoying its beauties and advantages." Letter to Forest Hills Inn, 30 December 1912, RSF, series 3, box 18, folder 149.

19. Preface to bound volumes 1–5 of the *Bulletin*. In October 1922 the name was changed to the *Forest Hills Bulletin*, to reflect its coverage of the broader area of Forest Hills. The *Bulletin*'s last issue was 13 December 1924. Bound and indexed copies of issues from 25 September 1915 to 4 September 1920 can be found in the New York City Public Library, the Russell Sage Foundation Archives at the RAC, and the archives in the Gardens Company office at Forest Hills Gardens.

20. *Bulletin* 1, no. 2 (9 October 1915).

21. The SFHC paid $9,000 for the twenty-two acres it retained for Forest Hills Gardens and $7,900 for the ten acres sold to the West Side Tennis Club (tract 3). Earlier, in February 1912, the Homes Company had purchased about thirty acres near Station Square southwest on Continental Avenue to Groton Street (tract 2) for $5,250 per acre. OA, series B, no. 3516.

22. *Bulletin* 2, no. 11 (10 February 1917).

23. Present-day Flushing Meadows Park, site of the 1964 World's Fair, was in those years a tidal marsh known as Flushing Swamp, an ideal breeding ground for mosquitoes.

24. Early residents noted that Olivia Sage "always took a special interest in our garden city. She usually passed through on her trips to and from her country home at Lawrence [Long Island], and until recent years, when physical weakness kept her in seclusion, was accustomed to make a brief tour of inspection." *Bulletin* 4, no. 5 (16 November 1918).

25. See Lucy Allen Smart, "History of Forest Hills from the Days of the Indians," *Bulletin* 10, no. 6 (13 December 1924). Permanent school buildings were erected in the 1920s.

26. *Bulletin* 5, no. 26 (4 September 1920).

27. Independence Day Program, 4 July 1915, RSF, series 3, box 19, folder 154. *Bulletin* 1, no. 21 (1 July 1916).

28. David Glassberg notes that historical pageants were a way of promoting what historians of the time called the "New History" of the Progressive Era, a version that celebrated the country's golden past but also showed that history unfolded in an orderly progress. The pageants thus were a vehicle for illustrating the "continuities between past, present and an ideal future." Depictions of the colonial era and the founding fathers were particularly popular. Dance played an important part in pageants, both abstract dance representing the idealized spirit of the community and historical forms such as Morris dancing and the minuet. Glassberg, *American Historical Pageantry: The Uses of Tradition in the Early Twentieth Century* (Chapel Hill: University of North Carolina Press, 1990), 50 (quot.), 126–27, 136–37, 146–47.

29. *Bulletin* 1, no. 21 (1 July 1916). Program for 1916 Fourth of July, RAC, series 3, box 19, folder 154. Dramas given in next few years were titled *The Masque of Liberty* (1917), *The Spirit of Play* (1918), and *The Golden Day* (1919). According to Glassberg, allegorical dramas made abstract values and symbols tangible. The religious and moral overtones of these productions helped explain a community's present and were a guide to its future. Thus "the old and the new belonged in the same tradition and were part of a continuous process of social evolution." Glassberg, *American Historical Pageantry*, 271.

30. Glassberg, *American Historical Pageantry*, 283. Glassberg argues that pageants were a "medium for the reform of public behavior on the holidays as well as a medium for the dissemination of other reform ideals" (64). The American Pageant Association, formed in 1913, gave training courses and certified "pageant masters."

31. "Report of the General Manager," 20 January 1922, RSF, series 3, box 20, folder 160.

32. "Draft of Statement Prepared by Atterbury and Olmsted, June 10, 1921," RSF, series 3, box 20, folder 158.

33. Ibid.

34. "Draft of statement about approval of plans, to accompany letter of 6 June 1921. F. L. Olmsted," attached to letter from John Demarest to Robert de Forest, John Glenn, and Charles Norton, 27 June 1921, RSF, series 3, box 20, folder 158.

35. Demarest to de Forest, Glenn, and Norton, ibid.

36. *Bulletin* 7, no. 15 (1 April 1922).

37. Minutes, 24 April 1922, RSF, series 3, box 23, folder 183. In addition to its initial investment in land and capital improvements, the foundation had been making up the difference between fees collected from the property owners for maintenance and its actual cost, about $100,000 annually. Report of the Committee on Proposed Membership Corporation [1922], RG 2775, Forest Hills Gardens Corp., box 2, Rare and Manuscript Collections, Carl A. Kroch Library, Cornell University. The General Manager's report of 20 January 1922 compares costs for labor and material in 1914, 1920, and 1922, RSF, series 3, box 20, folder 160. Development continued to be slow even after the sale of Forest Hills Gardens. A clipping from the *Brooklyn Eagle* dated 26 October 1924 noted that two-thirds of the property was still undeveloped. RSF, series 3, box 20, folder 162.

38. John M. Glenn, Lilian Brandt, and F. Emerson Andrews, *Russell Sage Foundation, 1907–1940* (New York: Russell Sage Foundation, 1947), 1:272, 275. The foundation's major undertaking over the next ten years was its funding of the Regional Plan of New York and Its Environs, which resulted in publication of the ten-volume *Regional Survey of New York and Its Environs* and two volumes on the plan itself in 1927 and 1931. Olmsted served as a consultant on the project. The foundation's history notes that during this time there was "little margin of income available for new projects. . . . In this respect the pattern of the second period resembled that of the first decade when expansion was limited after the opening years by the need of capital for the development of Forest Hills Gardens" (1:278).

39. De Forest to Glenn, 11 February 1922, RSF, series 3, box 17, folder 146.

40. "Sale of Forest Hills Gardens by the Russell Sage Foundation," Supplement to *Bulletin* 8, no. 5 (9 December 1922); By-Laws of Forest Hills Gardens Corporation as amended 14 December 1988, 1.

41. *Bulletin* 9, no. 5 (8 December 1923).

8. The Legacy of Forest Hills Gardens

1. Robert A. M. Stern, Gregory Gilmartin, and John Massengale, *New York 1900: Metropolitan Architecture and Urbanism, 1890–1915* (New York: Rizzoli, 1983), 428.

2. The 1970 census was the first to record that more Americans resided in suburbs than in central cities or rural areas. In its 1999 *State of the Cities* report, the U.S. Department of Housing and Urban Development documented that from 1970 to 1980, 95 percent of growth in metropolitan areas took place in the suburbs; since 1980, the rate has slowed to 77 percent. A majority of the population, some 138,231,000 people, now live in the

suburbs. Iver Peterson, "Some Perched in Ivory Tower Gain Rosier View of Suburbs," *New York Times*, 5 December 1999, 1.

3. Memo to Clarence Arthur Perry from John Glenn, 13 May 1938, RSF, series 3, box 30, folder 159.

4. Robert de Forest to John Nolen, 13 April 1922, RSF, series 3, box 23, folder 183.

5. Frederick Law Olmsted to Thomas Adams, 23 July 1912, OA, series B, job file no. 3586.

6. "Statement of John M. Glenn," Russell Sage Foundation *Bulletin* (October 1937): 2, RSF, series 3, box 20, folder 158.

7. Clarence Arthur Perry, "Forest Hills Gardens as a Neighborhood Community," in *Regional Plan of New York and Its Environs*, vol. 7, *Neighborhood and Community Planning* (New York: Committee on Regional Plan of New York and Its Environs, 1929), 94.

8. Clarence Arthur Perry, *Housing for the Machine Age* (New York: Russell Sage Foundation, 1939), 211.

9. *Forest Hills Gardens News* (first quarter 1999): 1.

10. See *Gardens News* (May 1990): 1; *Forest Hills Gardens News* (first quarter 1999): 5; and *Forest Hills Gardens News* (Spring/Summer 2000): 2.

11. A casual perusal of the real estate listings in the *New York Times* between 1997 and 2001 demonstrates the strength of the market in Forest Hills Gardens: 8 Greenway North (7 bedrooms), $1.1 million, 11 November 1997; 46 Ingram Street (5 bedrooms) $525,000, 28 May 1998; 251 Greenway South (5 bedrooms), $700,000, 12 November 1998; 93 Groton Street (6 bedrooms), $530,000, 14 January 1999; 25 Olive Place (5 bedrooms), $1.17 million, 23 March 2000; 80 Groton Street (5 bedrooms), $865,000, 6 April 2000; 45 Markwood Road (3 bedrooms), $650,000, 18 January 2001; and 15 Middlemay Circle (6 bedrooms), $775,000, 16 August 2001. In 1998 the largest house in the community, 8 Markwood Road, designed by Grosvenor Atterbury in 1916, was noted in *Architectural Digest* as being on the market for $4.2 million.

The Gardens Corporation does not keep statistics on residents, but it is likely that Forest Hills Gardens has followed a similar change in demographics as that experienced in other New York suburbs over the past decades. Hispanics, Indians, Koreans, and Iranians have come to New York's suburbs in successive waves as older, white residents have moved to the Sunbelt and to rural areas. See Rosalyn Baxandall and Elizabeth Ewen, *Picture Windows: How the Suburbs Happened* (New York: Basic Books, 2000), for a discussion of this process on Long Island. My observations of the community and informal talks with Gardens Corporation employees and with William Coleman, the town's unofficial historian, together with a review of the names of new residents printed in the newsletters, suggest that Forest Hills Gardens is becoming an ethnically and racially diverse community.

12. John Gardner argues that while influential planners and housing reformers of the 1920s and 1930s (including Clarence Stein, Henry Wright, Arthur Comey, Henry Churchill, Elbert Peets, Lewis Mumford, Edith Wood, Tracy Auger, and Catherine Bauer) were familiar with the planning principles of the garden city movement and the model communities in England and the continent based on this model, the so-called garden cities of the

United States had nothing in common with them "when it came to land acquisition, housing tenure, and administration." Gardner, "The Garden City and Planned Industrial Suburbs," in *From Tenements to the Taylor Homes: In Search of an Urban Housing Policy in Twentieth-Century America*, ed. John F. Bauman, Roger Biles, and Kristin M. Szylvian (University Park: Pennsylvania State University Press, 2000), 45.

13. It has been remarked that the sponsors of these model communities saw them as opportunities to "reconstruct the working class into an idealized image of the American middle class by molding the built environment." Eric J. Karolak, "'No Idea of Doing Anything Wonderful': The Labor-Crisis Origins of National Housing Policy and the Reconstruction of the Working-Class Community, 1917–1919," in Bauman et al., *From Tenements to the Taylor Homes*, 61.

14. See James Howard Kunstler, *The Geography of Nowhere: The Rise and Decline of America's Man-Made Landscape* (New York: Simon and Schuster, 1993).

15. See Marc A. Weiss, *The Rise of the Community Builders: The American Real Estate Industry and Urban Land Planning* (New York: Columbia University Press, 1987). For brief historical overviews, see Daniel Schaffer, "The American Garden City: Lost Ideals," and Robert Fishman, "The American Garden City: Still Relevant?," in *The Garden City: Past, Present, and Future*, ed. Stephen V. Ward (London: E & F N Spon, 1992), 127–45 and 146–64. During the 1990s, both Columbia and Reston finally developed the town centers called for in their original plans.

16. Andres Duany and Elizabeth Plater-Zyberk, "The Second Coming of the American Small Town," *Wilson Quarterly* 16, no. 4 (Autumn 1992): 21.

17. The new urbanism draws on the physical characteristics of traditional towns. Common elements used in the designs of these new communities include clearly articulated boundaries; an intimate scale of building with a mix of housing types grouped in a higher density than found in the conventional suburb; pedestrian-friendly sidewalks and pathways; architectural guidelines based on forms and materials related to the local milieu; a rational network of narrow, through-streets; a mixed-use town center and other well-defined public gathering spaces; a streetscape with landscape plantings, lighting, and street furniture that enhance the character of the place and encourage social interaction. Principles of planning and design are summarized in mandatory codes or pattern books that regulate design and construction and establish the framework for development and future growth. One of the first overviews of this revival of town planning is John A. Dutton, *New American Urbanism: Forming the Suburban Metropolis* (Milan: Skira Architectural Library, 2000).

18. Scully quoted in Douglas Frantz and Catherine Collins, *Celebration, U.S.A.: Living in Disney's Brave New Town* (New York: Henry Holt, 1999), 8. See also Andrew Ross, *The Celebration Chronicles: Life, Liberty, and the Pursuit of Property Value in Disney's New Town* (New York: Ballentine Books, 1999). A lottery for the right to purchase one of the town's first 359 home sites was held on 18 November 1995.

19. Celebration's "Covenant, Conditions, and Restrictions" state that when 75 percent of the town's housing units were sold, residents could elect three of the five directors of the homeowners association. The following year residents would elect six of seven directors; a year later the Celebration Company would end its representation on the board. However,

the company retains "veto power over all changes in governance" as long as it owns property in Celebration. Ross, *Celebration Chronicles*, 230. Celebration's plan did differ in several respects from what had become the neo-traditional standard. The Disney Company envisioned Celebration's eighteen-acre downtown as an attraction for tourists as well as residents. Therefore the plan incorporated several wide main thoroughfares to move traffic in and out of the town center and provided more commercial space than typical for a community of its size. Other exceptional features are the emphasis on educational and health institutions as cornerstones of community life, the attention to environmental issues of the wetlands surrounding the development, and the creation of the Celebration Foundation to facilitate volunteerism among residents and to help connect Celebration with neighboring communities.

20. John Beardsley, "A Mickey Mouse Utopia," *Landscape Architecture* 87 (February 1997): 76–93; Michael Pollan, "Sticks and Stone: Mickey for Mayor?," *House & Garden,* October 1996, 62–72; Douglas Frantz, "Trouble at the Happiest School on Earth," *New York Times*, 1 August 1999, A1, 4; and Franz, "Town That Disney Built Hit by First Violent Crime," *New York Times*, 13 August 1998, A10.

21. Jackie Flanigan quoted in "City Limits: Can a Planned Community Approach the Utopian Ideal?," *Washington Post,* 7 September 1999, C3.

22. Frantz and Collins, *Celebration, U.S.A*, 119.

23. Ross, *Celebration Chronicles*, 104.

24. Clarence S. Stein, *New Towns for America* (1957; Cambridge: MIT Press, 1966), 226.

25. Gated communities, with their restricted access and apparent total withdrawal from the larger community, are the fastest-growing sector of residential development. There were an estimated 20,000 gated communities in the United States in 1997. See Edward J. Blakely and Mary Gail Snyder, *Fortress America: Gated Communities in the United States* (Washington, D.C., and Cambridge, Mass.: Brookings Institution Press and Lincoln Institute of Land Policy, 1997), 7. Some gated communities have incorporated elements of neo-traditional town planning, but they are controlled environments in which security and privacy are primary concerns, very different from the broader concerns of the new urbanism. Forest Hills Gardens has boundary markers, usually brick posts, at the head of several streets on its borders. These were not part of Olmsted and Atterbury's original design but were added in the 1920s "to mark and preserve the identity of the Gardens and its standards," as concern grew over the quality of development in surrounding areas. "Why Boundary Markers," undated memo, RG 2775, Forest Hills Gardens Corp., box 1, Rare and Manuscript Collections, Carl A. Kroch Library, Cornell University.

26. Charles Beveridge, founding editor of the Frederick Law Olmsted Sr. Papers, estimates that plans were prepared, although not necessarily implemented, for approximately 250 residential communities and subdivisions. Memo to the Trustees, National Association for Olmsted Parks, 10 April 1996.

27. Olmsted, Vaux, & Co., "Preliminary Report upon the Proposed Suburban Village at Riverside, Near Chicago, by Olmsted, Vaux, & Co., Landscape Architects," reprinted in *The Papers of Frederick Law Olmsted*, vol. 6, *The Years of Olmsted, Vaux, & Co., 1865–1874*, ed.

David Schuyler and Jane Turner Censer (Baltimore: Johns Hopkins University Press, 1992), 279, 275.

28. Frederick Law Olmsted Jr., "Notes on the Palos Verdes Project," 19 February 1922, OA, no. 5920.

29. Olmsted, Memo to Messrs. Dawson, Langdon, and Gibbs, 25 January 1925, OA, series B, no. 2921.

30. Olmsted to J. S. Torrance, December 1911, OA, series B, no. 5354.

31. Olmsted to Country Club Development Company of Daytona, Florida, 1 October 1924, OA, series B, no. 7353.

32. Olmsted to Torrance.

33. Olmsted, "Report on Tuckers Town for the Bermuda Development Company," July 1922, OA, series B, no. 7034.

34. Franklin J. Sherman, *Building Up Greater Queens Borough: An Estimate of Its Development and the Outlooks* (New York: J. J. Littel & Ives, 1929), 65.

INDEX